# JavaScript Data Structures and Algorithms

## An Introduction to Understanding and Implementing Core Data Structure and Algorithm Fundamentals

Sammie Bae

Apress®

# JavaScript Data Structures and Algorithms

Sammie Bae
Hamilton, ON, Canada

ISBN-13 (pbk): 978-1-4842-3987-2
https://doi.org/10.1007/978-1-4842-3988-9

ISBN-13 (electronic): 978-1-4842-3988-9

Library of Congress Control Number: 2019930417

Managing Director, Apress Media LLC: Welmoed Spahr
Acquisitions Editor: Louise Corrigan
Development Editor: Chris Nelson
Coordinating Editor: Nancy Chen

Cover designed by eStudioCalamar

Distributed to the book trade worldwide by Springer Science+Business Media New York, 233 Spring Street, 6th Floor, New York, NY 10013. Phone 1-800-SPRINGER, fax (201) 348-4505, e-mail orders-ny@springer-sbm.com, or visit www.springeronline.com. Apress Media, LLC is a California LLC and the sole member (owner) is Springer Science + Business Media Finance Inc (SSBM Finance Inc). SSBM Finance Inc is a Delaware corporation.

For information on translations, please e-mail rights@apress.com, or visit www.apress.com/rights-permissions.

Apress titles may be purchased in bulk for academic, corporate, or promotional use. eBook versions and licenses are also available for most titles. For more information, reference our Print and eBook Bulk Sales web page at www.apress.com/bulk-sales.

Any source code or other supplementary material referenced by the author in this book is available to readers on GitHub via the book's product page, located at www.apress.com/9781484239872. For more detailed information, please visit www.apress.com/source-code.

Printed on acid-free paper

*This book is dedicated to Dr. Hamid R. Tizhoosh for inspiring me in my studies and to my mother, Min Kyoung Seo, for her kindness and support.*

# Table of Contents

# About the Author

**Sammie Bae** is a data engineer at Yelp and previously worked for the data platform engineering team at NVIDIA. He developed a deep interest in JavaScript during an internship at SMART Technologies (acquired by Foxconn), where he developed Node.js-based JavaScript APIs for serial port communication between electronic board drivers and a web application. Despite how relevant JavaScript is to the modern software engineering industry, currently no books besides this one teach algorithms and data structures using JavaScript. Sammie understands how difficult these computer science concepts are and aims to provide clear and concise explanations in this book.

# About the Technical Reviewer

 **Phil Nash** is a developer evangelist for Twilio, serving developer communities in London and all over the world. He is a Ruby, JavaScript, and Swift developer; Google Developers Expert; blogger; speaker; and occasional brewer. He can be found hanging out at meetups and conferences, playing with new technologies and APIs, or writing open source code.

# Acknowledgments

Thank you, Phil Nash, for the valuable feedback that helped me improve the technical content of this book with clear explanations and concise code.

Special thanks to the Apress team. This includes James Markham, Nancy Chen, Jade Scard, and Chris Nelson. Finally, I want to thank Steve Anglin for reaching out to me to publish with Apress.

# Introduction

The motivation for writing this book was the lack of resources available about data structures and algorithms written in JavaScript. This was strange to me because today many of the job opportunities for software development require knowledge of JavaScript; it is the only language that can be used to write the entire stack, including the front-end, mobile (native and hybrid) platforms, and back-end. It is crucial for JavaScript developers to understand how data structures work and how to design algorithms to build applications.

Therefore, this book aims to teach data structure and algorithm concepts from computer science for JavaScript rather than for the more typical Java or C++. Because JavaScript follows the prototypal inheritance pattern, unlike Java and C++ (which follow the inheritance pattern), there are some changes in writing data structures in JavaScript. The classical inheritance pattern allows inheritance by creating a blueprint-like form that objects follow during inheritance. However, the prototypal inheritance pattern means copying the objects and changing their properties.

This book first covers fundamental mathematics for Big-O analysis and then lays out the basic JavaScript foundations, such as primitive objects and types. Then, this book covers implementations and algorithms for fundamental data structures such as linked lists, stacks, trees, heaps, and graphs. Finally, more advanced topics such as efficient string search algorithms, caching algorithms, and dynamic programming problems are explored in great detail.

# CHAPTER 1

# Big-O Notation

*O(1) is holy.*

—Hamid Tizhoosh

Before learning how to implement algorithms, you should understand how to analyze the effectiveness of them. This chapter will focus on the concept of Big-O notation for time and algorithmic space complexity analysis. By the end of this chapter, you will understand how to analyze an implementation of an algorithm with respect to both time (execution time) and space (memory consumed).

## Big-O Notation Primer

The Big-O notation measures the worst-case complexity of an algorithm. In Big-O notation, $n$ represents the number of inputs. The question asked with Big-O is the following: "What will happen as $n$ approaches infinity?"

When you implement an algorithm, Big-O notation is important because it tells you how efficient the algorithm is. Figure 1-1 shows some common Big-O notations.

© Sammie Bae 2019
S. Bae, *JavaScript Data Structures and Algorithms*, https://doi.org/10.1007/978-1-4842-3988-9_1

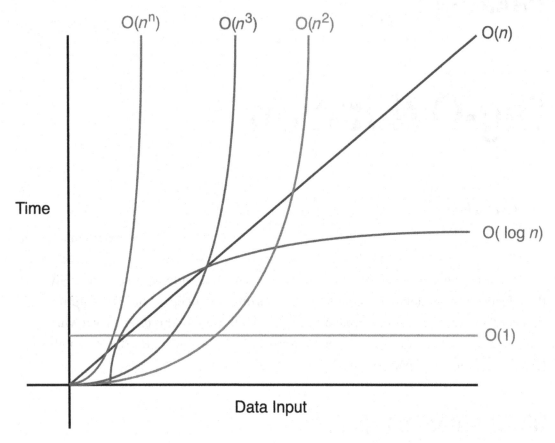

**Figure 1-1.** *Common Big-O complexities*

The following sections illustrate these common time complexities with some simple examples.

## Common Examples

O(1) does not change with respect to input space. Hence, O(1) is referred to as being *constant time*. An example of an O(1) algorithm is accessing an item in the array by its index. O($n$) is *linear time* and applies to algorithms that must do $n$ operations in the worst-case scenario.

An example of an O($n$) algorithm is printing numbers from 0 to $n$-1, as shown here:

```
1 function  exampleLinear(n) {
2               for  (var  i = 0 ; i <  n; i++ ) {
```

```
3                              console.log(i);
4                     }
5  }
```

Similarly, O($n^2$) is quadratic time, and O($n^3$) is cubic time. Examples of these complexities are shown here:

```
1 function  exampleQuadratic(n) {
2                 for  (var  i = 0 ; i <  n; i++ ) {
3                            console.log(i);
4                          for  (var  j =  i; j <  n; j++ ) {
5                                  console.log(j);
6                     }
7                 }
8  }
```

```
1 function  exampleCubic(n) {
2                 for  (var  i = 0 ; i <  n; i++ ) {
3                            console.log(i);
4                          for  (var  j =  i; j <  n; j++ ) {
5                                  console.log(j);
6                                    for  (var  k =  j;
                                     j <  n; j++ ) {
7                                          console.log(k);
8                                    }
9                          }
10             }
11 }
```

Finally, an example algorithm of logarithmic time complexity is printing elements that are a power of 2 between 2 and $n$. For example, exampleLogarithmic(10) will print the following:

```
2,4,8,16,32,64
```

The efficiency of logarithmic time complexities is apparent with large inputs such as a million items. Although $n$ is a million, exampleLogarithmic will print only 19 items because $\log_2(1{,}000{,}000) = 19.9315686$. The code that implements this logarithmic behavior is as follows:

```
1 function exampleLogarithmic(n) {
2                 for (var i = 2 ; i <= n; i= i*2 ) {
3                         console.log(i);
4                 }
5 }
```

# Rules of Big-O Notation

Let's represent an algorithm's complexity as f($n$). $n$ represents the number of inputs, f($n$)$_{time}$ represents the time needed, and f($n$)$_{space}$ represents the space (additional memory) needed for the algorithm. The goal of algorithm analysis is to understand the algorithm's efficiency by calculating f($n$). However, it can be challenging to calculate f($n$). Big-O notation provides some fundamental rules that help developers compute for f($n$).

- *Coefficient rule*: If f($n$) is O(g($n$)), then kf($n$) is O(g($n$)), for any constant k > 0. The first rule is the *coefficient rule*, which eliminates coefficients not related to the input size, $n$. This is because as $n$ approaches infinity, the other coefficient becomes negligible.

- *Sum rule*: If f($n$) is O(h($n$)) and g($n$) is O(p($n$)), then f($n$)+g($n$) is O(h($n$)+p($n$)). The sum rule simply states that if a resultant time complexity is a sum of two different time complexities, the resultant Big-O notation is also the sum of two different Big-O notations.

- *Product rule*: If f($n$) is O(h($n$)) and g($n$) is O(p($n$)), then f($n$)g($n$) is O(h($n$)p($n$)). Similarly, the product rule states that Big-O is multiplied when the time complexities are multiplied.

- *Transitive rule*: If f($n$) is O(g($n$)) and g($n$) is O(h($n$)), then f($n$) is O(h($n$)). The transitive rule is a simple way to state that the same time complexity has the same Big-O.

- *Polynomial rule*: If f($n$) is a polynomial of degree k, then f($n$) is O($n^k$). Intuitively, the polynomial rule states that polynomial time complexities have Big-O of the same polynomial degree.

- *Log of a power rule*: log($n$k) is O(log($n$)) for any constant k > 0. With the log of a power rule, constants within a log function are also ignored in Big-O notation.

Special attention should be paid to the first three rules and the polynomial rule because they are the most commonly used. I'll discuss each of those rules in the following sections.

## Coefficient Rule: "Get Rid of Constants"

Let's first review the coefficient rule. This rule is the easiest rule to understand. It simply requires you to ignore any non-input-size-related constants. Coefficients in Big-O are negligible with large input sizes. Therefore, this is the most important rule of Big-O notations.

If f($n$) is O(g($n$)), then kf($n$) is O(g($n$)), for any constant k > 0.

This means that both 5f($n$) and f($n$) have the same Big-O notation of O(f($n$)). Here is an example of a code block with a time complexity of O($n$):

```
1    function a(n){
2        var count =0;
3        for (var i=0;i<n;i++){
4            count+=1;
5        }
6        return count;
7    }
```

This block of code has f($n$) = $n$. This is because it adds to count $n$ times. Therefore, this function is O($n$) in time complexity:

```
1    function a(n){
2        var count =0;
3        for (var i=0;i<5*n;i++){
```

```
4              count+=1;
5          }
6          return count;
7      }
```

This block has $f(n) = 5n$. This is because it runs from 0 to $5n$. However, the first two examples both have a Big-O notation of $O(n)$. Simply put, this is because if $n$ is close to infinity or another large number, those four additional operations are meaningless. It is going to perform it $n$ times. Any constants are negligible in Big-O notation.

The following code block demonstrates another function with a linear time complexity but with an additional operation on line 6:

```
1   function a(n){
2       var count =0;
3       for (var i=0;i<n;i++){
4              count+=1;
5          }
6          count+=3;
7          return count;
8      }
```

Lastly, this block of code has $f(n) = n+1$. There is +1 from the last operation (count+=3). This still has a Big-O notation of $O(n)$. This is because that 1 operation is not dependent on the input $n$. As $n$ approaches infinity, it will become negligible.

## Sum Rule: "Add Big-Os Up"

The sum rule is intuitive to understand; time complexities can be added. Imagine a master algorithm that involves two other algorithms. The Big-O notation of that master algorithm is simply the sum of the other two Big-O notations.

If $f(n)$ is $O(h(n))$ and $g(n)$ is $O(p(n))$, then $f(n)+g(n)$ is $O(h(n)+p(n))$.

It is important to remember to apply the coefficient rule after applying this rule.

The following code block demonstrates a function with two main loops whose time complexities must be considered independently and then summed:

```
1    function a(n){
2         var count =0;
3         for (var i=0;i<n;i++){
4              count+=1;
5         }
6         for (var i=0;i<5*n;i++){
7              count+=1;
8         }
9         return count;
10   }
```

In this example, line 4 has f($n$) = $n$, and line 7 has f($n$) = 5$n$. This results in 6$n$. However, when applying the coefficient rule, the final result is O($n$) = $n$.

## Product Rule: "Multiply Big-Os"

The product rule simply states how Big-Os can be multiplied.

If f($n$) is O(h($n$)) and g($n$) is O(p($n$)), then f($n$)g($n$) is O(h($n$)p($n$)).

The following code block demonstrates a function with two nested for loops for which the product rule is applied:

```
1    function (n){
2         var count =0;
3         for (var i=0;i<n;i++){
4              count+=1;
5              for (var i=0;i<5*n;i++){
6                   count+=1;
7              }
8         }
9         return count;
10   }
```

In this example, $f(n) = 5n*n$ because line 7 runs $5n$ times for a total of $n$ iterations. Therefore, this results in a total of $5n^2$ operations. Applying the coefficient rule, the result is that $O(n)=n^2$.

## Polynomial Rule: "Big-O to the Power of k"

The polynomial rule states that polynomial time complexities have a Big-O notation of the same polynomial degree.

Mathematically, it's as follows:

> If $f(n)$ is a polynomial of degree k, then $f(n)$ is $O(n^k)$.

The following code block has only one for loop with quadratic time complexity:

```
1    function a(n){
2        var count =0;
3        for (var i=0;i<n*n;i++){
4            count+=1;
5        }
6        return count;
7    }
```

In this example, $f(n) = n\char`^2$ because line 4 runs $n*n$ iterations.

This was a quick overview of the Big-O notation. There is more to come as you progress through the book.

## Summary

Big-O is important for analyzing and comparing the efficiencies of algorithms. The analysis of Big-O starts by looking at the code and applying the rules to simplify the Big-O notation. The following are the most often used rules:

- Eliminating coefficients/constants (coefficient rule)

- Adding up Big-Os (sum rule)

- Multiplying Big-Os (product rule)

- Determining the polynomial of the Big-O notation by looking at loops (polynomial rule)

# Exercises

Calculate the time complexities for each of the exercise code snippets.

---

## EXERCISE 1

```
1    function someFunction(n) {
2
3        for (var i=0;i<n*1000;i++) {
4            for (var j=0;j<n*20;j++) {
5                console.log(i+j);
6            }
7        }
8
9    }
```

---

## EXERCISE 2

```
1    function someFunction(n) {
2
3        for (var i=0;i<n;i++) {
4            for (var j=0;j<n;j++) {
5                for (var k=0;k<n;k++) {
6                    for (var l=0;l<10;l++) {
7                        console.log(i+j+k+l);
8                    }
9                }
10            }
11        }
12
13    }
```

---

## EXERCISE 3

```
1    function someFunction(n) {
2
3        for (var i=0;i<1000;i++) {
4            console.log("hi");
5        }
6
7    }
```

## EXERCISE 4

```
1    function someFunction(n) {
2
3        for (var i=0;i<n*10;i++) {
4            console.log(n);
5        }
6
7    }
```

## EXERCISE 5

```
1    function someFunction(n) {
2
3        for (var i=0;i<n;i*2) {
4            console.log(n);
5        }
6
7    }
```

---

**EXERCISE 6**

---

```
1    function someFunction(n) {
2
3        while (true){
4            console.log(n);
5        }
6    }
```

---

## Answers

1. $O(n^2)$

   There are two nested loops. Ignore the constants in front of $n$.

2. $O(n^3)$

   There are four nested loops, but the last loop runs only until 10.

3. $O(1)$

   Constant complexity. The function runs from 0 to 1000. This does not depend on $n$.

4. $O(n)$

   Linear complexity. The function runs from 0 to $10n$. Constants are ignored in Big-O.

5. $O(\log_2 n)$

   Logarithmic complexity. For a given $n$, this will operate only $\log_2 n$ times because i is incremented by multiplying by 2 rather than adding 1 as in the other examples.

6. $O(\infty)$

   Infinite loop. This function will not end.

# CHAPTER 2

# JavaScript: Unique Parts

This chapter will briefly discuss some exceptions and cases of JavaScript's syntax and behavior. As a dynamic and interpreted programming language, its syntax is different from that of traditional object-oriented programming languages. These concepts are fundamental to JavaScript and will help you to develop a better understanding of the process of designing algorithms in JavaScript.

## JavaScript Scope

The *scope* is what defines the access to JavaScript variables. In JavaScript, variables can belong to the global scope or to the local scope. Global variables are variables that belong in the global scope and are accessible from anywhere in the program.

## Global Declaration: Global Scope

In JavaScript, variables can be declared without using any operators. Here's an example:

```
1  test = "sss";
2  console.log(test); // prints "sss"
```

However, this creates a global variable, and this is one of the worst practices in JavaScript. Avoid doing this at all costs. Always use `var` or `let` to declare variables. Finally, when declaring variables that won't be modified, use `const`.

## Declaration with var: Functional Scope

In JavaScript, `var` is one keyword used to declare variables. These variable declarations "float" all the way to the top. This is known as *variable hoisting*. Variables declared at the bottom of the script will not be the last thing executed in a JavaScript program during runtime.

© Sammie Bae 2019
S. Bae, *JavaScript Data Structures and Algorithms*, https://doi.org/10.1007/978-1-4842-3988-9_2

Here's an example:

```
1  function scope1(){
2          var top = "top";
3          bottom = "bottom";
4          console.log(bottom);
5
6          var bottom;
7  }
8  scope1(); // prints "bottom" - no error
```

How does this work? The previous is the same as writing the following:

```
1  function scope1(){
2          var top = "top";
3          var  bottom;
4          bottom = "bottom"
5          console.log(bottom);
6  }
7  scope1(); // prints "bottom" - no error
```

The bottom variable declaration, which was at the last line in the function, is floated to the top, and logging the variable works.

The key thing to note about the var keyword is that the scope of the variable is the closest function scope. What does this mean?

In the following code, the scope2 function is the function scope closest to the print variable:

```
1  function scope2(print){
2          if(print){
3                  var insideIf = '12';
4          }
5          console.log(insideIf);
6  }
7  scope2(true); // prints '12' - no error
```

To illustrate, the preceding function is equivalent to the following:

```
1  function scope2(print){
2         var insideIf;
3
4         if(print){
5                 insideIf = '12';
6         }
7         console.log(insideIf);
8  }
9  scope2(true); // prints '12' - no error
```

In Java, this syntax would have thrown an error because the insideIf variable is generally available only in that if statement block and not outside it.

Here's another example:

```
1  var a = 1;
2  function four() {
3    if (true) {
4      var a = 4;
5    }
6
7    console.log(a); // prints '4'
8  }
```

4 was printed, not the global value of 1, because it was redeclared and available in that scope.

# Declaration with let: Block Scope

Another keyword that can be used to declare a variable is let. Any variables declared this way are in the closest block scope (meaning within the {} they were declared in).

```
1  function scope3(print){
2         if(print){
3                 let insideIf = '12';
4         }
```

```
5              console.log(insideIf);
6  }
7  scope3(true); // prints ''
```

In this example, nothing is logged to the console because the insideIf variable is available only inside the if statement block.

# Equality and Types

JavaScript has different data types than in traditional languages such as Java. Let's explore how this impacts things such as equality comparison.

## Variable Types

In JavaScript, there are seven primitive data types: boolean, number, string, undefined, object, function, and symbol (symbol won't be discussed). One thing that stands out here is that undefined is a primitive value that is assigned to a variable that has just been declared. typeof is the primitive operator used to return the type of a variable.

```
1  var is20 = false; // boolean
2  typeof is20; // boolean
3
4  var  age = 19;
5  typeof age; // number
6
7  var  lastName = "Bae";
8  typeof lastName; // string
9
10 var fruits = ["Apple", "Banana", "Kiwi"];
11 typeof fruits; // object
12
13 var me = {firstName:"Sammie", lastName:"Bae"};
14 typeof me; // object
15
16 var nullVar = null;
17 typeof nullVar; // object
18
```

```
19  var function1 = function(){
20          console.log(1);
21  }
22  typeof function1 // function
23
24  var blank;
25  typeof blank; // undefined
```

# Truthy/Falsey Check

True/false checking is used in `if` statements. In many languages, the parameter inside the `if()` function must be a boolean type. However, JavaScript (and other dynamically typed languages) is more flexible with this. Here's an example:

```
1  if(node){
2          ...
3  }
```

Here, `node` is some variable. If that variable is empty, null, or undefined, it will be evaluated as `false`.

Here are commonly used expressions that evaluate to `false`:

- `false`
- `0`
- Empty strings (`''` and `""`)
- `NaN`
- `undefined`
- `null`

Here are commonly used expressions that evaluate to `true`:

- `true`
- Any number other than 0
- Non-empty strings
- Non-empty object

Here's an example:

```
1  var printIfTrue = ";
2
3  if (printIfTrue) {
4          console.log('truthy');
5  } else {
6          console.log('falsey'); // prints 'falsey'
7  }
```

## === VS ==

JavaScript is a scripting language, and variables are not assigned a type during declaration. Instead, types are interpreted as the code runs.

Hence, === is used to check equality more strictly than ==. === checks for both the type and the value, while == checks only for the value.

```
1  "5" == 5 // returns true
2  "5" === 5 // returns false
```

"5" == 5 returns true because "5" is coerced to a number before the comparison. On the other hand, "5" === 5 returns false because the type of "5" is a string, while 5 is a number.

## Objects

Most strongly typed languages such as Java use isEquals() to check whether two objects are the same. You may be tempted to simply use the == operator to check whether two objects are the same in JavaScript.

However, this will not evaluate to true.

```
1  var o1 = {};
2  var o2 = {};
3
4  o1 == o2 // returns false
5  o1 === o2 // returns false
```

Although these objects are equivalent (same properties and values), they are not equal. Namely, the variables have different addresses in memory.

This is why most JavaScript applications use utility libraries such as lodash[1] or underscore,[2] which have the isEqual(*object1, object2*) function to check two objects or values strictly. This occurs via implementation of some property-based equality checking where each property of the object is compared.

In this example, each property is compared to achieve an accurate object equality result.

```
1  function isEquivalent(a, b) {
2      // arrays of property names
3      var aProps = Object.getOwnPropertyNames(a);
4      var bProps = Object.getOwnPropertyNames(b);
5
6      // If their property lengths are different, they're different objects
7      if (aProps.length != bProps.length) {
8          return false;
9      }
10
11     for (var  i = 0; i < aProps.length; i++) {
12         var propName = aProps[i];
13
14         // If the values of the property are different, not equal
15         if (a[propName] !== b[propName]) {
16             return false;
17         }
18     }
19
20     // If everything matched, correct
21     return  true;
22  }
23  isEquivalent({'hi':12},{'hi':12}); // returns true
```

---

[1]https://lodash.com/
[2]http://underscorejs.org/

However, this would still work for objects that have only a string or a number as the property.

```
1  var obj1 = {'prop1': 'test','prop2': function (){} };
2  var obj2 = {'prop1': 'test','prop2': function (){} };
3
4  isEquivalent(obj1,obj2); // returns false
```

This is because functions and arrays cannot simply use the == operator to check for equality.

```
1  var function1 = function(){console.log(2)};
2  var function2 = function(){console.log(2)};
3  console.log(function1 == function2); // prints 'false'
```

Although the two functions perform the same operation, the functions have different addresses in memory, and therefore the equality operator returns false. The primitive equality check operators, == and ===, can be used only for strings and numbers. To implement an equivalence check for objects, each property in the object needs to be checked.

# Summary

JavaScript has a different variable declaration technique than most programming languages. var declares the variable within the function scope, let declares the variable in the block scope, and variables can be declared without any operator in the global scope; however, global scope should be avoided at all times. For type checking, typeof should be used to validate the expected type. Finally, for equality checks, use == to check the value, and use === to check for the type as well as the value. However, use these only on non-object types such as numbers, strings, and booleans.

# CHAPTER 3

# JavaScript Numbers

This chapter will focus on JavaScript number operations, number representation, `Number` objects, common number algorithms, and random number generation. By the end of this chapter, you will understand how to work with numbers in JavaScript as well as how to implement prime factorization, which is fundamental for encryption.

Number operations of a programming language allow you to compute numerical values. Here are the number operators in JavaScript:

```
+ : addition
- : subtraction
/ : division
* : multiplication
% : modulus
```

These operators are universally used in other programming languages and are not specific to JavaScript.

## Number System

JavaScript uses a 32-bit floating-point representation for numbers, as shown in Figure 3-1. In this example, the value is 0.15625. The sign bit (the 31st bit) indicates that the number is negative if the sign bit is 1. The next 8 bits (the 30th to 23rd bits) indicate the exponent value, e. Finally, the remaining 23 bits represent the fraction value.

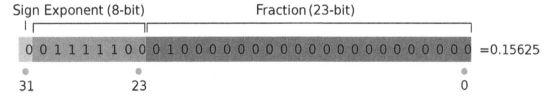

*Figure 3-1.* *The 32-bit floating-point number system*

© Sammie Bae 2019
S. Bae, *JavaScript Data Structures and Algorithms*, https://doi.org/10.1007/978-1-4842-3988-9_3

With the 32 bits, the value is computed by this esoteric formula:

$$value = (-1)^{sign} \times 2^{e-127} \times \left(1 + \sum_{t=1}^{23} b_{23-t} 2^{-t}\right)$$

Figure 3-1 shows the following break down of the 32 bits:

$$sign = 0$$
$$e = (0111100)_2 = 124 \text{ (in base 10)}$$

$$1 + \sum_{i=1}^{23} b_{23-i} 2^{-i} = 1 + 0 + 0.25 + 0$$

This results in the following:

$$value = 1 \times 2^{124-127} \times 1.25 = 1 \times 2^{-3} \times 1.25 = 0.15625$$

With decimal fractions, this floating-point number system causes some rounding errors in JavaScript. For example, 0.1 and 0.2 cannot be represented precisely.

Hence, 0.1 + 0.2 === 0.3 yields false.

```
1   0.1 + 0.2 === 0.3; // prints 'false'
```

To really understand why 0.1 cannot be represented properly as a 32-bit floating-point number, you must understand binary. Representing many decimals in binary requires an infinite number of digits. This because binary numbers are represented by $2^n$ where $n$ is an integer.

While trying to calculate 0.1, long division will go on forever. As shown in Figure 3-2, 1010 represents 10 in binary. Trying to calculate 0.1 (1/10) results in an indefinite number of decimal points.

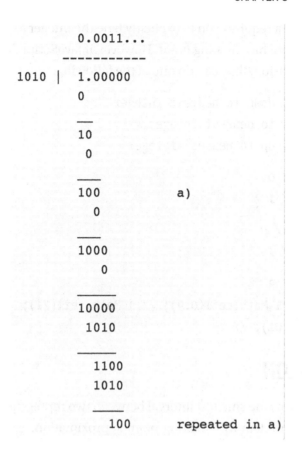

**Figure 3-2.** *Long division for 0.1*

# JavaScript Number Object

Luckily, there are some built-in properties of the Number object in JavaScript that help work around this.

# Integer Rounding

Since JavaScript uses floating point to represent all numbers, integer division does not work.

Integer division in programming languages like Java simply evaluates division expressions to their quotient.

For example, 5/4 is 1 in Java because the quotient is 1 (although there is a remainder of 1 left). However, in JavaScript, it is a floating point.

```
1  5/4; // 1.25
```

This is because Java requires you to explicitly type the integer as an integer. Hence, the result cannot be a floating point. However, if JavaScript developers want to implement integer division, they can do one of the following:

```
Math.floor - rounds down to nearest integer
Math.round - rounds to nearest integer
Math.ceil  - rounds up to nearest integer

Math.floor(0.9); // 0
Math.floor(1.1); // 1

Math.round(0.49); // 0
Math.round(0.5); // 1

Math.round(2.9); // 3
Math.ceil(0.1); // 1 Math.ceil(0.9); // 1 Math.ceil(21);
// 21 Math.ceil(21.01); // 22
```

## Number.EPSILON

Number.EPSILON returns the smallest interval between two representable numbers. This is useful for the problem with floating-point approximation.

```
1  function numberEquals(x, y) {
2      return Math.abs(x - y) < Number.EPSILON;
3  }
4
5  numberEquals(0.1 + 0.2, 0.3); // true
```

This function works by checking whether the difference between the two numbers are smaller than Number.EPSILON. Remember that Number.EPSILON is the smallest difference between two *representable* numbers. The difference between 0.1+0.2 and 0.3 will be smaller than Number.EPSILON.

## Maximums

Number.MAX_SAFE_INTEGER returns the largest integer.

```
1  Number.MAX_SAFE_INTEGER + 1 === Number.MAX_SAFE_INTEGER + 2; // true
```

This returns true because it cannot go any higher. However, it does not work for floating-point decimals.

```
1  Number.MAX_SAFE_INTEGER + 1.111 === Number.MAX_SAFE_INTEGER + 2.022;
   // false
```

Number.MAX_VALUE returns the largest floating-point number possible. Number.MAX_VALUE is equal to 1.7976931348623157e+308.

```
1  Number.MAX_VALUE + 1 === Number.MAX_VALUE + 2; // true
```

Unlike like Number.MAX_SAFE_INTEGER, this uses double-precision floating-point representation and works for floating points as well.

```
1  Number.MAX_VALUE + 1.111 === Number.MAX_VALUE + 2.022; // true
```

## Minimums

Number.MIN_SAFE_INTEGER returns the smallest integer.
   Number.MIN_SAFE_INTEGER is equal to -9007199254740991.

```
1  Number.MIN_SAFE_INTEGER - 1 === Number.MIN_SAFE_INTEGER - 2; // true
```

This returns true because it cannot get any smaller. However, it does not work for floating-point decimals.

```
1   Number.MIN_SAFE_INTEGER - 1.111 === Number.MIN_SAFE_INTEGER - 2.022;
   // false
```

Number.MIN_VALUE returns the smallest floating-point number possible.
   Number.MIN_VALUE is equal to 5e-324. This is not a negative number since it is the smallest *floating-point* number possible and means that Number.MIN_VALUE is actually bigger than Number.MIN_- SAFE_INTEGER.
   Number.MIN_VALUE is also the closest floating point to zero.

```
1  Number.MIN_VALUE - 1 == -1; // true
```

This is because this is similar to writing 0 - 1 == -1.

# Infinity

The only thing greater than `Number.MAX_VALUE` is `Infinity`, and the only thing smaller than `Number.MAX_SAFE_INTEGER` is `-Infinity`.

```
1  Infinity > Number.MAX_SAFE_INTEGER; // true
2  -Infinity < Number.MAX_SAFE_INTEGER // true;
3  -Infinity -32323323 == -Infinity -1; // true
```

This evaluates to `true` because nothing can go smaller than `-Infinity`.

## Size Summary

This inequality summarizes the size of JavaScript numbers from smallest (left) to largest (right):

```
-Infinity < Number.MIN_SAFE_INTEGER < Number.MIN_VALUE < 0 < Number.MAX_
SAFE_IN- TEGER < Number.MAX_VALUE < Infinity
```

## Number Algorithms

One of the most discussed algorithms involving numbers is for testing whether a number is a prime number. Let's review this now.

## Primality Test

A primality test can be done by iterating from 2 to *n*, checking whether modulus division (remainder) is equal to zero.

```
1  function isPrime(n){
2      if (n <= 1) {
3              return false;
4      }
5
6      // check from 2 to n-1
7      for (var i=2; i<n; i++) {
8              if (n%i == 0) {
9                      return false;
10          }
```

```
11         }
12
13         return true;
14  }
```

**Time Complexity:** $O(n)$

The time complexity is $O(n)$ because this algorithm checks all numbers from 0 to $n$.

This is an example of an algorithm that can be easily improved. Think about how this method iterates through 2 to $n$. Is it possible to find a pattern and make the algorithm faster? First, any multiple of 2s can be ignored, but there is more optimization possible.

Let's list some prime numbers.

```
2,3,5,7,11,13,17,19,23,29,31,37,41,43,47,53,59,61,67,71,73,79,83,89,97
```

This is difficult to notice, but all primes are of the form $6k \pm 1$, with the exception of 2 and 3 where k is some integer. Here's an example:

```
5 = (6-1) , 7 = ((1*6) + 1), 13 = ((2*6) + 1) etc
```

Also realize that for testing the prime number $n$, the loop only has to test until the square root of $n$. This is because if the square root of $n$ is not a prime number, $n$ is not a prime number by mathematical definition.

```
1   function isPrime(n){
2       if (n <= 1) return false;
3       if (n <= 3) return true;
4
5       // This is checked so that we can skip
6       // middle five numbers in below loop
7       if (n%2 == 0 || n%3 == 0) return false;
8
9       for (var i=5; i*i<=n; i=i+6){
10          if (n%i == 0 || n%(i+2) == 0)
11              return false;
12      }
13
14      return true;
15  }
```

**Time Complexity:** $O(sqrt(n))$

This improved solution cuts the time complexity down significantly.

# Prime Factorization

Another useful algorithm to understand is for determining prime factorization of a number. Prime numbers are the basis of encryption (covered in Chapter 4) and hashing (covered in Chapter 11), and *prime factorization* is the process of determining which prime numbers multiply to a given number. Given 10, it would print 5 and 2.

```javascript
1  function primeFactors(n){
2          // Print the number of 2s that divide n
3          while (n%2 == 0) {
4              console.log(2);
5              n = n/2;
6          }
7
8          // n must be odd at this point. So we can skip one element
           (Note i = i +2)
9          for (var i = 3; i*i <= n; i = i+2) {
10             // While i divides n, print i and divide n
11             while (n%i == 0) {
12                 console.log(i);
13                 n = n/i;
14             }
15         }
16         // This condition is to handle the case when n is a prime number
17         // greater than 2
18         if (n > 2) {
19             console.log(n);
20         }
21  }
22  primeFactors(10); // prints '5' and '2'
```

**Time Complexity:** $O(sqrt(n))$

This algorithm works by printing any number that is divisible by i without a remainder. In the case that a prime number is passed into this function, it would be handled by printing whether $n$ is greater than 2.

# Random Number Generator

Random number generation is important to simulate conditions. JavaScript has a built-in function for generating numbers: `Math.random()`.

> `Math.random()` returns a float between 0 and 1.

You may wonder how you get random integers or numbers greater than 1.

To get floating points higher than 1, simply multiply `Math.random()` by the range. Add or subtract from it to set the base.

```
Math.random() * 100; // floats between 0   and   100
Math.random() * 25 + 5; // floats between 5   and   30
Math.random() * 10 - 100; // floats between -100 and -90
```

To get random integers, simply use `Math.floor()`, `Math.round()`, or `Math.ceil()` to round to an integer.

```
Math.floor(Math.random() * 100); // integer between 0 and 99
Math.round(Math.random() * 25) + 5; // integer between 5 and 30
Math.ceil(Math.random() * 10) - 100; // integer between -100 and -90
```

# Exercises

1.  Given three numbers x, y, and p, compute (x^y) % p. (This is modular exponentiation.)

    Here, x is the base, y is exponent, and p is the modulus.

    Modular exponentiation is a type of exponentiation performed over a modulus, which is useful in computer science and used in the field of public-key encryption algorithms.

    At first, this problem seems simple. Calculating this is a one-line solution, as shown here:

29

```
1  function modularExponentiation ( base, exponent, modulus ) {
2          return Math.pow(base,exponent) % modulus;
3  }
```

This does exactly what the question asks. However, it cannot handle large exponents.

Remember that this is implemented with encryption algorithms. In strong cryptography, the base is often at least 256 bit (78 digits).

Consider this case, for example:

Base: $6x10^{77}$, Exponent: 27, Modulus: 497

In this case, $(6x10^{77})^{27}$ is a very large number and cannot be stored in a 32-bit floating point.

There is another approach, which involves some math. One must observe the following mathematical property:

For arbitrary $a$ and $b$,

```
c % m = (a   b) % m
c % m = [(a % m)   (b % m)] % m
```

Using this mathematical property, you can iterate 1 to the exponent, recalculating each time by multiplying the current modulus value with the last.

Here is the pseudocode:

1  Set value = 1, current exponent = 0.
2  Increment current exponent by 1.
3  Set value = (base   value) mod modulus until current
   exponent is reached exponent

Example: Base: 4, Exponent: 3, Modulus: 5

```
4^3 % 5 = 64 % 5 = 4
```

value = (lastValue x base ) % modulus:

value = (1 x 4) % 5 = 4 % 5 = 4

value = (4 x 4) % 5 = 16 % 5 = 1

value = (1 x 4) % 5 = 4 % 5 = 4

Finally, here is the code:

```
1  function modularExponentiation ( base, exponent, modulus ) {
2          if (modulus == 1) return 0;
3
4          var value = 1;
5
6          for ( var i=0; i<exponent; i++ ){
7                  value = (value * base) % modulus;
8          }
9          return value;
10 }
```

**Time Complexity:** O($n$)

The time complexity is O($n$) where $n$ is equal to the exponent value.

2. Print all primes less than n.

To do this, use the isPrime function covered in this chapter. Simply iterate from 0 to $n$ and print any prime numbers where isPrime() evaluates to true.

```
1  function allPrimesLessThanN(n){
2          for (var i=0; i<n; i++) {
3                  if (isPrime(i)){
4                          console.log(i);
5                  }
6          }
7  }
8
9  function isPrime(n){
10     if (n <= 1) return false;
11     if (n <= 3) return true;
12
```

```
13        // This is checked so that we can skip
14        // middle five numbers in below loop
15        if (n%2 == 0 || n%3 == 0) return false;
16
17        for (var i=5; i*i<=n; i=i+6){
18            if (n%i == 0 || n%(i+2) == 0)
19                return false;
20        }
21
22        return true;
23  }
24
25  allPrimesLessThanN(15);
26
27  // prints 2, 3, 5, 7, 11, 13
```

**Time Complexity:** $O(nsqrt(n))$

This is because isPrime (covered earlier in this chapter) with a time complexity of $O(sqrt(n))$ is run $n$ times.

3.  Check for a set of prime factors.

    Let's define ugly numbers as those whose only prime factors are 2, 3, or 5. The sequence 1, 2, 3, 4, 5, 6, 8, 9, 10, 12, 15, ... shows the first 11 ugly numbers. By convention, 1 is included.

    To do this, divide the number by the divisors (2, 3, 5) until it cannot be divided without a remainder. If the number can be divided by all the divisors, it should be 1 after dividing everything.

```
1  function maxDivide (number, divisor) {
2          while (number % divisor == 0) {
3                  number /= divisor;
4          }
5          return number;
6  }
7
8  function isUgly (number){
9          number = maxDivide(number, 2);
```

```
10              number = maxDivide(number, 3);
11              number = maxDivide(number, 5);
12              return number === 1;
13   }
```

Iterate this over *n*, and now the list of ugly numbers can be returned.

```
1    function arrayNUglyNumbers (n) {
2            var counter = 0, currentNumber = 1,
             uglyNumbers = [];
3
4            while ( counter != n ) {
5
6                    if ( isUgly(currentNumber) ) {
7                            counter++;
8                            uglyNumbers.push(currentNumber);
9                    }
10
11                   currentNumber++;
12           }
13
14           return uglyNumbers;
15   }
```

**Time Complexity for maxDivide(number, divisor):**
$O(\log_{divisor}(number))$

The time complexity of maxDivide is a logarithmic function which depends on divisor and the number. When testing primes of 2, 3, and 5, the logarithmic of 2 ($\log_2 (n)$) yields the highest time complexity.

**Time Complexity for isUgly:** $O(\log_2(n))$

**Time Complexity for arrayNUglyNumbers:** $O(n(\log_2(n)))$

The isUgly function is limited by the time complexity of maxDivide(number, 2). Hence, arrayNUglyNumbers has *n* times that time complexity.

# Summary

Recall that all numbers in JavaScript are in 32-bit floating point format. To get the smallest possible floating point increment, you should use `Number.EPILSON`. The maximum and minimum numbers of JavaScript can be summarized by the following inequality:

```
-Infinity < Number.MIN_SAFE_INTEGER < Number.MIN_VALUE < 0
< Number.MAX_SAFE_INTEGER < Number.MAX_VALUE < Infinity
```

Prime number validation and prime factorization are concepts used in various computer science applications such as encryption, as covered in Chapter 4. Finally, random number generation in JavaScript works via `Math.random()`.

# CHAPTER 4

# JavaScript Strings

This chapter will focus on working with strings, the JavaScript String object, and the String object's built-in functions. You will learn how to access, compare, decompose, and search strings for commonly used real-life purposes. In addition, the chapter will explore string encoding, decoding, encryption, and decryption. By the end of this chapter, you will understand how to effectively work with JavaScript strings and have a fundamental understanding of string encoding and encryption.

## JavaScript String Primitive

JavaScript's native String primitive comes with various common string functions.

## String Access

For accessing characters, you use .chartAt().

```
1  'dog'.charAt(1); // returns "o"
```

.charAt(index) takes an index (which starts at 0) and returns the character at that index location in the string.

For string (multiple-character) access, you can use .substring(startIndex, endIndex), which will return the characters between the specified indices.

```
1  'YouTube'.substring(1,2); // returns 'o'
2  YouTube'.substring(3,7); // returns 'tube'
```

If you do not pass a second parameter (endIndex), it will return all the character values from the specified start position until the end.

```
1  return 'YouTube'.substring(1); // returns 'outube'
```

© Sammie Bae 2019
S. Bae, *JavaScript Data Structures and Algorithms*, https://doi.org/10.1007/978-1-4842-3988-9_4

# String Comparison

Most programming languages have a function that allows you to compare strings. In JavaScript, this can be done simply by using less-than and greater-than operators.

```
1  var a = 'a';
2  var b = 'b';
3  console.log(a < b); // prints 'true'
```

This can be really useful for comparing strings when sorting algorithms, which is covered later in the book.

However, if you are comparing two strings of different lengths, it starts comparing from the start of the string until the length of the smaller string.

```
1  var a = 'add';
2  var b = 'b';
3
4  console.log(a < b); // prints 'true'
```

In this example, a and b are compared. Since a is smaller than b, a < b evaluates to true.

```
1  var a = 'add';
2  var b = 'ab';
3  console.log(a < b); // prints 'false'
```

In this example, after 'a' and 'b' are compared, 'd' and 'b' are compared. Processing cannot continue because everything in 'ab' has been looked at. This is the same as comparing 'ad' with 'ab'.

```
1  console.log('add'<'ab' == 'ad'<'ab'); // prints 'true'
```

# String Search

To find a specific string within a string, you can use .indexOf(searchValue[, fromIndex]). This takes a parameter that is the string to be searched as well as an optional parameter for the starting index for the search. It returns the position of the matching string, but if nothing is found, then -1 is returned. Note that this function is case sensitive.

```
1  'Red Dragon'.indexOf('Red');      // returns 0
2  'Red Dragon'.indexOf('RedScale'); // returns -1
3  'Red Dragon'.indexOf('Dragon', 0); // returns 4
4  'Red Dragon'.indexOf('Dragon', 4); // returns 4
5  'Red Dragon'.indexOf('', 9);      // returns 9
```

To check for the occurrence of a search string inside a larger string, simply check whether -1 was returned from .indexOf.

```
1  function existsInString (stringValue, search) {
2         return stringValue.indexOf(search) !== -1;
3  }
4  console.log(existsInString('red','r')); // prints 'true';
5  console.log(existsInString('red','b')); // prints 'false';
```

You can use an additional parameter to search after a certain index in a string. An example is counting occurrences of certain letters . In the following example, the occurrences of the character 'a' will be counted:

```
1  var str        = "He's my king from this day until his last day";
2  var count      = 0;
3  var pos        = str.indexOf('a');
4  while (pos !== -1) {
5    count++;
6    pos = str.indexOf('a', pos + 1);
7  }
8  console.log(count); // prints '3'
```

Finally, startsWith returns true (boolean) if the string starts with the specified input, and endsWith checks whether the string ends with the specified input.

```
1  'Red Dragon'.startsWith('Red'); // returns true
2  'Red Dragon'.endsWith('Dragon'); // returns true
3  'Red Dragon'.startsWith('Dragon'); // returns false
4  'Red Dragon'.endsWith('Red'); // returns false
```

# String Decomposition

For decomposing a string into parts, you can use `.split(separator)`, which is a great utility function. It takes one parameter (the separator) and creates an array of substrings.

```
1  var test1 = 'chicken,noodle,soup,broth';
2  test1.split(","); // ["chicken", "noodle", "soup", "broth"]
```

Passing an empty separator will create an array of all the characters.

```
1  var test1 = 'chicken';
2  test1.split(""); // ["c", "h", "i", "c", "k", "e", "n"]
```

This is useful for when there are items listed in a string. The string can be turned into an array to easily iterate through them.

# String Replace

`.replace(string, replaceString)` replaces a specified string within a string variable with another string.

```
1  "Wizard of Oz".replace("Wizard","Witch"); // "Witch of Oz"
```

# Regular Expressions

Regular expressions (*regexes*) are a set of characters that define a search pattern. Learning how to use regexes is a massive task of its own, but as a JavaScript developer, it is important you know the basics of regexes.

JavaScript also comes with the native object `RegExp`, which is used for regular expressions.

The constructor for the `RegExp` object takes two parameters: the regular expression and the optional match settings, as shown here:

```
i       Perform case-insensitive matching
g       Perform a global match (find all matches rather than stopping after
        first match)
m       Perform multiline matching
```

RegExp has the following two functions:

- search(): Tests for matches in a string. This returns the index of the match.

- match(): Tests for matches. This returns all the matches.

The JavaScript String object also has the following two regex-related functions that accept the RegExp object as an argument:

- exec(): Tests for matches in a string. This returns the first match.

- test(): Tests for matches in a string. This returns true or false.

# Basic Regex

Here are the basic regex rules:

^: Indicates the start of a string/line
\d: Finds any digit
[abc]: Finds any character between the brackets
[^abc]: Finds any character *not* between the brackets
[0-9]: Finds any digit between the brackets
[^0-9]: Finds any digit *not* between the brackets
(x|y): Finds any of the alternatives specified

The following returns index 11, which is the index of the character D, which is the first character of the matched regex:

```
1  var str = "JavaScript DataStructures";
2  var n = str.search(/DataStructures/);
3  console.log(n); // prints '11'
```

# Commonly Used Regexes

Regexes are immensely helpful for checking the validity of user input in JavaScript. One common type of input check is to validate whether it has any numeric characters.

The following are five regexes that developers often use.

## Any Numeric Characters

/\d+/

```
1  var reg = /\d+/;
2  reg.test("123"); // true
3  reg.test("33asd"); // true
4  reg.test("5asdasd"); // true
5  reg.test("asdasd"); // false
```

## Only Numeric Characters

/^\d+$/

```
1  var reg = /^\d+$/;
2  reg.test("123"); // true
3  reg.test("123a"); // false
4  reg.test("a"); // false
```

## Floating Numeric Characters

/^[0-9]*.[0-9]*[1-9]+$/

```
1  var reg = /^[0-9]*.[0-9]*[1-9]+$/;
2  reg.test("12"); // false
3  reg.test("12.2"); // true
```

## Only Alphanumeric Characters

/[a-zA-Z0-9]/

```
1  var reg = /[a-zA-Z0-9]/;
2  reg.test("somethingELSE"); // true
3  reg.test("hello"); // true
4  reg.test("112a"); // true
5  reg.test("112"); // true
6  reg.test("^"); // false
```

## Query String

```
/(([^?=&]+)(=([^&]*))/
```

In web applications, web URLs often pass in parameters in the URL for routing or database query purposes.

For example, for the URL http://your.domain/product.aspx?category=4& product_id=2140&query=lcd+tv, the URL might respond to a back-end SQL query like the following:

```
1  SELECT LCD, TV FROM database WHERE Category = 4 AND Product_id=2140;
```

To parse these parameters, regexes can be useful.

```
1  var  uri = 'http://your.domain/product.aspx?category=4&product_id=2140&
   query=lcd+tv' ;
2  var  queryString =  {};
3  uri.replace(
4              new RegExp ("([^?=&]+)(=([^&]*))?" , "g" ),
5              function ($0, $1, $2, $3) { queryString[$1] =  $3; }
6  );
7  console.log('ID: ' + queryString['product_id' ]); // ID: 2140
8  console.log('Name: ' + queryString['product_name' ]); // Name: undefined
9  console.log('Category: ' + queryString['category' ]); // Category: 4
```

# Encoding

Encoding is a general concept in computer science that represents characters in a specialized format for efficient transmission or storage.

All computer file types are encoded in specific structures.

For example, when you upload a PDF, the encoding may look like this:

```
1  JVBERi0xLjMKMSAwIG9iago8PCAvVHlwZSAvQ2F0YWxvZwovT3VObGluZXMgMiAwIFIKL1Bh
   Z2VzIDMgMCBS\
2  ID4+CmVuZG9iagoyIDAgb2JqCjw8IC9UeXBlIC9PdXRsaW5lcyAvQ291bnQgMCA+PgplbmR
   vYmoKMyAwIG9i\
3  ago8PCAvVHlwZSAvUGFnZXMKL0tpZHMgWzYgMCBSCloKLONvdW50IDEKL1Jlc291cmNlcyA8
   PAovUHJvY1Nl\
```

```
 4   dCAoIDAgUgovRm9udCA8PCAKL0YxIDggMCBSCj4+Cj4+Ci9NZWRpYUJveCBbMC4wMDAgMC4w
     MDAgNjEyLjAw\

 5   MCA3OTIuMDAwXQogPj4KZW5kb2JqCjQgMCBvYmoKWy9QREYgL1RleHQgXQplbmRvYmoKNSAw
     IG9iago8PAov\

 6   Q3JlYXRvciAoRE9NUERGKQovQ3JlYXRpb25EYXRlIChEOjIwMTUwNzIwMTMzMzIzKzAyJzAw
     JykKL01vZERh\

 7   dGUgKEQ6MjAxNTA3MjAxMzMzMjMrMDInMDAnKQo+PgplbmRvYmoKNiAwIG9iago8PCAvVHlw
     ZSAvUGFnZQov\

 8   UGFyZW50IDMgMCBSCi9Db250ZW50cyA3IDAgUgo+PgplbmRvYmoKNyAwIG9iago8PCAvRmls
     dGVyIC9GbGF0\

 9   ZUR1Y29kZQovTGVuZ3RoIDY2ID4+CnN0cmVhbQp4nOMyODMwMFBAJovSuZxCFIxN9AwMzRTM
     DS31DCxNFUJS\

10   FPTdDBWMgKIKIWkKCtEaIanFJZqxCiFeCq4hAO4PDOMKZW5kc3RyZWFtCmVuZG9iago4IDA
     gb2JqCjw8IC9U\

11   eXBlIC9Gb250Ci9TdWJ0eXBlIC9UeXBlMQovTmFtZSAvRjEKL0Jhc2VGb250IC9UaW1lcy1
     Cb2xkCi9FbmNv\

12   ZGluZyAvV2luQW5zaUVuY29kaW5nCj4+CmVuZG9iago4cmVmCjAgOQowMDAwMDAwMDAwIDY
     1NTM1IGYgCjAw\

13   MDAwMDAwMDggMDAwMDAgbiAKMDAwMDAwMDA3MyAwMDAwMCBuIAowMDAwMDAwMTE5IDAwMDA
     wIG4gCjAwMDAw\

14   MDAyNzMgMDAwMDAgbiAKMDAwMDAwMDMwMiAwMDAwMCBuIAowMDAwMDAwNDE2IDAwMDAwIG4
     gCjAwMDAwMDA0\

15   NzkgMDAwMDAgbiAKMDAwMDAwMDYxNiAwMDAwMCBuIApocmFpbGVyCjw8Ci9TaXplIDkKL1J
     vb3QgMSAwIFIK\

16   L0luZm8gNSAwIFIKPj4Kc3RhcnR4cmVmCjcyNQol1JUVPRgo=.....
```

This is a Base64-encoded PDF string. Data like this is often passed to the server when a PDF file is uploaded.

## Base64 Encoding

The btoa() function creates a Base64-encoded ASCII string from a string. Each character in the string is treated as a byte (8 bits: eight 0 and 1s).

The .atob() function decodes a string of data that has been encoded using Base64 encoding. For example, the string "hello I love learning to computer program" in a Base64-encoded string looks like this: aGVsbG8gSSBsb3ZlIGxlYXJuaW5nIHRvIGNvbXB1dGVyIHByb2dyYW0.

```
1  btoa('hello I love learning to computer program');
2  //  aGVsbG8gSSBsb3ZlIGxlYXJuaW5nIHRvIGNvbXB1dGVyIHByb2dyYW0
```

```
1  atob('aGVsbG8gSSBsb3ZlIGxlYXJuaW5nIHRvIGNvbXB1dGVyIHByb2dyYW0');
2  // hello I love learning to computer program
```

Learn more about Base64 at https://en.wikipedia.org/wiki/Base64.

# String Shortening

Have you ever wondered how URL-shortening sites such as Bit.ly work? A simplified URL compression algorithm follows a certain structure, as shown here for www.google.com:

1.  The database creates a unique integer-based ID for the URL. In Figure 4-1, www.google.com has the entry 11231230 in the database.

### Relational Database

| Id | url |
|----|-----|
| 0 | www.youtube.com |
| ... | .... |
| 11231230 | www.google.com |

*Figure 4-1.  Database entries*

2.  The integer ID is shortened into a string. When shortened with Base62 encoding, 11231230 will be VhU2.

### Relational Database

| Id | url | Shortened Id |
|----|-----|--------------|
| 0 | www.youtube.com | a |
| ... | .... | .... |
| 11231230 | www.google.com | VhU2 |

*Figure 4-2.  Database entries after shortening*

For the shortening part, the following algorithm can be used. There are 62 possible letters and numbers, consisting of 26 lowercase letters, 26 uppercase letters, and 10 numbers (0 to 9).

```
1  var  DICTIONARY = "abcdefghijklmnopqrstuvwxyzABCDEFGHIJKLMNOPQRSTUVWXYZ
   0123456789" .split("");
2
3  function  encodeId(num) {
4              var  base = DICTIONARY.length;
5              var  encoded = " ;
6
7              if  (num === 0 ) {
8                  return  DICTIONARY[0 ];
9              }
10
11                   while  (num > 0 ) {
12                      encoded +=  DICTIONARY[(num %  base)];
13                      num = Math .floor(num /  base);
14          }
15
16              return  reverseWord(encoded);
17  }
18
19  function  reverseWord(str) {
20              var  reversed = "" ;
21              for  (var  i =  str.length - 1 ; i >= 0 ; i-- ) {
22                              reversed +=  str.charAt(i);
23          }
24          return  reversed;
25  }
26
27  function  decodeId(id) {
28              var  base = DICTIONARY.length;
29              var  decoded = 0 ;
30
```

```
31              for  (var  index = 0 ; index <  id.split("" ).length;
                index++ ) {
32                      decoded =  decoded * base + DICTIONARY.
                        indexOf(id.charAt(index));
33              }
34
35              return  decoded;
36  }
37
38  console.log(encodeId(11231230 )); // prints 'VhU2'
39  console.log(decodeId('VhU2' )); // prints '11231230'
```

# Encryption

Encryption is extremely important when protecting people's information online. Have you ever seen the warning in Figure 4-3 in the Google Chrome browser?

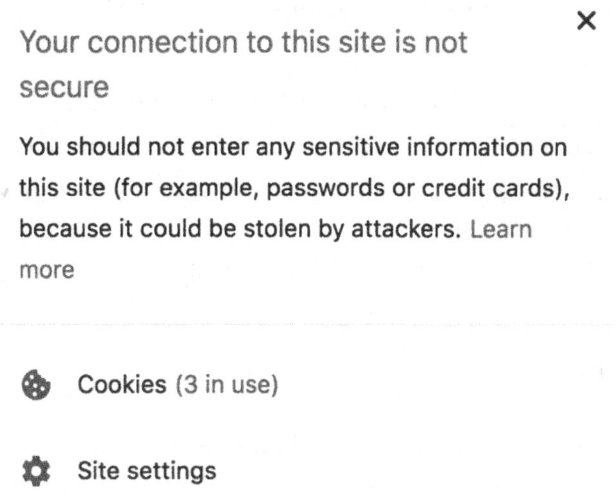

*Figure 4-3.* SSL warning

This likely means the web site you are trying to access does not have the proper Secure Sockets Layer (SSL) certificate.

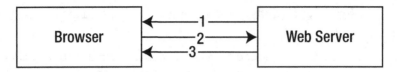

**Figure 4-4.** *TSL process*

TSL is a standard security technology for establishing an encrypted link between the server and the client (browser). The following are the simplified steps of the TSL process. In this process, asymmetric encryption is used for different keys for encryption and decryption by the server. The browser only uses symmetric encryption, which uses a single key to both encrypt and decrypt the data.

1.  The server sends its asymmetric public key to the browser.

2.  The browser creates a symmetric key for the current session, which is encrypted by the server's asymmetric public key.

3.  The server decrypts the browser's session via its private key and retrieves the session key.

4.  Both systems have the session key and will use this to transmit data securely.

This is secure because only the browser and the server know the session key. If the browser was to connect to the same server the next day, a new session key would be created.

The SSL warning message is a sign that the browser and server may not be encrypting the data on that connection.

The most commonly used public-key encryption algorithm is the RSA algorithm.

## RSA Encryption

RSA is an encryption algorithm based on the difficulty of factoring large integers. In RSA, two large prime numbers and a supplementary value are generated as the public key. Anyone can use the public key to encrypt a message, but only those with the prime factors can decode the message.

There are three phases in the process: key generation, encryption, and decryption.

Key generation: The public key (shared) and private key (kept secret) are generated. The construction method of the keys generated should be also secret.

Encryption: The secret message can be encrypted via the public key.

Decryption: Only the private key can be used to decrypt the message.

Here's an overview of the algorithm:

1. Select two (usually large) prime numbers, *p* and *q*.

    a. The product of *p* and *q* is denoted as *n*.

    b. The product of (*p*-1) and (*q*-1) is denoted as *phi*.

2. Choose two exponents, *e* and *d*.

    a. *e* is typically 3. Other values greater than 2 can be used.

    b. *d* is a value such that (e × d) % phi = 1.

```
Encryption process is as shown:
        m - message:
        m^e % n = c
        c - encrypted message
```

```
Decryption process is as shown:
        c^d % n = m
```

This is the implementation of calculating *d*:

```
1  function modInverse(e, phi) {
2      var m0 = phi, t, q;
3      var x0 = 0, x1 = 1;
4
5      if (phi == 1)
6          return 0;
7
8      while (e > 1) {
9          // q is quotient
10         q = Math.floor(e / phi);
11
12         t = phi;
13
```

```
14              // phi is remainder now, process same as
15              // Euclid's algo
16              phi = e % phi, e = t;
17
18              t = x0;
19
20              x0 = x1 - q * x0;
21
22              x1 = t;
23          }
24
25      // Make x1 positive
26      if (x1 < 0)
27          x1 += m0;
28
29      return x1;
30  }
31  modInverse(7,40); // 23
```

Key pairs of a public key and a private key also need to be generated.

```
1   function RSAKeyPair(p, q) {
2               // Need to check that they are primes
3               if (! (isPrime(p) && isPrime(q)))
4                       return;
5
6               // Need to check that they're not the same
7               if (p==q)
8                       return;
9
10      var n = p * q,
11              phi = (p-1)*(q-1),
12              e = 3,
13              d = modInverse(e,phi);
14
```

```
15          // Public key: [e,n], Private key: [d,n]
16          return [[e,n], [d,n]]
17  }
```

Let's pick 5 and 11 as the primes and see an example where message is 50.

```
1  RSAKeyPair(5,11); //Public key: [3,55], Private key: [27,55]
```

```
p = 5, 11
n = p x q = 55
phi = (5-1) x (11-1) = 4 x 10 = 40
e = 3
(e x d) % phi = 1 (3 x d) % 40 = 1
(81) % 40 = 1. 81 = 3 x d = 3 x 27
d = 27
```

```
Encryption:
        m - message: 50
        m^e % n = c
        50^3 % 55 = 40
```

```
Encrypted message.,c:
        40
Decryption:
c^d % n = m
40^27 % 55 = 50
```

This fully encrypts 50, and the receiver can decrypt that back to 50. Typically the prime numbers chosen are very large for the RSA algorithm. This is because the prime factorization of large numbers takes a long time to compute. Today's standard is to use a 4,096-bit prime product. Computing its prime factors would take years even for advanced computers to compute. Figure 4-5 shows the largest possible value for a 4,096-bit number.

1 044 388 881 413 152 506 691 752 710 716 624 382 579 964 249 047 383 780 ⋱
384 233 483 283 953 907 971 557 456 848 826 811 934 997 558 340 890 106 ⋱
714 439 262 837 987 573 438 185 793 607 263 236 087 851 365 277 945 956 ⋱
976 543 709 998 340 361 590 134 383 718 314 428 070 011 855 946 226 376 ⋱
318 839 397 712 745 672 334 684 344 586 617 496 807 908 705 803 704 071 ⋱
284 048 740 118 609 114 467 977 783 598 029 006 686 938 976 881 787 785 ⋱
946 905 630 190 260 940 599 579 453 432 823 469 303 026 696 443 059 025 ⋱
015 972 399 867 714 215 541 693 835 559 885 291 486 318 237 914 434 496 ⋱
734 087 811 872 639 496 475 100 189 041 349 008 417 061 675 093 668 333 ⋱
850 551 032 972 088 269 550 769 983 616 369 411 933 015 213 796 825 837 ⋱
188 091 833 656 751 221 318 492 846 368 125 550 225 998 300 412 344 784 ⋱
862 595 674 492 194 617 023 806 505 913 245 610 825 731 835 380 087 608 ⋱
622 102 834 270 197 698 202 313 169 017 678 006 675 195 485 079 921 636 ⋱
419 370 285 375 124 784 014 907 159 135 459 982 790 513 399 611 551 794 ⋱
271 106 831 134 090 584 272 884 279 791 554 849 782 954 323 534 517 065 ⋱
223 269 061 394 905 987 693 002 122 963 395 687 782 878 948 440 616 007 ⋱
412 945 674 919 823 050 571 642 377 154 816 321 380 631 045 902 916 136 ⋱
926 708 342 856 440 730 447 899 971 901 781 465 763 473 223 850 267 253 ⋱
059 899 795 996 090 799 469 201 774 624 817 718 449 867 455 659 250 178 ⋱
329 070 473 119 433 165 550 807 568 221 846 571 746 373 296 884 912 819 ⋱
520 317 457 002 440 926 616 910 874 148 385 078 411 929 804 522 981 857 ⋱
338 977 648 103 126 085 903 001 302 413 467 189 726 673 216 491 511 131 ⋱
602 920 781 738 033 436 090 243 804 708 340 403 154 190 336

*Figure 4-5.* $2^{4096}$

# Summary

Various natively implemented string functions were covered in this chapter and are summarized in Table 4-1.

**Table 4-1.**  *String Function Summary*

| Function | Usage |
| --- | --- |
| charAt(index) | Accesses a single character at index |
| substring(startIndex, endIndex) | Accesses part of string from startIndex to endIndex |
| str1 > str2 | Returns true if str1 is lexicographically bigger than str2 |
| indexOf(str, startIndex) | Index of the desired str starting at startIndex |
| str.split(delimiter) | Breaks a string into an array with the specified delimiter |
| str.replace(original,new) | Replaces original with new |

In addition, a JavaScript native Regex object can be used for commonly used string validation. Table 4-2 provides a summary.

**Table 4-2.**  *Regex Summary*

| Regex Pattern | Usage |
| --- | --- |
| /\d+/ | Any numeric characters |
| /^\d+$/ | Only numeric characters |
| /^[0-9]*.[0-9]*[1-9]+$/ | Float numeric characters |
| /[a-zA-Z0-9]/ | Only alphanumeric characters |

# CHAPTER 5

# JavaScript Arrays

This chapter will focus on working with JavaScript arrays. As a JavaScript developer, you will use the array often; it is the most commonly used data structure. Arrays in JavaScript come with a lot of built-in methods. In fact, there are various ways to do the same type of array operations for each use case. By the end of this chapter, you will understand how to work with arrays and be able to choose the right method for the situation.

## Introducing Arrays

Arrays are one of the most fundamental data structures. If you have ever programmed before, you've most likely used an array.

```
1   var array1 = [1,2,3,4];
```

For any data structure, developers are interested in time and space complexity associated with the four fundamental operations: access, insertion, deletion, and search. (For a review of Big-O notations, please refer to Chapter 1.)

## Insertion

Insertion means adding a new element inside a data structure. JavaScript implements array insertion with the .push(element) method. This method adds a new element at the end of the array.

```
1   var array1 = [1,2,3,4];
2   array1.push(5); //array1 = [1,2,3,4,5]
3   array1.push(7); //array1 = [1,2,3,4,5,7]
4   array1.push(2); //array1 = [1,2,3,4,5,7,2]
```

© Sammie Bae 2019

S. Bae, *JavaScript Data Structures and Algorithms*, https://doi.org/10.1007/978-1-4842-3988-9_5

The time complexity of this operation is O(1) in theory. It should be noted that, practically, this depends on the JavaScript engine that runs the code. This applies to all natively supported JavaScript objects.

## Deletion

JavaScript implements array deletion with the .pop() method. This method removes the last-added element of the array. This also returns the removed element.

```
1   var array1 = [1,2,3,4];
2   array1.pop(); //returns 4, array1 = [1,2,3]
3   array1.pop(); //returns 3, array1 = [1,2]
```

The time complexity of .pop is O(1) similarly to .push.

Another way to remove an element from an array is with the .shift() method. This method will remove the first element and return it.

```
1   array1 = [1,2,3,4];
2   array1.shift(); //returns 1, array1 = [2,3,4]
3   array1.shift(); //returns 2, array1 = [3,4]
```

## Access

Accessing an array at a specified index only takes O(1) because this process uses that index to get the value directly from the address in memory. It is done by specifying the index (remember that indexing starts at 0).

```
1   var array1 = [1,2,3,4];
2   array1[0]; //returns 1
3   array1[1]; //returns 2
```

## Iteration

Iteration is the process of accessing each of the items contained within a data structure. There are multiple ways to iterate through an array in JavaScript. They all have a time complexity of O($n$) since the iteration is visiting $n$ number of elements.

# for (Variables; Condition; Modification)

for is the most common method of iteration. It is most often used in this form:

```
1  for ( var i=0, len=array1.length; i<len; i++ ) {
2      console.log(array1[i]);
3  }
```

The previous code simply means initialize the variable i, check whether the condition is false before executing the body (i<len), and then modify (i++) until the condition is false. Similarly, you can use a while loop. However, the counter will have to be set outside.

```
1  var counter=0;
2  while(counter<array1.length){
3      // insert code here
4      counter++;
5  }
```

You can implement an infinite loop using a while loop, as shown here:

```
1  while(true){
2      if (breakCondition) {
3          break;
4      }
5  }
```

Similarly, a for loop can implement an infinite loop by not setting a condition, as shown here:

```
1  for ( ; ;) {
2      if (breakCondition) {
3          break
4      }
5  }
```

# for ( in )

Another way to iterate a JavaScript array is to call the indices one by one. The variable specified before in is the index of the array, as follows:

```
1    var array1 = ['all','cows','are','big'];
2
3    for (var index in array1) {
4        console.log(index);
5    }
```

This prints the following: 0,1,2,3.
To print the content, use this:

```
1    for (var index in array1) {
2        console.log(array1[index]);
3    }
```

This prints all, cows, are, and big.

# for ( of )

The variable specified before of is the element (the value) of the array, as follows:

```
1    for (var element of array1) {
2        console.log(element);
3    }
```

This prints out all, cows, are, and big.

# forEach()

The big difference between forEach and other methods of iteration is that forEach cannot break out of the iteration or skip certain elements in the array. forEach is more expressive and explicit by going through each element.

```
1  var array1 = ['all','cows','are','big'];
2
3  array1.forEach( function (element, index){
4      console.log(element);
5  });
6
7  array1.forEach( function (element, index){
8      console.log(array1[index]);
9  });
```

Both print all, cows, are, and big.

# Helper Functions

The following sections discuss other commonly used helper functions for processing. In addition, working with arrays will be covered.

## .slice(begin,end)

This helper function returns a portion of an existing array without modifying the array. .slice() takes two parameters: the beginning index and the ending index of the array.

```
1  var array1 = [1,2,3,4];
2  array1.slice(1,2); //returns [2], array1 = [1,2,3,4]
3  array1.slice(2,4); //returns [3,4], array1 = [1,2,3,4]
```

If only the beginning index is passed, the ending will be assumed to be the maximum index.

```
1  array1.slice(1); //returns [2,3,4], array1 = [1,2,3,4]
2  array1.slice(1,4); //returns [2,3,4], array1 = [1,2,3,4]
```

If nothing is passed, this function simply returns a copy of the array. It should be noted that array1.slice() === array1 evaluates to false. This is because although the contents of the arrays are the same, the memory addresses at which those arrays reside are different.

```
1  array1.slice(); //returns [1,2,3,4], array1 = [1,2,3,4]
```

This is useful for copying an array in JavaScript. Remember that arrays in JavaScript are reference-based, meaning that if you assign a new variable to an array, changes to that variable apply to the original array.

```
1   var array1 = [1,2,3,4],
2         array2 = array1;
3
4   array1 // [1,2,3,4]
5   array2 // [1,2,3,4]
6
7   array2[0] = 5;
8
9   array1 // [5,2,3,4]
10  array2 // [5,2,3,4]
```

The changing element of `array2` changed the original array by accident because it is a reference to the original array. To create a new array, you can use `.from()`.

```
1   var array1 = [1,2,3,4];
2   var array2 = Array.from(array1);
3
4   array1 // [1,2,3,4]
5   array2 // [1,2,3,4]
6
7   array2[0] = 5;
8
9   array1 // [1,2,3,4]
10  array2 // [5,2,3,4]
```

`.from()` takes $O(n)$, where $n$ is the size of the array. This is intuitive because copying the array requires copying all $n$ elements of the array.

# .splice(begin,size,element1,element2…)

This helper function returns and changes the contents of an array by removing existing elements and/or adding new elements.

.splice() takes three parameters: the beginning index, the size of things to be removed, and the new elements to add. New elements are added at the position specified by the first parameter. It returns the removed elements.

```
1  var array1 = [1,2,3,4];
2  array1.splice(); //returns [], array1 = [1,2,3,4]
3  array1.splice(1,2); //returns [2,3], array1 = [1,4]
```

This example demonstrates removal. [2,3] was returned because it selected two items starting from an index of 1.

```
1  var array1 = [1,2,3,4];
2  array1.splice(); //returns [], array1 = [1,2,3,4]
3  array1.splice(1,2,5,6,7); //returns [2,3],array1 = [1,5,6,7,4]
```

Anything (any object type) can be added to the array. This is the beauty (and odd part) of JavaScript.

```
1  var array1 = [1,2,3,4];
2  array1.splice(1,2,[5,6,7]); //returns [2,3], array1 = [1,[5,6,7],4]
3  array1 = [1,2,3,4];
4  array1.splice(1,2,{'ss':1}); //returns [2,3], array1 = [1,{'ss':1},4]
```

.splice() is, worst case, $O(n)$. Similarly to copying, if the range specified is the whole array, each $n$ item has to be removed.

## .concat()

This adds new elements to the array at the end of the array and returns the array.

```
1  var array1 = [1,2,3,4];
2  array1.concat(); //returns [1,2,3,4], array1 = [1,2,3,4]
3  array1.concat([2,3,4]); //returns [1,2,3,4,2,3,4],array1 = [1,2,3,4]
```

## .length Property

The .length property returns the size of the array. Changing this property to a lower size can delete elements from the array.

```
1  var array1 = [1,2,3,4];
2  console.log(array1.length); //prints 4
3  array1.length = 3; // array1 = [1,2,3]
```

## Spread Operator

The spread operator, denoted by three periods (...), is used to expand arguments where zero arguments are expected.

```
1  function addFourNums(a, b, c, d) {
2      return a + b + c + d;
3  }
4  var numbers = [1, 2, 3, 4];
5  console.log(addFourNums(...numbers)); // 10
```

Both the Math.max and Math.min functions take an unlimited number of parameters, so you can use the spread operator for the following operations.

To find the maximum in an array, use this:

```
1  var array1 = [1,2,3,4,5];
2  Math.max(array1); // 5
```

To find the minimum in an array, use this:

```
1  var array2 = [3,2,-123,2132,12];
2  Math.min(array2); // -123
```

## Exercises

All the code for the exercises can be found on GitHub.[1]

---

### FIND TWO ARRAY ELEMENTS IN AN ARRAY THAT ADD UP TO A NUMBER

Problem: Given the array arr, find and return two indices of the array that add up to weight or return -1 if there is no combination that adds up to weight.

---

[1]https://github.com/Apress/js-data-structures-and-algorithms

For example, in an array like [1,2,3,4,5], what numbers add up to 9?

The answers are 4 and 5, of course.

The simple solution is to try every combination by having two for loops, as shown here:

```
1    function findSum(arr, weight) {
2        for (var i=0,arrLength=arr.length; i<arrLength; i++){
3            for (var j=i+1; j<arrLength; j++) {
4                if (arr[i]+arr[j]==weight){
5                    return [i,j];
6                }
7            }
8        }
9        return -1;
10   }
```

This solution iterates through an array looking to see whether a matching pair exists.

Two for loops over $n$ elements of the array yields a high time complexity. However, no extra memory was created. Similar to how time complexity describes the time required relative to input size, $n$, to finish the algorithm, the space complexity describes the additional memory needed for implementation. The space complexity, O(1), is constant.

**Time Complexity:** $O(n^2)$

**Space Complexity:** O(1)

Let's think about how to do this in linear time of O($n$).

What if any previously seen array elements were stored and could be checked easily?

Here's the input:

```
1    var arr = [1,2,3,4,5];
2    var weight = 9;
```

Here, 4 and 5 are the combination, and their indices are [3,4]. How could it be determined that a solution exists when 5 is visited?

If the current value is at 5 and the weight is 9, the remaining required weight is just 4 (9-5=4). Since 4 is shown before 5 in the array, this solution can work in O($n$). Finally, to store the seen elements, use a JavaScript object as a hash table. The implementation and use of a hash table will be discussed in later chapters. Storing into and retrieving a JavaScript object property is O(1) in time.

```
1    function findSumBetter(arr, weight) {
2        var hashtable = {};
3
4        for (var i=0, arrLength=arr.length; i<arrLength; i++) {
5            var currentElement = arr[i],
6                difference = weight - currentElement;
7
8            // check the right one already exists
9            if (hashtable[currentElement] != undefined) {
10                return [i, hashtable[weight-currentElement]];
11            } else {
12                // store index
13                hashtable[difference] = i;
14            }
15        }
16        return -1;
17   }
```

**Time Complexity:** O(*n*)

**Space Complexity:** O(*n*)

Storing into a hash table and looking an item up from a hash table is only O(1). Space complexity has increased to O(*n*) to store the visited array indices inside the hash table.

---

## IMPLEMENT THE ARRAY.SLICE() FUNCTION FROM SCRATCH

Let's review what the .slice() function does.

.slice() takes two parameters: the beginning index and the last ending index of the array. It returns a portion of an existing array without modifying the array function arraySlice (array, beginIndex, endIndex).

```
1 function arraySlice(array, beginIndex, endIndex) {
2 // If no parameters passed, return the array
3    if (! beginIndex && ! endIndex) {
4        return array;
5    }
6
```

```
7 // If only beginning index is found, set endIndex to size
8  endIndex =  array.length;
9
10 var  partArray =  [];
11
12 // If both begin and end index specified return the part of the array
13 for  (var  i =  beginIndex; i <  endIndex; i++ ) {
14    partArray.push(array[i]);
15  }
16
17          return  partArray;
18  }
19  arraySlice([1 , 2 , 3 , 4 ], 1 , 2 ); // [2]
20  arraySlice([1 , 2 , 3 , 4 ], 2 , 4 ); // [3,4]
```

**Time Complexity:** $O(n)$

**Space Complexity:** $O(n)$

The time complexity is $O(n)$ because all n items in the array must be accessed. Space complexity is also $O(n)$ to hold all $n$ items when copying the array.

---

## FIND THE MEDIAN OF TWO SORTED ARRAYS OF THE SAME SIZE

Recall that *median* in an even number of a set is the average of the two middle numbers. If the array is sorted, this is simple.

Here's an example:

[1,2,3,4] has the median of (2+3)/2 = 2.5.

```
1    function medianOfArray(array) {
2        var length = array.length;
3        // Odd
4        if (length % 2 == 1) {
5            return array[Math.floor(length/2)];
6        } else {
7        // Even
8            return (array[length/2]+array[length/2 - 1])/2;
```

```
 9        }
10    }
```

Now, you can iterate through both of the arrays and compare which is bigger to track the median. If the two arrays are the same size, the total size will be an even number.

This is because both two even numbers and two odd numbers add up to an even number. Please refer to Chapter 8 for more background.

Since both of the arrays are sorted, this function can be recursively called. Each time, it checks which median is greater.

If the second array's median is greater, the first array is cut in half, and only the higher half is passed recursively.

If the first array's median is greater, the second array is cut in half, and only the higher half is passed in as the first array for the next function call because the array2 parameter in the function must always be bigger than the array1 parameter. Finally, the size of the array represented as pos is required to check whether the size of the array is even or odd.

Here's another example:

array1 = [1,2,3] and array2 = [4, 5, 6]

Here, the median of array1 is 2, and the median of array2 is 5. So, the median must be present within [2,3] and [4,5]. Since there are only four elements left, the median can be computed as follows:

max(arr1[0], arr2[0]) + min(arr1[1], arr2[1]) / 2;

```
 1 function  medianOfArray(array) {
 2     var  length =  array.length;
 3     // Odd
 4     if  (length % 2 == 1 ) {
 5         return  array[Math .floor(length / 2 )];
 6     } else  {
 7     // Even
 8         return  (array[length / 2 ] +  array[length / 2 - 1 ]) / 2 ;
 9     }
10  }
11 // arr2 is the bigger array
12 function  medianOfTwoSortedArray(arr1, arr2, pos) {
```

```
13    if  (pos <= 0 ) {
14        return -1 ;
15    }
16    if  (pos == 1 ) {
17        return  (arr1[0] +  arr2[0]) / 2 ;
18    }
19    if  (pos == 2 ) {
20        return  (Math .max(arr1[0], arr2[0]) + Math .min(arr1[1],
          arr2[1])) / 2 ;
21    }
22
23    var  median1 =  medianOfArray(arr1),
24        median2 =  medianOfArray(arr2);
25
26    if  (median1 ==  median2) {
27        return  median1;
28    }
29
30    var  evenOffset =  pos % 2 == 0 ? 1 : 0 ,
31        offsetMinus = Math .floor(pos / 2 ) -  evenOffset,
32        offsetPlus = Math .floor(pos / 2 ) +  evenOffset;
33
34
35    if  (median1 <  median2) {
36        return  medianOfTwoSortedArray(arr1.slice(offsetMinus), arr2.
          slice(offsetMinus), offsetPlus);
37    } else  {
38        return  medianOfTwoSortedArray(arr2.slice(offsetMinus), arr1.
          slice(offsetMinus), offsetPlus);
39    }
40  }
41
42  medianOfTwoSortedArray([1 , 2 , 3 ], [4 , 5 , 6 ], 3 ); // 3.5
43  medianOfTwoSortedArray([11 , 23 , 24 ], [32 , 33 , 450 ], 3 ); // 28
44  medianOfTwoSortedArray([1 , 2 , 3 ], [2 , 3 , 5 ], 3 ); // 2.5
```

**Time Complexity:** $O(log_2(n))$

By cutting the array size by half each time, logarithmic time complexity is achieved.

## FIND COMMON ELEMENTS IN K-SORTED ARRAYS

```
1    var arr1    = [1, 5, 5, 10];
2    var arr2    = [3, 4, 5, 5, 10];
3    var arr3    = [5, 5, 10, 20];
4    var output  = [5 ,10];
```

In this example with three arrays, $k=3$.

To do this, simply iterate over each array and count instances of every element. However, do not track repeated ones (5 and 5.5 should be counted once in one array iteration). To do this, check whether the last element is the same before incrementing. This will work only if it is sorted.

After all three arrays have been iterated, iterate through the hash table's properties. If the value matches 3, it means that the number showed up in all three arrays. This can be generalized to $k$ number of arrays by putting the $k$-loop check into another `for` loop.

```
 1 function commonElements(kArray) {
 2     var hashmap = {},
 3        last, answer = [];
 4
 5     for (var i = 0 , kArrayLength = kArray.length; i < kArrayLength;
       i++ ) {
 6         var currentArray = kArray[i];
 7            last = null ;
 8         for (var j = 0 , currentArrayLen = currentArray.length;
 9              j < currentArrayLen;  j++ ) {
10            var currentElement = currentArray[j];
11            if (last != currentElement) {
12                if (! hashmap[currentElement]) {
13                    hashmap[currentElement] = 1 ;
14                } else {
15            hashmap[currentElement]++ ;
16                }
17            }
18        last = currentElement;
19        }
20     }
21
```

```
22      // Iterate through hashmap
23      for (var prop in hashmap) {
24          if (hashmap[prop] == kArray.length) {
25              answer.push(parseInt (prop));
26          }
27      }
28      return answer;
29  }
30
31  commonElements([[1 ,2 ,3 ],[1 ,2 ,3 ,4 ],[1 ,2 ]]); // [ 1, 2 ]
```

**Time Complexity:** O(*kn*)

**Space Complexity:** O(*n*)

Here, *n* is longest array length, and *k* is the number of arrays.

# JavaScript Functional Array Methods

Some parts of JavaScript can be written just like a functional programming language. Unlike imperative programming, JavaScript does not focus on the state of the program. It does not use loops, only function (method) calls. You can learn more about functional programming in JavaScript from *Beginning Functional JavaScript* by Anto Aravinth (Apress, 2017).

In this section, only three functional array methods in JavaScript will be explored: map, filter, and reduce. These methods do not change the original array contents.

## Map

The map function applies passed function transformation to every element in the array and returns a new array with those transformations applied.

For example, you can multiply every element by 10, as shown here:

```
1  [1,2,3,4,5,6,7].map(function (value){
2      return value*10;
3  });
4  // [10, 20, 30, 40, 50, 60, 70]
```

## Filter

The `filter` function returns only those elements of the array that meet a passed condition parameter. Again, this does not change the original array.

For example, this filters elements greater than 100:

```
1   [100,2003,10,203,333,12].filter(function (value){
2       return value > 100;
3   });
4   // [2003, 203, 333]
```

## Reduce

The `reduce` function combines all the elements in the array into one value using a passed transformation function parameter.

For example, this adds all the elements:

```
1   var sum = [0,1,2,3,4].reduce( function (prevVal, currentVal, index,
    array) {
2       return prevVal + currentVal;
3   });
4   console.log(sum); // prints 10
```

This function also can take `initialValue` as its second argument, which initializes the reduce value. For example, providing an `initialValue` of 1 in the previous example will yield 11, as shown here:

```
1   var sum = [0,1,2,3,4].reduce( function (prevVal, currentVal, index,
    array) {
2       return prevVal + currentVal;
3   }, 1);
4   console.log(sum); // prints 11
```

## Multidimensional Arrays

Unlike Java and C++, JavaScript does not have multidimensional arrays (see Figure 5-1).

Column

| 0,0 | 0,1 | 0,2 | 0,3 |
|-----|-----|-----|-----|
| 1,0 | 1,1 | 1,2 | 1,3 |
| 2,0 | 2,1 | 2,2 | 2,3 |
| 3,0 | 3,1 | 3,2 | 3,3 |

Row

***Figure 5-1.*** *Multidimensional array*

Instead, there are "jagged" arrays. A *jagged array* is an array whose elements are arrays. The elements of a jagged array can be of different dimensions and sizes (see Figure 5-2).

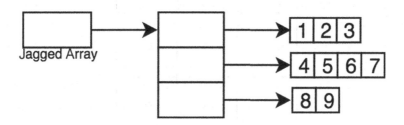

***Figure 5-2.*** *Jagged array*

Here is a helper function to create a jagged array like the one in Figure 5-3:

```
1    function Matrix(rows, columns) {
2        var jaggedarray = new Array(rows);
3        for (var i=0; i < columns; i +=1) {
4            jaggedarray[i]=new Array(rows);
5        }
6        return jaggedarray;
7    }
8    console.log(Matrix(3,3));
```

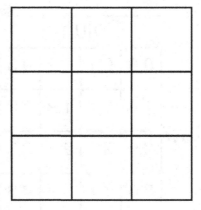

**Figure 5-3.**  *Three-by-three matrix*

To access elements in a jagged array, specify a row and a column (see Figure 5-4).

| 1 | 2 | 3 |
|---|---|---|
| 4 | 5 | 6 |
| 7 | 8 | 9 |

**Figure 5-4.**  *Three-by-three matrix of numbers*

```
1   var matrix3by3 = [[1,2,3],[4,5,6],[7,8,9]];
2   matrix3by3[0]; // [1,2,3]
3   matrix3by3[1]; // [4,5,6]
4   matrix3by3[1]; // [7,8,9]
5
6   matrix3by3[0][0]; // 1
7   matrix3by3[0][1]; // 2
8   matrix3by3[0][2]; // 3
9
10  matrix3by3[1][0]; // 4
11  matrix3by3[1][1]; // 5
```

```
12    matrix3by3[1][2]; // 6
13
14    matrix3by3[2][0]; // 7
15    matrix3by3[2][1]; // 8
16    matrix3by3[2][2]; // 9
```

# Exercises

All the code for the exercises can be found on GitHub.[2]

---

**SPIRAL PRINT**

Let's create an example problem with a matrix. Given a matrix, print the elements in a spiral order, like in Figure 5-5.

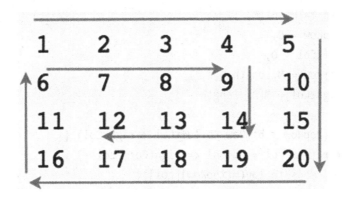

*Figure 5-5.* *Spiral print*

This looks like a daunting task at first. However, the problem can be broken down to five main components.

- Printing from left to right

- Printing from top to bottom

- Printing from right to left

- Printing from bottom to top

- Keeping a limit on these four operations

---

[2]https://github.com/Apress/js-data-structures-and-algorithms

In other words, keep four key variables that indicate the following:

- Top row

- Bottom row

- Left column

- Right column

Each time one of the four `print` functions is successfully executed, simply increment one of the four variables. For example, after printing the top row, increment it by 1.

```
1    var M = [
2        [1, 2, 3, 4, 5],
3        [6, 7, 8, 9, 10],
4        [11, 12, 13, 14, 15],
5        [16, 17, 18, 19, 20]
6    ];
7    function spiralPrint(M) {
8        var topRow = 0,
9            leftCol = 0,
10           btmRow = M.length - 1,
11           rightCol = M[0].length - 1;
12
13       while (topRow < btmRow && leftCol < rightCol) {
14           for (var col = 0; col <= rightCol; col++) {
15               console.log(M[topRow][col]);
16           }
17           topRow++;
18           for (var row = topRow; row <= btmRow; row++) {
19               console.log(M[row][rightCol]);
20           }
21           rightCol--;
22           if (topRow <= btmRow) {
23               for (var col = rightCol; col >= 0; col--) {
24                   console.log(M[btmRow][col]);
25               }
26               btmRow--;
27           }
28           if (leftCol <= rightCol) {
```

```
29                    for (var row = btmRow; row > topRow; row--) {
30                            console.log(M[row][leftCol]);
31                    }
32                    leftCol++;
33                }
34            }
35    }
36    spiralPrint(M);
```

**Time Complexity:** 0(*mn*)

**Space Complexity:** 0(1)

Here, *m* is the number of rows, and *n* is the number of columns. Each item in the matrix is visited only once.

---

## TIC-TAC-TOE CHECK

Given a matrix representing a tic-tac-toe board, determine whether someone won, whether it was a tie, or whether the game has not ended yet.[3]

Here are some examples.

Here, X won:

```
OX-
-XO
OX
```

Here it is as a matrix: [['O', 'X', '-'], ['-' ,'X', 'O'], ['O', 'X', '-']].

Here, O won:

```
O-X
-O-
-XO
```

Here it is as a matrix: [['O','-','X'], ['-','O','-'], ['-','X','O']].

To do this, check all three rows using a for loop, check all columns using a for loop, and check diagonals.

---

[3]To read more about the rules of tic-tac-toe, visit https://en.wikipedia.org/wiki/Tic-tac-toe.

```
1    function checkRow ( rowArr, letter ) {
2        for ( var i=0; i < 3; i++) {
3            if (rowArr[i]!=letter) {
4                return false;
5            }
6        }
7        return true;
8    }
9
10   function checkColumn ( gameBoardMatrix, columnIndex, letter ) {
11       for ( var i=0; i < 3; i++) {
12           if (gameBoardMatrix[i][columnIndex]!=letter) {
13               return false;
14           }
15       }
16       return true;
17   }
18
19   function ticTacToeWinner ( gameBoardMatrix, letter) {
20
21       // Check rows
22       var rowWin = checkRow(gameBoardMatrix[0], letter)
23       || checkRow(gameBoardMatrix[1], letter)
24       || checkRow(gameBoardMatrix[2], letter);
25
26       var colWin = checkColumn(gameBoardMatrix, 0, letter)
27       || checkColumn(gameBoardMatrix, 1, letter)
28       || checkColumn(gameBoardMatrix, 2, letter);
29
30       var diagonalWinLeftToRight = (gameBoardMatrix[0][0]==letter &&
         gameBoardMatrix[1][1]==letter && gameBoardMatrix[2][2]==letter);
31       var diagonalWinRightToLeft = (gameBoardMatrix[0][2]==letter &&
         gameBoardMatr ix[1][1]==letter && gameBoardMatrix[2][0]==letter);
32
33       return rowWin || colWin || diagonalWinLeftToRight ||
         diagonalWinRightToLeft;
34   }
35
```

```
36    var board = [['O','-','X'],['-','O','-'],['-','X','O']];
37    ticTacToeWinner(board, 'X'); // false
38    ticTacToeWinner(board, 'O'); // true
```

## PATH FINDING

In Figure 5-6, given the location x, find the exit e.

```
%e%%%%%%%%
%...%.%...%
%.%.%.%.%%%
%.%.......%
%.%%%%.%%.%
%.%.....%.%
%%%%%%%%x%
```

**Figure 5-6.** *Finding a path*

\n is the set of characters used to break a line in JavaScript, like in many standard programming languages. Combining it with backticks, you can create line breaks during the variable-to-string assignment.

```
1    var board =
2    `%e%%%%%%%%\n
3    %...%.%...%\n
4    %.%.%.%.%%%\n
5    %.%.......%\n
6    %.%%%%.%%.%\n
7    %.%.....%.%\n
8    %%%%%%%%x%`;
```

**var** rows = board.split("\n")

Then use .map over the array to divide by certain characters into each column.

```
function generateColumnArr (arr) {
    return arr.split("");
}
var mazeMatrix = rows.map(generateColumnArr);
```

This will generate the proper matrix where each row is an array of the characters and the board is the array of those rows.

Now, first find the entrance, *e*, and exit, *x*. This function will return the row position, *i*, and the column position, *j*, of the character to be searched for:

```
1 function findChar(char , mazeMatrix) {
2                var row = mazeMatrix.length,
3                    column = mazeMatrix[0 ].length;
4
5                for (var i = 0 ; i <  row; i++ ) {
6                        for (var j = 0 ; j < column; j++ ) {
7                                if (mazeMatrix[i][j] ==
                                   char ) {
8                                return [i, j];
9                                }
10                       }
11        }
12 }
```

Of course, there also needs to be a function to print the matrix nicely as a string, as shown here:

```
1 function printMatrix(matrix) {
2                var mazePrintStr = "" ,
3                    row = matrix.length,
4                    column = matrix[0 ].length;
5
6                for (var i = 0 ; i < row; i++ ) {
7
8                        for (var j = 0 ; j < column; j++ ) {
9                                mazePrintStr += mazeMatrix[i][j];
10                       }
11
12                mazePrintStr += "\n" ;
13
14        }
15        console.log(mazePrintStr);
16 }
```

Finally, define a function called path. This recursively checks up, right, down, and left.

```
        Up:      path(x+1,y)
        Right:   path(x,y+1)
        Down:    path(x-1,y)
        Left:    path(x,y-1)
function mazePathFinder(mazeMatrix) {
    var row = mazeMatrix.length,
        column = mazeMatrix[0].length,
        startPos = findChar('e', mazeMatrix),
        endPos = findChar('x', mazeMatrix);

    path(startPos[0], startPos[1]);

    function path(x, y) {
        if (x > row - 1 || y > column - 1 || x < 0 || y < 0) {
            return false;
        }
        // Found
        if (x == endPos[0] && y == endPos[1]) {
            return true;
        }
        if (mazeMatrix[x][y] == '%' || mazeMatrix[x][y] == '+') {
            return false;
        }
        // Mark the current spot
        mazeMatrix[x][y] = '+';
        printMatrix(mazeMatrix);

        if (path(x, y - 1) || path(x + 1, y) || path(x, y + 1) || path(x - 1, y)) {
            return true;
        }
        mazeMatrix[x][y] = '.';
        return false;
    }
}
```

Figure 5-7 shows the console output.

```
%+%%%%%%%
%...%.%...%
%.%.%.%.%%%
%.%.......%
%.%%%.%%.%
%.%.....%.%
%%%%%%%%x%


%+%%%%%%%
%+..%.%...%
%.%.%.%.%%%
%.%.......%
%.%%%.%%.%
%.%.....%.%
%%%%%%%%x%


...


%+%%%%%%%
%+++%.%...%
%.%+%.%.%%%
%.%+++++++%
%.%%%.%%+%
%.%.....%.%
%%%%%%%%x%


%+%%%%%%%
%+++%.%...%
%.%+%.%.%%%
%.%+++++++%
%.%%%.%%+%
%.%.....%+%
%%%%%%%%x%
```

**Figure 5-7.** *Console output*

**Time Complexity:** $O(mn)$

**Space Complexity:** $O(1)$

Here, $m$ is the row length, and $n$ is the column length. Each element is visited only once.

---

# MATRIX ROTATION

Rotate a matrix to the left by 90 degrees.

For example, the following:

```
101
001
111
```

rotates to this:

```
111
001
101
```

Figure 5-8 shows the rotation.

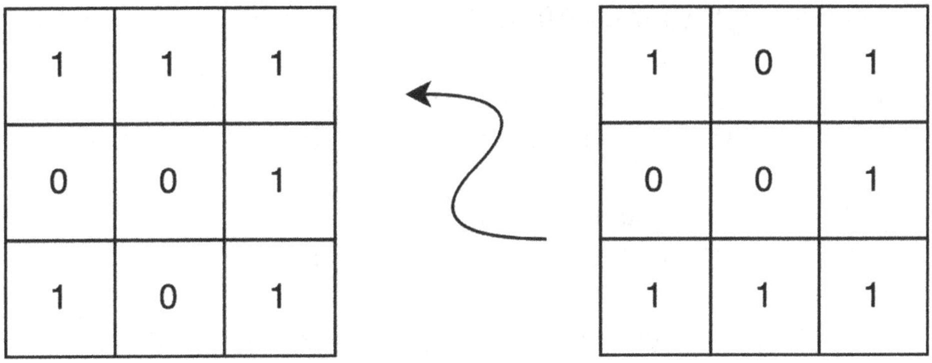

***Figure 5-8.*** *Matrix counterclockwise rotation*

As shown in Figure 5-8, when rotated 90 degrees left, the following happens:

1.  The third column of the matrix becomes the first row of the result.

2.  The second column of the matrix becomes the second row of the result.

3.  The first column of the matrix becomes the third row of the result.

The following rotation turns the third column of the original:

```
1   var matrix = [[1,0,1],[0,0,1],[1,1,1]];
2
3
4   function rotateMatrix90Left (mat){
5       var N = mat.length;
6
7       // Consider all squares one by one
8       for (var x = 0; x < N / 2; x++) {
9           // Consider elements in group of 4 in
10          // current square
11          for (var y = x; y < N-x-1; y++) {
12              // store current cell in temp variable
13              var temp = mat[x][y];
14
15              // move values from right to top
16              mat[x][y] = mat[y][N-1-x];
17
18              // move values from bottom to right
19              mat[y][N-1-x] = mat[N-1-x][N-1-y];
20
21              // move values from left to bottom
22              mat[N-1-x][N-1-y] = mat[N-1-y][x];
23
24              // assign temp to left
25              mat[N-1-y][x] = temp;
26          }
27      }
28  }
29  rotateMatrix90Left(matrix);
30  console.log(matrix); // [[1,1,1],[0,0,1],[1,0,1]]
```

**Time Complexity:** $O(mn)$

**Space Complexity:** $O(1)$

Here, $m$ is the row length, and $n$ is the column length. Each element is visited only once. The space complexity is $O(1)$ because the original array is modified instead of creating a new array.

# Summary

Various natively implemented array functions were covered in this chapter and are summarized in Table 5-1.

*Table 5-1.* *Array Function Summary*

| Function | Usage |
| --- | --- |
| push(element) | Adds an element to the end of the array |
| pop() | Removes the last element of the array |
| shift() | Removes the first element of the array |
| slice(beginIndex, endIndex) | Returns a part of the array from beginIndex to endIndex |
| splice(beginIndex, endIndex) | Returns a part of the array from beginIndex to endIndex and modifies the original array by removing those elements |
| concat(arr) | Adds new elements (from arr) into the array at the end of array |

In addition to the standard while and for loop mechanisms, an iteration of array elements can use the alternative loop mechanisms shown in Table 5-2.

***Table 5-2.*** *Iteration Summary*

| Function | Usage |
| --- | --- |
| for (**var** prop in arr) | Iterates by the index of the array element |
| for (**var** elem of arr) | Iterates by the value of the array element |
| arr.forEach(fnc) | Applies the fnc value on each element |

Finally, recall that JavaScript utilizes jagged arrays, an array of arrays, to get multidimensional array behavior. With two-dimensional arrays, two-dimensional surfaces such as a tic-tac-toe board and maze can easily be represented.

# CHAPTER 6

# JavaScript Objects

JavaScript objects are what makes the JavaScript programming language so versatile. Before diving into data structures and algorithms, let's review how JavaScript objects work. This chapter will focus on what JavaScript objects are, how they are declared, and how their properties can be changed. In addition, this chapter will cover how JavaScript classes are implemented using prototypal inheritance.

## JavaScript Object Property

JavaScript objects can be created via the object literal {} or via the syntax **new** Object();. Additional properties can be added or accessed in one of two ways: object. propertyName or object['propertyName'].

```
1   var javaScriptObject = {};
2   var testArray = [1,2,3,4];
3
4   javaScriptObject.array = testArray;
5   console.log(javaScriptObject); // {array: [1,2,3,4]}
6
7   javaScriptObject.title = 'Algorithms';
8   console.log(javaScriptObject); // {array: [1,2,3,4],
    title:'Algorithms'}
```

As shown in the previous code, the title property was dynamically added in line 7 to the JavaScript object. Similarly, functions in JavaScript classes are added this way by dynamically adding them to the object.

© Sammie Bae 2019
S. Bae, *JavaScript Data Structures and Algorithms*, https://doi.org/10.1007/978-1-4842-3988-9_6

# Prototypal Inheritance

In most strongly typed languages such as Java, the methods of a class are defined at the same time as the class. However, in JavaScript, the function has to be added as a JavaScript Object property of that class.

Here is an example of a class in JavaScript using this.functionName = function(){}:

```
1    function ExampleClass(){
2        this.name = "JavaScript";
3        this.sayName = function(){
4            console.log(this.name);
5        }
6    }
7
8    //new object
9    var example1 = new ExampleClass();
10   example1.sayName(); //"JavaScript"
```

This class dynamically adds the sayName function in the constructor. This pattern is known as *prototypal inheritance.*

Prototypal inheritance is the only method of inheritance in JavaScript. To add functions of a class, simply use the .prototype property and specify the name of function.

When you use the .prototype property, you are essentially dynamically extending the JavaScript Object property of the object. This is the standard because JavaScript is dynamic and classes can add new function members as needed later. This isn't possible for compiled languages such as Java because they will throw an error on compilation. This unique property of JavaScript lets developers take advantage of the prototypical inheritance.

Here's an example of using .prototype:

```
1    function ExampleClass(){
2        this.array = [1,2,3,4,5];
3        this.name = "JavaScript";
4    }
5
```

```
6    //new object
7    var example1 = new ExampleClass();
8
9    ExampleClass.prototype.sayName = function() {
10       console.log(this.name);
11   }
12
13   example1.sayName(); //"JavaScript"
```

To reiterate, adding functions to a class dynamically is how JavaScript implements prototypical inheritance. Functions of a class are added either in the constructor or via .prototype.

# Constructor and Variables

Because variables of a class in JavaScript are properties of that class object, any properties declared with this.propertyName will be available publicly. This means that the object's properties can be directly accessed in other scopes.

```
1    function ExampleClass(name, size){
2        this.name = name;
3        this.size = size;
4    }
5
6    var example = new ExampleClass("Public",5);
7    console.log(example); // {name:"Public", size: 5}
8
9    // accessing public variables
10   console.log(example.name); // "Public"
11   console.log(example.size); // 5
```

To mimic a private variable, instead of using this.propertyName, you can declare a local variable and have getter/setters that allow access to that variable. This way, the variable is available only to the constructor's scope. Notably, however, these mimicked private variables are now accessible only through the defined interfacing functions (getter getName and setter setName). These getters and setters cannot be added outside of the constructor.

```
1    function ExampleClass(name, size) {
2        var privateName = name;
3        var privateSize = size;
4
5        this.getName = function() {return privateName;}
6        this.setName = function(name) {privateName = name;}
7
8        this.getSize = function() {return privateSize;}
9        this.setSize = function(size) {privateSize = size;}
10   }
11
12   var example = new ExampleClass("Sammie",3);
13   example.setSize(12);
14   console.log(example.privateName); // undefined
15   console.log(example.getName()); // "Sammie"
16   console.log(example.size); // undefined
17   console.log(example.getSize()); // 3
```

# Summary

In JavaScript, unlike other object-oriented programming languages, prototypical inheritance is the preferred method of inheritance. Prototypical inheritance works by adding new functions to a JavaScript class via .prototype. Private variables are explicitly declared in Java and C++. However, a private variable is not supported in JavaScript, and to mimic the functionality of a private variable, you need to create a variable that is scoped to the constructor function. Declaring a variable as part of that object in the constructor via this.variableName automatically makes that property public.

# Exercises

## ADDING A PROPERTY TO AN OBJECT

Add an exampleKey property to an empty JavaScript object in two different ways and set it to exampleValue.

As discussed earlier in this chapter, a property can be added to an object in two ways. There is no performance advantage or disadvantage of using one way over the other; the choice comes down to style.

```
1   var emptyJSObj = {};
2   emptyJSObj['exampleKey'] = 'exampleValue';
3   emptyJSObj.exampleKey = 'exampleValue';
```

## DEFINING CLASSES

Create two classes: Animal and Dog. The Animal class should take two parameters in the constructor (name and animalType). Set them as its public properties.

In addition, the Animal class should have two functions: sayName and sayAnimalType. sayName prints name, and sayAnimalType prints animalType initialized in the constructor.

Finally, the Dog class inherits from the Animal class.

1.  Let's first define the Animal class and the specified required functions.

```
1    function Animal(name, animalType) {
2        this.name = name;
3        this.animalType = animalType;
4    }
5    Animal.prototype.sayName = function () {
6        console.log(this.name);
7    }
8    Animal.prototype.sayAnimalType  = function () {
9        console.log(this.animalType);
10   }
```

2.  For the Dog class to inherit this, define the Dog class and then copy its
    prototype, as shown in the following code block:

```
1   function Dog(name) {
2       Animal.call(this, name, "Dog");
3   }
4   // copy over the methods
5   Dog.prototype = Object.create(Animal.prototype);
6   var myAnimal = new Animal("ditto", "pokemon");
7   myAnimal.sayName(); // "ditto"
8   myAnimal.sayAnimalType(); // "pokemon"
9   var myDog = new Dog("candy", "dog");
10  myDog.sayName(); // "candy"
11  myDog.sayAnimalType(); // "dog"
```

# CHAPTER 7

# JavaScript Memory Management

In any program, a variable takes up some memory. In low-level programming languages such as C, the programmer must allocate and deallocate memory manually. In contrast, the V8 JavaScript engine and other modern JavaScript engines have garbage collectors that delete unused variables for the programmer. Despite this memory management done by the JavaScript engine, however, there are common pitfalls that developers can fall into. This chapter will show some basic examples of these pitfalls and present techniques to help the garbage collector minimize the key JavaScript memory problems.

## Memory Leaks

A *memory leak* is a failure in a program to release discarded memory, causing impaired performance and sometimes even failure. Memory leaks can happen when JavaScript engines' garbage collectors do not free memory properly.

Follow the key principles outlined in this chapter to avoid memory leaks during JavaScript development.

## Reference to an Object

If there is a reference to an object, it is in memory. In this example, say that the memory() function returns some array with 5KB of data.

```
1    var foo = {
2        bar1: memory(), // 5kb
3        bar2: memory() // 5kb
4    }
5
```

© Sammie Bae 2019
S. Bae, *JavaScript Data Structures and Algorithms*, https://doi.org/10.1007/978-1-4842-3988-9_7

```
6    function clickEvent(){
7        alert(foo.bar1[0]);
8    }
```

You might expect the clickEvent() function to use 5KB of memory since it is only referencing bar1 from the foo object. However, the truth is that it is using 10KB of memory since it has to load the whole foo object into the function's into scope to access the bar1 property.

## Leaking DOM

If a variable pointing to a DOM element is declared outside of an event callback, then it is in memory and leaks DOM if the element is deleted.

In this example, there are two DOM elements selected by document. getElementByID.

```
1    <div id="one">One</div>
2    <div id="two">Two</div>
```

The following JavaScript code demonstrates the DOM memory leak. When one is clicked, it removes two. When one is clicked again, it still tries to reference the removed two.

```
1    var one = document.getElementById("one");
2    var two = document.getElementById("two");
3    one.addEventListener('click', function(){
4        two.remove();
5        console.log(two); // will print the html even after deletion
6    });
```

The event listener on the one element will cause the two to disappear from the web page when clicked. However, even if the DOM is deleted in the HTML, reference to it will remain if used in an event callback. When the two element is no longer in use, this is a memory leak and should be avoided.

This can easily be fixed so that it won't cause a memory leak, as shown here:

```
1   var one = document.getElementById("one");
2
3   one.addEventListener('click', function(){
4       var two = document.getElementById("two");
5       two.remove();
6   });
```

Another way to address this is by unregistering the click handler once it has been used, as shown here:

```
1   var one = document.getElementById("one");
2       function callBackExample() {
3           var two = document.getElementById("two");
4           two.remove();
5           one.removeEventListener("click",callBackExample);
6       }
7       one.addEventListener("click",callBackExample);
8   });
```

# Global window Object

If an object is on the global window object, it is in memory. The window object is a global object in a browser and comes with various built-in methods such as alert() and setTimeout(). Any additional objects declared as a property of window will not be cleared because window is a required object for the browser to run. Remember that any global variable declared will be set as a property of the window object.

In this example, there are two global variables declared.

```
1   var a = "apples"; //global with var
2   b = "oranges"; //global without var
3
4   console.log(window.a); // prints "apples"
5   console.log(window.b); // prints "oranges"
```

It is good to avoid global variables whenever possible. This will help save memory.

# Limiting Object References

An object is cleared when all references are cleared. Always remember to limit the amount of scope the function pulls and pass the property of an object only into functions instead of the entire object. This is because the object's memory footprint can be very large (e.g., an array of 100,000 integers for data visualization project); if only one of the object's properties is needed, you should avoid using the entire object as a parameter.

For example, *do not* do this:

```
1   var test = {
2         prop1: 'test'
3   }
4
5   function printProp1(test){
6         console.log(test.prop1);
7   }
8
9   printProp1(test); //'test'
```

Instead, pass the property like this:

```
1   var test = {
2         prop1: 'test'
3   }
4
5   function printProp1(prop1){
6         console.log(prop1);
7   }
8
9   printProp1(test.prop1); //'test'
```

# The delete Operator

Always remember that the delete operator can be used to delete an unwanted *object property* (though it does not work on nonobjects).

```
1   var test = {
2         prop1: 'test'
```

```
3    }
4    console.log(test.prop1); // 'test'
5    delete test.prop1;
6    console.log(test.prop1); // _undefined_
```

# Summary

Although memory in JavaScript is not allocated by the programmer, there are still numerous ways to mitigate memory leaks where applicable. If the object is in reference, it is in memory. Similarly, HTML DOM elements should not be referenced once deleted. Finally, only reference objects in a function that are needed. In many cases, it is more applicable to pass in a property of the object rather than the object itself. Also, be extremely mindful when declaring a global variable.

# Exercises

In this chapter, exercises are about identifying memory inefficiencies and optimizing a given piece of code.

---

### ANALYZING AND OPTIMIZING A PROPERTY CALL

Analyze and optimize the call for printProperty.

```
1    function someLargeArray() {
2        return new Array(1000000);
3    }
4    var exampleObject = {
5        'prop1': someLargeArray(),
6        'prop2': someLargeArray()
7    }
8    function printProperty(obj){
9        console.log(obj['prop1']);
10   }
11   printProperty(exampleObject);
```

**Problem:** An excessive amount of memory is used in `printProperty` because the entire object is brought into the `printProperty` function. To fix this, only the property being printed should be brought in as a parameter of the function.

## Answer:

```
1    function someLargeArray() {
2        return new Array(1000000);
3    }
4    var exampleObject = {
5        'prop1': someLargeArray(),
6        'prop2': someLargeArray()
7    }
8    function printProperty(prop){
9        console.log(prop);
10    }
11    printProperty(exampleObject['prop1']);
```

## ANALYZING AND OPTIMIZING SCOPE

Analyze and optimize the global scope for the following code block:

```
1    var RED     = 0,
2        GREEN   = 1,
3        BLUE    = 2;
4
5    function redGreenBlueCount(arr) {
6        var counter = new Array(3) .fill(0);
7        for (var i=0; i < arr.length; i++) {
8            var curr = arr[i];
9            if (curr == RED) {
10                counter[RED]++;
11            } else if (curr == GREEN) {
12                counter[GREEN]++;
13            } else if (curr == BLUE) {
14                counter[BLUE]++;
15            }
```

```
16      }
17      return counter;
18  }
19  redGreenBlueCount([0,1,1,1,2,2,2]); // [1, 3, 3]
```

**Problem:** Global variables are used where not necessary. Albeit small, the global variables RED, GREEN, and BLUE bloat the global scope and should be moved inside the redGreenBlueCount function.

## Answer:

```
1   function redGreenBlueCount(arr) {
2       var RED     = 0,
3           GREEN   = 1,
4           BLUE    = 2,
5           counter = new Array(3) .fill(0);
6       for (var i=0; i < arr.length; i++) {
7           var curr = arr[i];
8           if (curr == RED) {
9               counter[RED]++;
10          } else if (curr == GREEN) {
11              counter[GREEN]++;
12          } else if (curr == BLUE) {
13              counter[BLUE]++;
14          }
15      }
16      return counter;
17  }
18  redGreenBlueCount([0,1,1,1,2,2,2]); // [1, 3, 3]
```

## ANALALYZING AND REPAIRING MEMORY ISSUES

Analyze and fix memory issues for the following code.

**HTML:**

```
<button id="one">Button 1</button>
<button id="two">Button 2</button>
```

**JavaScript:**

```
1   var one = document.querySelector("#one");
2   var two = document.querySelector("#two");
3   function callBackExample () {
4       one.removeEventListener("",callBackExample);
5   }
6   one.addEventListener('hover', function(){
7       two.remove();
8       console.log(two); // will print the html even after deletion
9   });
10  two.addEventListener('hover', function(){
11      one.remove();
12      console.log(one); // will print the html even after deletion
13  });
```

**Problem:** This is the "leaking DOM" issue discussed earlier in the chapter. When elements are removed, they are still referenced by the callback function. To address this, put the one and two variables into a callback's scope and remove the event listener after.

**Answer:**

**HTML:**

```
<button id="one"> Button 1 </button>
<button id="two"> Button 2 </button>
```

**JavaScript:**

```
1   var one = document.querySelector("#one");
2   var two = document.querySelector("#two");
3   function callbackOne() {
4       var two = document.querySelector("#two");
5       if (!two)
6           return;
7       two.remove();
8       one.removeEventListener("hover", callbackOne);
9   }
10
11  function callbackTwo() {
12      var one = document.querySelector("#one");
```

```
13      if (!one)
14          return;
15      one.remove();
16      two.removeEventListener("hover", callbackTwo);
17  }
18  one.addEventListener("click", callbackOne);
19  two.addEventListener("click", callbackTwo);
```

# CHAPTER 8

# Recursion

This chapter introduces the concept of recursion and recursive algorithms. First, the definition of recursion and fundamental rules for recursive algorithms will be explored. In addition, methods of analyzing efficiencies of recursive functions will be covered in detail using mathematical notations. Finally, the chapter exercises will help solidify this information.

## Introducing Recursion

In math, linguistics, and art, *recursion* refers to the occurrence of a thing defined in terms of itself. In computer science, a *recursive function* is a function that calls itself. Recursive functions are often elegant and solve complex problems through the "divide-and-conquer" method. Recursion is important because you will see it again and again in the implementation of various data structures. Figure 8-1 shows a visual illustration of recursion where the picture has smaller pictures of itself.

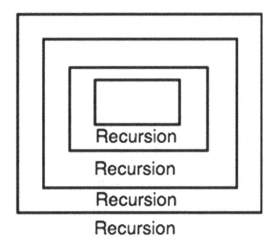

*Figure 8-1.* *Recursion illustrated*

© Sammie Bae 2019

S. Bae, *JavaScript Data Structures and Algorithms*, https://doi.org/10.1007/978-1-4842-3988-9_8

# Rules of Recursion

When recursive functions are implemented incorrectly, it causes fatal issues because the program will get stuck and not terminate. Infinite recursive calls result in stack overflow. *Stack overflow* is when the maximum number of call stacks of the program exceeds the limited amount of address space (memory).

For recursive functions to be implemented correctly, they must follow certain rules so that stack overflow is avoided. These rules are covered next.

## Base Case

In recursion, there must be a base case (also referred to as *terminating case*). Because recursive methods call themselves, they will never stop unless this base case is reached. Stack overflow from recursion is most likely the result of not having a proper base case. In the base case, there are *no* recursive function calls.

Let's examine the following function, which prints numbers counting down from n to 0 as an example:

```
1   function countDownToZero(n) {
2       // base case. Stop at 0
3       if (n < 0) {
4           return; // stop the function
5       } else {
6           console.log(n);
7           countDownToZero(n - 1); // count down 1
8       }
9   }
10  countDownToZero(12);
```

The base case for this function is when n is smaller or equal to 0. This is because the desired outcome was to stop counting at 0. If a negative number is given as the input, it will not print that number because of the base case. In addition to a base case, this recursive function also exhibits the divide-and-conquer method.

# Divide-and-Conquer Method

In computer science, the *divide-and-conquer* method is when a problem is solved by solving all of its smaller components. With the countdown example, counting down from 2 can be solved by printing 2 and then *counting down from 1*. Here, *counting down from 1* is the part solved by "dividing and conquering." It is necessary to make the problem smaller to reach the base case. Otherwise, if the recursive call does not converge to a base case, a stack overflow occurs.

Let's now examine a more complex recursive function known as the *Fibonacci sequence*.

# Classic Example: Fibonacci Sequence

The Fibonacci sequence is a list of infinite numbers, each of which is the sum of the past two terms (starting with 1).

> 1, 1, 2, 3, 5, 8, 13, 21 ...

How might you program something to print the Nth term of the Fibonacci sequence?

## Iterative Solution: Fibonacci Sequence

An iterative solution using a for loop may look something like this:

```
1   function getNthFibo(n) {
2       if ( n <= 1)  return n;
3       var sum = 0,
4           last = 1,
5           lastlast = 0;
6
7       for (var i = 1; i < n; i++) {
8           sum = lastlast + last;
9           lastlast = last;
10          last = sum;
11      }
12      return sum;
13  }
```

A `for` loop can be used to keep track of the last two elements of the Fibonacci sequence, and its sum yields the Fibonacci number.

Now, how might this be done recursively?

## Recursive Solution: Fibonacci

The following shows the recursive solution:

```
1    function getNthFibo(n) {
2        if (n <= 1) {
3            return n;
4        } else {
5            return getNthFibo(n - 1) + getNthFibo(n - 2);
6        }
7    }
```

**Base case:** The base case for the Fibonacci sequence is that the first element is 1.

**Divide and conquer:** By definition of the Fibonacci sequence, the Nth Fibonacci number is the sum of the $(n-1)$th and $(n-2)$th Fibonacci numbers. However, this implementation has a time complexity of $O(2^n)$, which is discussed in detail later in this chapter. We will explore a more efficient recursive algorithm for the Fibonacci sequence using tail recursion in the next section.

## Fibonacci Sequence: Tail Recursion

A *tail recursive* function is a recursive function in which the recursive call is the last executed thing in the function. First let's look at the iterative solution:

```
1    function getNthFibo(n) {
2        if ( n <= 1)  return n;
3        var sum = 0,
4            last = 1,
5            lastlast = 0;
6
7        for (var i = 1; i < n; i++) {
8            sum = lastlast + last;
9            lastlast = last;
```

```
10          last = sum;
11      }
12      return sum;
13  }
```

At each iteration, the following update happens: (lastlast, last) = (last, lastlast+last). With this structure, the following recursive function can be formed:

```
1   function getNthFiboBetter(n, lastlast, last) {
2       if (n == 0) {
3           return lastlast;
4       }
5       if (n == 1) {
6           return last;
7       }
8       return getNthFiboBetter(n-1, last, lastlast + last);
9   }
```

**Time Complexity:** $O(n)$

At most, this function executes $n$ times because it's decremented by $n$-1 each time with only single recursive call.

**Space Complexity:** $O(n)$

The space complexity is also $O(n)$ because of the stack call used for this function. This will be further explained in the "Recursive Call Stack Memory" section later in this chapter.

To conclude the rules of recursion, let's examine another example, which is more complex.

# Pascal's Triangle

In this example, a function for calculating a term of Pascal's triangle will be explored. *Pascal's triangle* is a triangle whose element value is the summation of its top two (left and right) values, as shown in Figure 8-2.

$$1$$
$$1\ 1$$
$$1\ 2\ 1$$
$$1\ 3\ 3\ 1$$
$$1\ 4\ 6\ 4\ 1$$
$$1\ 5\ 10\ 10\ 5\ 1$$

*Figure 8-2.* *Pascal's triangle*

**Base case:** The base case for Pascal's triangle is that the top element (row=1, col=1) is 1. Everything else is derived from this fact alone. Hence, when the column is 1, return 1, and when the row is 0, return 0.

**Divide and conquer:** By the mathematical definition of Pascal's triangle, a term of Pascal's triangle is defined as the sum of its upper terms. Therefore, this can be expressed as the following: pascalTriangle(row - 1, col) + pascalTriangle(row - 1, col - 1).

```
1   function pascalTriangle(row, col) {
2       if (col == 0) {
3           return 1;
4       } else if (row == 0) {
5           return 0;
6       } else {
7           return pascalTriangle(row - 1, col) + pascalTriangle(row - 1,
            col - 1);
8       }
```

```
 9    }
10    pascalTriangle(5, 2); // 10
```

This is the beauty of recursion! Look next at how short and elegant this code is.

# Big-O for Recursion

In Chapter 1, Big-O analysis of recursive algorithms was not covered. This was because recursive algorithms are much harder to analyze. To perform Big-O analysis for recursive algorithms, its recurrence relations must be analyzed.

# Recurrence Relations

In algorithms implemented iteratively, Big-O analysis is much simpler because loops clearly define when to stop and how much to increment in each iteration. For analyzing recursive algorithms, recurrence relations are used. Recurrence relations consist of two-part analysis: Big-O for base case and Big-O for recursive case.

Let's revisit the naive Fibonacci sequence example:

```
function getNthFibo(n) {
    if (n <= 1) {
        return n;
    } else {
        return getNthFibo(n - 1) + getNthFibo(n - 2);
    }
}
getNthFibo(3);
```

The base case has a time complexity of $O(1)$. The recursive case calls itself twice. Let's represent this as $T(n) = T(n - 1) + T(n - 2) + O(1)$.

- **Base case:** $T(n) = O(1)$

- **Recursive case:** $T(n) = T(n - 1) + T(n - 2) + O(1)$

Now, this relation means that since $T(n) = T(n - 1) + T(n - 2) + O(1)$, then (by replacing $n$ with $n-1$), $T(n - 1) = T(n - 2) + T(n - 3) + O(1)$. Replacing $n-1$ with $n-2$ yields $T(n - 2) = T(n - 3) + T(n - 4) + O(1)$. Therefore, you can see that for every call, there are two more calls for each call. In other words, this has a time complexity of $O(2^n)$.

It helps to visualize it as such:

```
F(6)                    * <-- only once
F(5)                    *
F(4)                    **
F(3)                    ****
F(2)                    ********
F(1)                ****************            <-- 16
F(0)  ******************************** <-- 32
```

Calculating Big-O this way is difficult and prone to error. Thankfully, there is a concept known as the *master theorem* to help. The master theorem helps programmers easily analyze the time and space complexities of recursive algorithms.

## Master Theorem

The master theorem states the following:

> Given a recurrence relation of the form $T(n) = aT(n/b) + O(n^c)$
> where a >= 1 and b >=1, there are three cases.

$a$ is the coefficient that is multiplied by the recursive call. $b$ is the "logarithmic" term, which is the term that divides the $n$ during the recursive call. Finally, $c$ is the polynomial term on the nonrecursive component of the equation.

The first case is when the polynomial term on the nonrecursive component $O(n^c)$ is smaller than $log_b(a)$.

> **Case 1:** $c < log_b(a)$ then $T(n) = O(n^{(log_b(a))})$.
>
> For example, $T(n) = 8T(n/2) + 1000n^2$
>
> **Identify a, b, c:** $a = 8$, $b = 2$, $c = 2$
>
> **Evaluate:** $log_2(8) = 3$. $c < 3$ is satisfied.
>
> **Result:** $T(n) = O(n^3)$

The second case is when c is *equal* to $log_b(a)$.

> **Case 2:** $c = log_b(a)$ then $T(n) = O(n^c log(n))$.
>
> For example, $T(n) = 2T(n/2) + 10n$.

**Identify a, b, c:** $a = 2$, $b = 2$, $c = 1$

**Evaluate:** $log_2(2) = 1$. $c = 1$ is satisfied.

**Result:** $T(n) = O(n^c log(n)) = T(n) = O(n^1 log(n)) = T(n) = O(nlog(n))$

The third and final case is when $c$ is *greater* than $log_b(a)$.

**Case 3:** $c > log_b(a)$ *then* $T(n) = O(f(n))$.

For example, $T(n) = 2T(n/2) + n^2$.

**Identify a,b,c:** $a = 2$, $b = 2$, $c = 2$

**Evaluate:** $log_2(2) = 1$. $c > 1$ is satisfied.

**Result:** $T(n) = f(n) = O(n^2)$

This section covered a lot about analyzing the time complexity of recursive algorithms. Space complexity analysis is just as important. The memory used by recursive function calls should also be noted and analyzed for space complexity analysis.

# Recursive Call Stack Memory

When a recursive function calls itself, that takes up memory, and this is really important in Big-O *space* complexity analysis.

For example, this simple function for printing from $n$ to 1 recursively takes $O(n)$ in space:

```
1  function printNRecursive(n) {
2      console.log(n);
3      if (n > 1){
4          printNRecursive(n-1);
5      }
6  }
7  printNRecursive(10);
```

A developer can run this on a browser or any JavaScript engine and will see the result shown in Figure 8-3 in the call stack.

▶, ⌒ ↕ ↑ | ▶/ ⓪ | ☐ Async

Scope | Watch

▼ Call Stack

▶ printNRecursive ................................. testing.html:115

printNRecursive .................................... testing.html:117

printNRecursive .................................... testing.html:117

printNRecursive .................................... testing.html:117

printNRecursive .................................... testing.html:117

printNRecursive .................................... testing.html:117

printNRecursive .................................... testing.html:117

printNRecursive .................................... testing.html:117

printNRecursive ................................... testing.html:117

▼ Local

  n: 1

  ▶ this: Window

▶ Global                                            Window

*Figure 8-3.* *Call stack in Developer Tools*

As shown in Figures 8-3 and 8-4, each recursive call must be stored in memory until the base case is resolved. Recursive algorithms take extra memory because of the call stack.

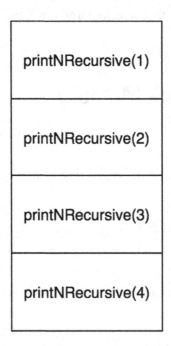

*Figure 8-4.* *Call stack memory*

Recursive functions have an additional space complexity cost that comes from the recursive calls that need to be stored in the operating system's memory stack. The stack is accumulated until the base case is solved. In fact, this is often why an iterative solution may be preferred over the recursive solution. In the worst case, if the base case is implemented incorrectly, the recursive function will cause the program to crash because of a stack overflow error that occurs when there are more than the allowed number of elements in the memory stack.

# Summary

Recursion is a powerful tool to implement complex algorithms. Recall that all recursive functions consist of two parts: the base case and the divide-and-conquer method (solving subproblems).

Analyzing the Big-O of these recursive algorithms can be done empirically (not recommended) or by using the master theorem. Recall that the master theorem needs the recurrence relation in the following form: $T(n) = aT(n/b) + O(n^c)$. When using the master theorem, identify $a$, $b$, and $c$ to determine which of the three cases of the master theorem it belongs to.

Finally, when implementing and analyzing recursive algorithms, consider the additional memory caused by the call stack of the recursive function calls. Each recursive call requires a place in the call stack at runtime; when the call stack accumulate $n$ calls, then the space complexity of the function is $O(n)$.

# Exercises

These exercises on recursion cover varying problems to help solidify the knowledge gained from this chapter. The focus should be to identify the correct base case first before solving the entire problem. You will find all the code for the exercises on GitHub.[1]

---
**CONVERT DECIMAL (BASE 10) TO BINARY NUMBER**
---

To do this, keep dividing the number by 2 and each time calculate the modulus (remainder) and division.

**Base case:** The base case for this problem is when the $n$ is less than 2. When it is less than 2, it can be only 0 or 1.

---

[1]https://github.com/Apress/js-data-structures-and-algorithms

```
1    function base10ToString(n) {
2        var binaryString = "";
3
4        function base10ToStringHelper(n) {
5            if (n < 2) {
6                binaryString += n;
7                return;
8            } else {
9                base10ToStringHelper(Math.floor(n / 2));
10               base10ToStringHelper(n % 2);
11           }
12       }
13       base10ToStringHelper(n);
14
15       return binaryString;
16   }
17
18   console.log(base10ToString(232)); // 11101000
```

**Time Complexity:** $O(log_2(n))$

Time complexity is logarithmic because the recursive call divides the $n$ by 2, which makes the algorithm fast. For example, for $n = 8$, it executes only three times. For $n=1024$, it executes 10 times.

**Space Complexity:** $O(log_2(n))$

---

## PRINT ALL PERMUTATIONS OF AN ARRAY

This is a classical recursion problem and one that is pretty hard to solve. The premise of the problem is to swap elements of the array in every possible position.

First, let's draw the recursion tree for this problem (see Figure 8-5).

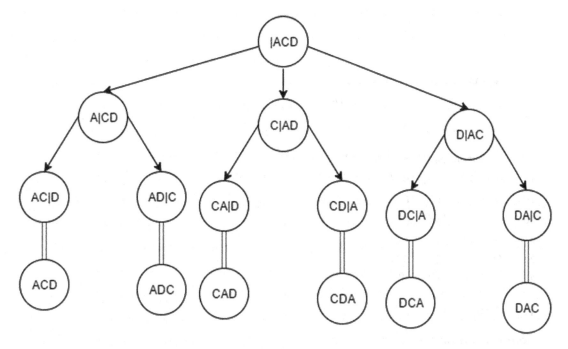

***Figure 8-5.*** *Permutation of array recursion tree*

**Base case:** beginIndex is equal to endIndex.

When this occurs, the function should print the current permutation.

**Permutations:** We will need a function to swap elements:

```
1   function swap(strArr, index1, index2) {
2       var temp = strArr[index1];
3       strArr[index1] = strArr[index2];
4       strArr[index2] = temp;
5   }
```

```
1   function permute(strArr, begin, end) {
2       if (begin == end) {
3           console.log(strArr);
4       } else {
5           for (var i = begin; i < end + 1; i++) {
6               swap(strArr, begin, i);
7               permute(strArr, begin + 1, end);
8               swap(strArr, begin, i);
9           }
```

```
10          }
11      }
12
13      function permuteArray(strArr) {
14          permute(strArr, 0, strArr.length - 1);
15      }
16
17      permuteArray(["A", "C", "D"]);
18      // ["A", "C", "D"]
19      // ["A", "D", "C"]
20      // ["C", "A", "D"]
21      // ["C", "D", "A"]
22      // ["D", "C", "A"]
23      // ["D", "A", "C"]
```

**Time Complexity:** O($n!$)

**Space Complexity:** O($n!$)

There are n! permutations, and it creates n! call stacks.

---

## FLATTEN AN OBJECT

Given a JavaScript array like this:

```
1      var dictionary = {
2          'Key1': '1',
3          'Key2': {
4              'a' : '2',
5              'b' : '3',
6              'c' : {
7                  'd' : '3',
8                  'e' : '1'
9              }
10         }
11     }
```

flatten it into `{'Key1': '1', 'Key2.a': '2','Key2.b' : '3', 'Key2.c.d' : '3', 'Key2.c.e' : '1'}`, where the child is denoted by . between the parent and child (see Figure 8-6).

To do this, iterate over any property and recursively check it for child properties, passing in the concatenated string name.

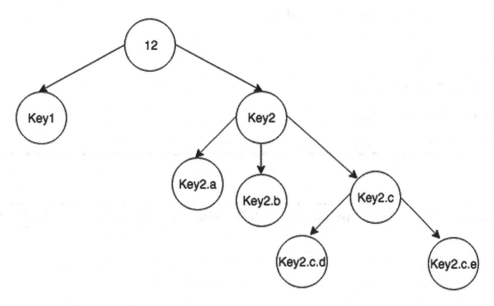

***Figure 8-6.*** *Flatten a dictionary recursion tree*

**Base case:** The base case for this problem is when input is not an object.

```
1    function flattenDictionary(dictionary) {
2        var flattenedDictionary = {};
3
4        function flattenDitionaryHelper(dictionary, propName) {
5            if (typeof dictionary != 'object') {
6                flattenedDictionary[propName] = dictionary;
7                return;
8            }
9            for (var prop in dictionary) {
10               if (propName == ")){
11                   flattenDitionaryHelper(dictionary[prop], propName+prop);
12               } else {
```

```
13                          flattenDitionaryHelper(dictionary[prop],
                            propName+'.'+prop);
14                  }
15              }
16          }
17
18      flattenDitionaryHelper(dictionary, ");
19      return flattenedDictionary;
20  }
```

**Time Complexity:** $O(n)$

**Space Complexity:** $O(n)$

Each property is visited only once and stored once per $n$ properties.

## WRITE A PROGRAM THAT RECURSIVELY DETERMINES IF A STRING IS A PALINDROME

A *palindrome* is a word spelled the same backward and forward such as *deified*, *racecar*, testset, and *aibohphobia* (the fear of palindromes).

```
1   function isPalindromeRecursive(word) {
2       return isPalindromeHelper(word, 0, word.length-1);
3   }
4
5   function isPalindromeHelper(word, beginPos, endPos) {
6       if (beginPos >= endPos) {
7           return true;
8       }
9       if (word.charAt(beginPos) != word.charAt(endPos)) {
10          return false;
11      } else {
12          return isPalindromeHelper(word, beginPos + 1, endPos - 1);
13      }
14  }
15
16  isPalindromeRecursive('hi'); // false
17  isPalindromeRecursive('iii'); // true
```

```
18   isPalindromeRecursive('ii'); // true
19   isPalindromeRecursive('aibohphobia'); // true
20   isPalindromeRecursive('racecar'); // true
```

The idea behind this one is that with two indexes (one in front and one in back) you check at each step until the front and back meet.

**Time Complexity:** $O(n)$

**Space Complexity:** $O(n)$

Space complexity here is still $O(n)$ because of the recursive call stack. Remember that the call stack remains part of memory even if it is not declaring a variable or being stored inside a data structure.

# CHAPTER 9

# Sets

This chapter focuses on working with sets. The concepts of sets from both a mathematical definition and on the implementation level are described and explored. Common set operations, as well as their implementations, are covered in great detail. By end of this chapter, you will understand how to use JavaScript's native Set object to utilize set operations.

## Introducing Sets

Sets are one of the most fundamental data structures. The idea of a set is simple: it is a group of definite, distinct objects. In layman's terms, in programming, a *set* is a group of unordered *unique* (no duplicate) elements. For example, a set of integers may be {1, 2, 3, 4}. Within this, its subsets are {}, {1}, {2}, {3}, {4}, {1, 2}, {1, 3}, {1, 4}, {2, 3}, {2, 4}, {3, 4}, {1, 2, 3}, {1, 2, 4}, {1, 3, 4}, and {2, 3, 4}. Sets are important for checking and adding a unique element in O(1) constant time. The reason that sets have constant time operations is that the implementations are based on that of hash tables (covered in Chapter 11).

Set is natively supported in JavaScript as follows:

```
1    var exampleSet = new Set();
```

The native Set object has only one property: size (integer). This property is the current number of elements within the set.

## Set Operations

The set is a powerful data structure for performing uniqueness checks. This section will cover the following key operations: *insertion, deletion,* and *contains.*

© Sammie Bae 2019
S. Bae, *JavaScript Data Structures and Algorithms*, https://doi.org/10.1007/978-1-4842-3988-9_9

# Insertion

Set has one primary function: to check for uniqueness. Set can add items, but duplicates are not allowed.

```
1   var exampleSet = new Set();
2   exampleSet.add(1); // exampleSet: Set {1}
3   exampleSet.add(1); // exampleSet: Set {1}
4   exampleSet.add(2); // exampleSet: Set {1, 2}
```

Notice that adding the duplicate element does not work for a set. As discussed in the introduction, insertion into a set occurs in constant time.

**Time Complexity:** O(1)

# Deletion

Set can also delete items from the set. Set.delete returns a boolean (true if that element exists and was deleted, false otherwise).

```
1   var exampleSet = new Set();
2   exampleSet.add(1); // exampleSet: Set {1}
3   exampleSet.delete(1); // true
4   exampleSet.add(2); // exampleSet: Set {2}
```

This is useful for being able to delete items in constant time in contrast to arrays where it would take O($n$) time to delete an item.

**Time Complexity:** O(1)

# Contains

Set.has does a quick O(1) lookup to check whether the element exists within the set.

```
1   var exampleSet = new Set();
2   exampleSet.add(1); // exampleSet: Set {1}
3   exampleSet.has(1); // true
4   exampleSet.has(2); // false
5   exampleSet.add(2); // exampleSet: Set {1, 2}
6   exampleSet.has(2); // true
```

**Time Complexity:** O(1)

# Other Utility Functions

In addition to the natively supported set functions, other essential operations are available; they are explored in this section.

## Intersection

First, the intersection of two sets consists of the common elements between those two sets. This function returns a set with common elements between two sets:

```
1   function intersectSets (setA, setB) {
2       var intersection = new Set();
3       for (var elem of setB) {
4           if (setA.has(elem)) {
5               intersection.add(elem);
6           }
7       }
8       return intersection;
9   }
10  var setA = new Set([1, 2, 3, 4]),
11      setB = new Set([2, 3]);
12  intersectSets(setA,setB); // Set {2, 3}
```

## isSuperSet

Second, a set is a "superset" of another set if it contains all the elements of the other set. This function checks whether a set is a superset of another. This is implemented simply by checking whether the other set contains all the elements of the reference set.

```
1   function isSuperset(setA, subset) {
2       for (var elem of subset) {
3           if (!setA.has(elem)) {
4               return false;
5           }
6       }
7       return true;
8   }
```

```
9    var setA = new Set([1, 2, 3, 4]),
10        setB = new Set([2, 3]),
11        setC = new Set([5]);
12   isSuperset(setA, setB); // true
13   // because setA has all elements that setB does
14   isSuperset(setA, setC); // false
15   // because setA does not contain 5 which setC contains
```

## Union

Third, the union of two sets combines the elements from both sets. This function returns a new set with both elements without duplicates.

```
1    function unionSet(setA, setB) {
2        var union = new Set(setA);
3        for (var elem of setB) {
4            union.add(elem);
5        }
6        return union;
7    }
8    var setA = new Set([1, 2, 3, 4]),
9        setB = new Set([2, 3]),
10       setC = new Set([5]);
11   unionSet(setA,setB); // Set {1, 2, 3, 4}
12    unionSet(setA,setC); // Set {1, 2, 3, 4, 5}
```

## Difference

Finally, the difference of set A from set B is all of the elements in set A that are not in set B. This function implements the difference operation by making use of the native delete method.

```
1    function differenceSet(setA, setB) {
2        var difference = new Set(setA);
3        for (var elem of setB) {
4            difference.delete(elem);
```

```
5        }
6        return difference;
7    }
8    var setA = new Set([1, 2, 3, 4]),
9        setB = new Set([2, 3]);
10   differenceSet(setA, setB); // Set {1, 4}
```

# Summary

A set is a fundamental data structure to represent unordered unique elements. In this chapter, JavaScript's native Set object was introduced. The Set object supports insertion, deletion, and contains check, which all have a time complexity of O(1). With these built-in methods, other fundamental set operations such as intersection, difference, union, and superset check are implemented. These will enable you to implement algorithms with fast uniqueness checks in future chapters.

Table 9-1 summarizes the set operations.

*Table 9-1.* *Set Summary*

| Operation | Function Name | Description |
| --- | --- | --- |
| Insertion | Set.add | Native JavaScript. Adds the element to the set if it's not already in the set. |
| Deletion | Set.delete | Native JavaScript. Deletes the element from the set if it's in the set. |
| Contains | Set.has | Native JavaScript. Checks whether an element exists within in the set. |
| Intersection (A∩B) | intersectSets | Returns a set with common elements of set A and set B. |
| Union (A∪B) | unionSet | Returns a set with all elements of set A and set B. |
| Difference (A-B) | differenceSet | Returns a set with all elements. |

# Exercises

---

## USING SETS TO CHECK FOR DUPLICATES IN AN ARRAY

Check whether there are any duplicates in an array of integers using sets. By converting the array into a set, the size of the set can be compared with the length of the array to check for duplicates easily.

```
1   function checkDuplicates(arr) {
2       var mySet = new Set(arr);
3       return mySet.size < arr.length;
4   }
5   checkDuplicates([1,2,3,4,5]); // false
6   checkDuplicates([1,1,2,3,4,5]); // true
```

**Time Complexity:** $O(n)$

**Space Complexity:** $O(n)$

In an array of length $n$, this function has to iterate through the entire array in the worst case and also store all those elements in the set.

---

## RETURNING ALL UNIQUE VALUES FROM SEPARATE ARRAYS

Given two integer arrays with some of the same values, return one array that has all the unique elements from both of the original arrays.

Using sets, unique elements can be stored easily. By concatenating two arrays and converting them to a set, only unique items are stored. Converting the set to an array results in an array with unique items only.

```
1   function uniqueList(arr1, arr2) {
2       var mySet = new Set(arr1.concat(arr2));
3       return Array.from(mySet);
4   }
5
```

```
6   uniqueList([1,1,2,2],[2,3,4,5]); // [1,2,3,4,5]
7   uniqueList([1,2],[3,4,5]); // [1,2,3,4,5]
8   uniqueList([],[2,2,3,4,5]); // [2,3,4,5]
```

**Time Complexity:** $O(n + m)$

**Space Complexity:** $O(n + m)$

The time and space complexity for this algorithm is $O(n + m)$ where $n$ is the length of `arr1` and $m$ is the length of `arr2`. This is because all elements inside both arrays need to be iterated through.

# CHAPTER 10

# Searching and Sorting

Searching data and sorting through data are fundamental algorithms. *Searching* refers to iterating over the data structure's elements to retrieve some data. *Sorting* refers to putting the data structure's elements in order. The searching and sorting algorithms are different for every data structure. This chapter focuses on searching and sorting for arrays. By the end of this chapter, you will understand how to use common sorting and searching algorithms for arrays.

## Searching

As mentioned, searching is the task of looking for a specific element inside a data structure. When searching in an array, there are two main techniques depending on whether the array is sorted. In this section, you'll learn about linear and binary searching. Linear searches are especially flexible because they can be used with both sorted and unsorted data. Binary searches are specifically used with sorted data. However, a linear search has a higher time complexity than a binary search.

## Linear Search

A linear search works by going through each element of the array one index after another sequentially. The following code example is an implementation of a linear search that iterates through the entire array of numbers to find out whether 4 and 5 exist within the array.

```
1    //iterate through the array and find
2    function linearSearch(array,n){
3        for(var i=0; i<array.length; i++) {
4            if (array[i]==n) {
```

© Sammie Bae 2019
S. Bae, *JavaScript Data Structures and Algorithms*, https://doi.org/10.1007/978-1-4842-3988-9_10

```
5                    return true;
6              }
7          }
8          return false;
9      }
10     console.log(linearSearch([1,2,3,4,5,6,7,8,9], 6)); // true
11     console.log(linearSearch([1,2,3,4,5,6,7,8,9], 10)); // false
```

**Time Complexity:** $O(n)$

As shown in Figure 10-1, when 6 is searched for, it goes through six iterations. When 10 is searched for, it must iterate through all $n$ elements before returning `false`; therefore, the time complexity is $O(n)$.

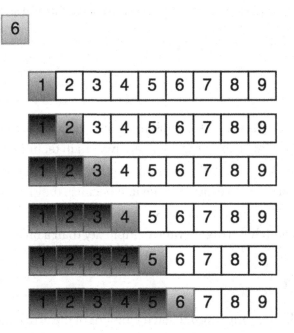

***Figure 10-1.*** *Linear search*

As another example, with an array of [1,2,3,4,5] and a search term of 3, it would take three iterations to complete (1, 2, 3). The reason why this algorithm has a Big-O of $O(n)$ is that, in the worst-case scenario, the entire array needs to be iterated. For example, if the search term is 5, it takes five iterations (1, 2, 3, 4, 5). If 6 is the search term, it goes through the entire array (1, 2, 3, 4, 5) and then returns `false` because it was not found.

As noted previously, a linear search algorithm like this is great because it works whether or not the array is sorted. In a linear search algorithm, every element of the array is checked. So, you should use a linear search when the array is not sorted. If the array is sorted, you can do the search faster via a binary search.

# Binary Search

Binary search is a searching algorithm that works on sorted data. Unlike the linear search algorithm, in which every element of the array is checked, binary searches can check the middle value to see whether the desired value is greater or smaller than it. If the desired value is smaller, this algorithm can search through the smaller parts, or it can search through the bigger parts if the desired value is bigger.

Figure 10-2 illustrates the process of a binary search. First, the search range is 1 to 9. Since the middle element, 5, is bigger than 3, the search range is restricted to 1 to 4. Finally, 3 is found as the middle element. Figure 10-3 illustrates searching for an item in the right half of the array.

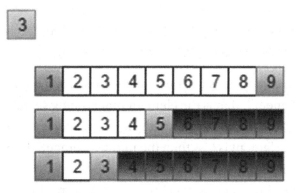

***Figure 10-2.***  *Binary search in the left half of the array*

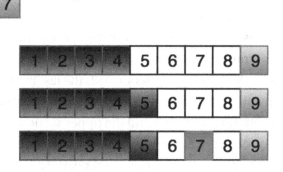

***Figure 10-3.***  *Binary search in the right half of the array*

The following code implements the binary search algorithm described:

```
1   function binarySearch(array,n){
2       var lowIndex = 0, highIndex = array1.length-1;
3
4       while(lowIndex<=highIndex){
5           var midIndex = Math.floor((highIndex+lowIndex) /2);
6           if (array[midIndex]==n) {
7               return midIndex;
8           } else if (n>array[midIndex]) {
9               lowIndex = midIndex;
10          } else {
11              highIndex = midIndex;
12          }
13      }
14      return -1;
15  }
16  console.log(binarySearch([1,2,3,4], 4)); // true
17  console.log(binarySearch([1,2,3,4], 5)); // -1
```

The binary search algorithm is fast but can be done only if the array is sorted. It checks the middle element if that is the element that is being searched for. If the search element is bigger than the middle element, the lower bound is set to the middle element plus one. If the search element is less than the middle element, the higher bound is set to the middle element minus one.

This way, the algorithm is continuously dividing the array into two sections: the lower half and the upper half. If the element is smaller than the middle element, it should look for it in the lower half; if the element is bigger than the middle element, it should look for it in the upper half.

Binary searches are used by humans without them even knowing. An example is a phone directory that is arranged from *A* to *Z* by last name.

If you are given the task of finding someone with the last name of Lezer, one would first go to the L section and open it halfway through. Lizar is on that page; this means that the lower section contains L + [a to i] and the upper section contains L + [i to z] last names. You would then check the middle of the lower section. Laar appears, so you would now check the upper section. This process repeats until Lezer is found.

# Sorting

Sorting is one of the most important topics in computer science; it is faster and easier to locate items in a sorted array than in an unsorted sorted array. You can use sorting algorithms to sort an array in memory for searching later in the program or to write to a file for later retrieval. In this section, different sorting techniques will be explored. We will start with the naive sorting algorithms and then explore efficient sorting algorithms. Efficient sorting algorithms have various trade-offs that should be considered during usage.

## Bubble Sort

Bubble sorting is the simplest sorting algorithm. It simply iterates over the entire array and swaps elements if one is bigger than the other, as shown in Figure 10-4 and Figure 10-5.

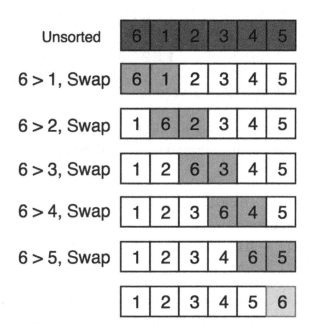

***Figure 10-4.*** *First run of the bubble sort*

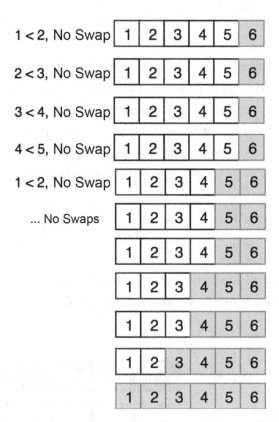

**Figure 10-5.**  *The rest of the bubble sort runs*

swap is a common function used in sorting. It simply switches two array element values and will be used as a helper function for most of the sorting algorithms mentioned.

```
1    function swap(array, index1, index2) {
2        var temp = array[index1];
3        array[index1] = array[index2];
4        array[index2] = temp;
5    }
```

The following bubbleSort code block illustrates the bubble sort algorithm previously described:

```
1    function bubbleSort(array) {
2        for (var i=0, arrayLength = array.length; i<arrayLength; i++) {
3            for (var j=0; j<=i; j++) {
```

```
4                if (array[i] < array[j]) {
5                    swap(array, i, j);
6                }
7            }
8        }
9        return array;
10   }
11   bubbleSort([6,1,2,3,4,5]); // [1,2,3,4,5,6]
```

**Time Complexity:** $O(n^2)$

**Space Complexity:** $O(1)$

Bubble sort is the worst type of sort because it compares every pair possible, whereas other sorting algorithms take advantage of the presorted parts of the array. Because bubble sort uses nested loops, it has a time complexity of $O(n^2)$.

## Selection Sort

Selection sorting works by scanning the elements for the smallest element and inserting it into the current position of the array. This algorithm is marginally better than bubble sort. Figure 10-6 shows this minimum selection process.

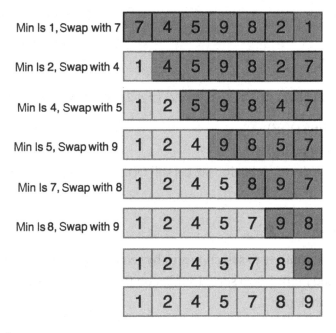

*Figure 10-6.* *Selection sort*

The following code implements the selection sort. In the code, there is one for loop to iterate through the array and one nested for loop to scan to get the minimum element.

```
1    function selectionSort(items) {
2        var len = items.length,
3            min;
4
5        for (var i=0; i < len; i++){
6            // set minimum to this position
7            min = i;
8            //check the rest of the array to see if anything is smaller
9            for (j=i+1; j < len; j++){
10                if (items[j] < items[min]){
11                    min = j;
12                }
13            }
14            //if the minimum isn't in the position, swap it
15            if (i != min){
16                swap(items, i, min);
17            }
18        }
19
20        return items;
21    }
22    selectionSort([6,1,23,4,2,3]); // [1, 2, 3, 4, 6, 23]
```

**Time Complexity:** $O(n^2)$
**Space Complexity:** $O(1)$
The time complexity for selection sort is still $O(n^2)$ because of the nested for loop.

# Insertion Sort

Insertion sort works similarly to selection sort by searching the array sequentially and moving the unsorted items into a sorted sublist on the left side of the array. Figure 10-7 shows this process in detail.

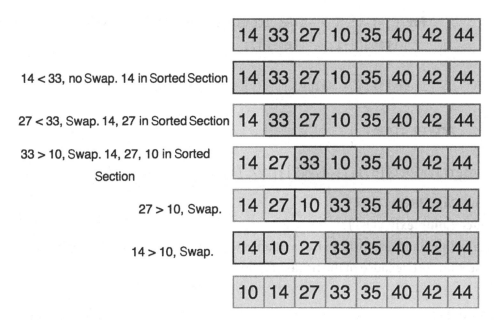

**Figure 10-7.** *Insertion sort*

The following code implements the insertion sort algorithm. The outer for loop iterates over the array indices, and the inner for loop moves the unsorted items into the sorted sublist on the left side of the array.

```
1   function insertionSort(items) {
2       var len = items.length, // number of items in the array
3           value,              // the value currently being compared
4           i,                  // index into unsorted section
5           j;                  // index into sorted section
6
7       for (i=0; i < len; i++) {
8           // store the current value because it may shift later
9           value = items[i];
10
11          // Whenever the value in the sorted section is greater than the value
12          // in the unsorted section, shift all items in the sorted section
13          // over by one. This creates space in which to insert the value.
14
```

```
15              for (j=i-1; j > -1 && items[j] > value; j--) {
16                  items[j+1] = items[j];
17              }
18              items[j+1] = value;
19          }
20          return items;
21      }
22      insertionSort([6,1,23,4,2,3]); // [1, 2, 3, 4, 6, 23]
```

**Time Complexity:** $O(n^2)$

**Space Complexity:** $O(1)$

Again, this sorting algorithm has a quadratic time complexity of $O(n^2)$ like bubble and insertion sort because of the nested for loop.

# Quicksort

Quicksort works by obtaining a pivot and partitioning the array around it (bigger elements on one side and smaller elements on the other side) until everything is sorted. The ideal pivot is the median of the array since it will partition the array evenly but getting the median of an unsorted array linear time to compute. Hence, a pivot is typically obtained by taking the median value of the first, middle, and last elements in the partition. This sort is a recursive one and uses the divide-and-conquer methodology to break the quadratic complexity barrier and get the time complexity down to $O(nlog_2(n))$. However, with a pivot that partitions everything on one side, the time complexity is worse case: $O(n^2)$.

Figure 10-8 shows the quicksort process's partitioning steps in great detail.

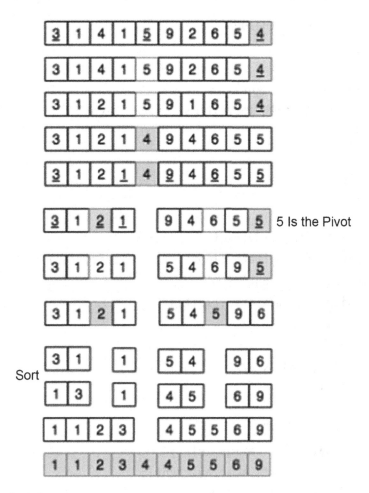

Sort

5 Is the Pivot

*Figure 10-8. Quicksort*

The following code shows an implementation of the quicksort algorithm:

```
1   function quickSort(items) {
2       return quickSortHelper(items, 0, items.length-1);
3   }
4
5   function quickSortHelper(items, left, right) {
6       var index;
7       if (items.length > 1) {
8           index = partition(items, left, right);
9
10          if (left < index - 1) {
```

```
11                    quickSortHelper(items, left, index - 1);
12                }
13
14            if (index < right) {
15                    quickSortHelper(items, index, right);
16                }
17            }
18        return items;
19    }
20
21    function partition(array, left, right) {
22        var pivot = array[Math.floor((right + left) / 2)];
23        while (left <= right) {
24            while (pivot > array[left]) {
25                left++;
26            }
27            while (pivot < array[right]) {
28                right--;
29            }
30            if (left <= right) {
31                var temp = array[left];
32                array[left] = array[right];
33                array[right]= temp;
34                left++;
35                right--;
36            }
37        }
38        return left;
39    }
40
41    quickSort([6,1,23,4,2,3]); // [1, 2, 3, 4, 6, 23]
```

**Time Complexity:** $O(nlog_2(n))$ on average, $O(n^2)$ for worst case

**Space Complexity:** $O(log_2(n))$

One downside about a quicksort algorithm is that it could potentially be $O(n^2)$ if a bad pivot is always picked. A bad pivot is one that it does not partition the array evenly. The ideal pivot is the median element of the array. In addition, a quicksort algorithm takes a bigger space complexity of $O(log_2(n))$ compared to other sorting algorithms because of the call stack in recursion.

Use a quicksort algorithm when the average performance should be optimal. This has to do with the fact that quicksort works better for the RAM cache.

# Quickselect

Quickselect is a selection algorithm to find the *k*th smallest element in an unordered list. Quickselect uses the same approach as a quicksort algorithm. A pivot is chosen, and the array is partitioned. Instead of recursing both sides like quicksort, however, it recurses only the side for the element. This reduces the complexity from $O(nlog_2(n))$ to $O(n)$.

Quickselect is implemented in the following code:

```
1    var array = [1,3,3,-2,3,14,7,8,1,2,2];
2    // sorted form: [-2, 1, 1, 2, 2, 3, 3, 3, 7, 8, 14]
3
4    function quickSelectInPlace(A, l, h, k){
5        var p = partition(A, l, h);
6        if(p==(k-1)) {
7            return A[p];
8        } else if(p>(k-1)) {
9            return quickSelectInPlace(A, l, p - 1,k);
10       } else {
11           return quickSelectInPlace(A, p + 1, h,k);
12       }
13   }
14
15   function medianQuickselect(array) {
16       return quickSelectInPlace(array,0,array.length-1, Math.
         floor(array.length/2));
17   }
18
19   quickSelectInPlace(array,0,array.length-1,5); // 2
```

```
20    // 2 - because it's the fifth smallest element
21    quickSelectInPlace(array,0,array.length-1,10); // 7
22    // 7 - because it's the tenth smallest element
```

**Time Complexity:** $O(n)$

# Mergesort

Mergesort works by dividing the array into subarrays until each array has one element. Then, each subarray is *concatenated* (merged) in a sorted order (see Figure 10-9).

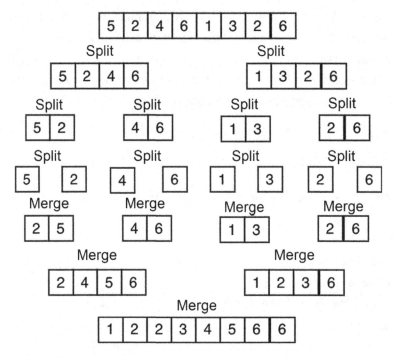

*Figure 10-9. Mergesort*

The merge function should add all the elements from both arrays in sorted order in a "result array." To do this, the index of each array can be created to keep track of elements already compared. Once one array exhausts all its elements, the rest can be appended to the result array.

```
1    function merge(leftA, rightA){
2        var results= [], leftIndex= 0, rightIndex= 0;
3
```

```
4        while (leftIndex < leftA.length && rightIndex < rightA.length) {
5            if( leftA[leftIndex]<rightA[rightIndex] ){
6                results.push(leftA[leftIndex++]);
7            } else {
8                results.push(rightA[rightIndex++]);
9            }
10       }
11       var leftRemains = leftA.slice(leftIndex),
12           rightRemains = rightA.slice(rightIndex);
13
14       // add remaining to resultant array
15       return results.concat(leftRemains).concat(rightRemains);
16   }
```

The merging function works by taking the two arrays (left and right) and merging them into one resultant array. The elements need to be compared as they get merged to preserve order.

Now, the mergeSort function has to partition the bigger array into two separate arrays and recursively call merge.

```
1    function mergeSort(array) {
2
3        if(array.length<2){
4            return array; // Base case: array is now sorted since it's
                                        just 1 element
5        }
6
7        var midpoint = Math.floor((array.length)/2),
8            leftArray = array.slice(0, midpoint),
9            rightArray = array.slice(midpoint);
10
11       return merge(mergeSort(leftArray), mergeSort(rightArray));
12   }
13   mergeSort([6,1,23,4,2,3]); // [1, 2, 3, 4, 6, 23]
```

**Time Complexity:** $O(nlog_2(n))$
**Space Complexity:** $O(n)$

Mergesort has a large space complexity of O(*n*) because of the need to create *n* number of arrays to be merged later. Use mergesort when a stable sort is needed. A stable sort is one that's guaranteed not to reorder elements with identical keys. Mergesort is guaranteed to be O(*nlog₂(n)*). A disadvantage of mergesort is that it uses O(*n*) in space.

## Count Sort

Count sort can be done in O(*k+n*) because it does not compare values. It works only for numbers and given a certain range. Instead of sorting by swapping elements, this count works by counting occurrences of each element in the array. Once occurrences of each element are counted, the new array can be created using those occurrences. This sorts the data without having to swap elements, as shown in Figure 10-10.

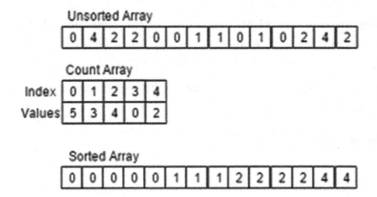

*Figure 10-10.  Count sort*

Here's an implementation using a JavaScript object:

```
1    function countSort(array) {
2        var hash = {}, countArr= [];
3        for(var i=0;i<array.length;i++){
4            if(!hash[array[i]]){
5                hash[array[i]] = 1;
6            }else{
7                hash[array[i]]++;
8            }
9        }
10
```

```
11        for(var key in hash){
12            // for any number of _ element, add it to array
13            for(var i=0;i<hash[key];i++) {
14                countArr.push(parseInt(key));
15            }
16        }
17
18        return countArr;
19    }
20    countSort([6,1,23,2,3,2,1,2,2,3,3,1,123,123,4,2,3]); // [1, 2, 3, 4, 6, 23]
```

**Time Complexity:** $O(k+n)$

**Space Complexity:** $O(k)$

Use count sort when you're sorting integers with a limited range. This will be the fastest sort for this case.

# JavaScript's Built-in Sort

JavaScript has a built-in sort() method for an array object, which sorts elements by ascending order. To use it, there is an optional parameter that you can pass in a comparator function.

However, the default comparator function sorts alphabetically, so it will not work for numbers.

```
1    var array1 = [12,3,4,2,1,34,23];
2    array1.sort(); // array1: [1, 12, 2, 23, 3, 34, 4]
```

In the previous example, notice that numbers starting with 1 came first (1, 12), then numbers starting with 2, and so forth. This is because no comparator function was passed and JavaScript converted the elements into a string and sorted it according to the alphabet.

To sort numbers correctly, use this:

```
1    var array1 = [12,3,4,2,1,34,23];
2
3    function comparatorNumber(a,b) {
4        return a-b;
5    }
6
```

```
7    array1.sort(comparatorNumber);
8    // array1: [1, 2, 3, 4, 12, 23, 34]
```

a-b indicates that it should be from smallest to biggest (ascending). Descending order can be done as follows:

```
1    var array1 = [12,3,4,2,1,34,23];
2
3    function comparatorNumber(a,b) {
4        return b-a;
5    }
6
7    array1.sort(comparatorNumber); // array1: [34, 23, 12, 4, 3, 2, 1]
```

The sort() function can be useful when you need a quick way to sort something without implementing it yourself.

# Summary

There are two ways to search inside an array: linear search and binary search. Binary search is faster with $O(log_2(n))$ time complexity, while linear search has $O(n)$ time complexity. However, the binary search can be performed only on a sorted array.

Table 10-1 summarizes time and space complexities of different sorting algorithms. The most efficient sorting algorithms are quicksort, mergesort, and count sort. Count sort, while the fastest, is limited to when the range of array's values are known.

**Table 10-1.** *Sorting Summary*

| Algorithm | Time Complexity | Space Complexity |
| --- | --- | --- |
| Quicksort | $O(nlog_2(n))$ | $O(nlog_2(n))$ |
| Mergesort | $O(nlog_2(n))$ | $O(nlog_2(n))$ |
| Bubble sort | $O(n^2)$ | $O(n^2)$ |
| Insertion sort | $O(n^2)$ | $O(n^2)$ |
| Selection sort | $O(n^2)$ | $O(n^2)$ |
| Count sort | $O(k + n)$ | $O(k)$ |

# Exercises

---

**USE THE IMPLEMENT SQUARE ROOT FUNCTION FOR AN INTEGER WITHOUT USING ANY MATH LIBRARIES**

---

The first solution that may come to mind is trying every possibility from 1 to the number, as follows:

```
1    function sqrtIntNaive(number){
2        if(number == 0 || number == 1)
3            return number;
4
5        var index = 1, square = 1;
6
7        while(square < number){
8            if (square == number){
9                return square;
10            }
11
12            index++;
13            square = index*index;
14        }
15        return index;
16    }
17    sqrtIntNaive(9);
```

**Time Complexity:** $O(n)$

This is essentially a linear search since it has to linearly check one by one the value for the square root.

The binary search algorithm can be applied to this problem. Instead of going up 1 by 1, partition the range into upper half and lower half between 1 and the given number as follows:

```
1    function sqrtInt(number) {
2        if(number == 0 || number == 1) return number;
3
4        var start = 1, end = number, ans;
5
```

```
6          while(start <= end) {
7              let mid = parseInt((start+end)/2);
8
9              if (mid*mid == number)
10                 return mid;
11
12             if(mid*mid<number){
13                 start = mid+1; // use the upper section
14                 ans = mid;
15             }else{
16                 end = mid-1; // use the lower section
17             }
18         }
19         return ans;
20     }
21     sqrtInt(9);
```

**Time Complexity:** $O(log_2(n))$

## Bonus: Find a Square Root of a Float

For this exercise, the only difference is using a threshold value to calculate accuracy to because the square root of a double will have decimals. Hence, the time complexity also stays the same.

```
1      function sqrtDouble(number) {
2          var threshold = 0.1;
3          //9 try middle,
4          var upper = number;
5          var lower = 0;
6          var middle;
7          while(upper-lower>threshold){
8              middle = (upper+lower)/2;
9              if(middle*middle>number){
10                 upper = middle;
11             }else{
12                 lower = middle;
13             }
14         }
15         return middle
16     }
17     sqrtDouble(9); // 3.0234375
```

## FIND IF TWO ELEMENTS OF AN ARRAY ADD UP TO A GIVEN NUMBER

The simple approach to this problem is to check every other element for each element in the array.

```
1    function findTwoSum(array, sum) {
2
3        for(var i=0, arrayLength = array.length; i<arrayLength;i++){
4            for(var j=i+1;j<arrayLength;j++){
5                if(array[j]+array[i] == sum){
6                    return true;
7                }
8            }
9        }
10       return false;
11   }
```

**Time Complexity:** $O(n^2)$

**Space Complexity:** $O(1)$

There is a lot of checking, and hence it takes quadratic time.

A better approach is to store the already visited numbers and check against them. This way, it can be done in linear time.

```
1    function findTwoSum(array, sum){
2        var store = {};
3
4        for(var i=0, arrayLength = array.length; i<arrayLength;i++){
5            if(store[array[i]]){
6                return true;
7            }else{
8                store[sum-array[i]] = array[i];
9            }
10       }
11       return false;
12   }
```

**Time Complexity:** $O(n)$

**Space Complexity:** $O(n)$

This algorithm cuts the time complexity to $O(n)$ but takes $O(n)$ space as well to store items into the `store` object.

---

## FIND AN ELEMENT WITHIN AN ARRAY THAT APPEARS ONLY ONCE

Given a sorted array in which all elements appear twice (one after one) and one element appears only once, find that element in $O(log_2n)$ complexity. This can be done by modifying the binary search algorithm and checking the addition indices.

```
Input:   arr = [1, 1, 3, 3, 4, 5, 5, 7, 7, 8, 8]      Output:  4
Input:   arr = [1, 1, 3, 3, 4, 4, 5, 5, 7, 7, 8]      Output:  8
```

```
1    function findOnlyOnce(arr, low, high) {
2        if (low > high) {
3            return null;
4        }
5        if (low == high) {
6            return arr[low];
7        }
8
9        var mid = Math.floor((high+low)/2);
10
11       if (mid%2 == 0) {
12           if (arr[mid] == arr[mid+1]) {
13               return findOnlyOnce(arr, mid+2, high);
14           } else {
15               return findOnlyOnce(arr, low, mid);
16           }
17       } else {
18           if (arr[mid] == arr[mid-1]) {
19               return findOnlyOnce(arr, mid+1, high);
20           } else {
21               return findOnlyOnce(arr, low, mid-1);
22           }
```

```
23        }
24    }
25    function findOnlyOnceHelper(arr) {
26        return findOnlyOnce(arr, 0, arr.length);
27    }
28    findOnlyOnceHelper([ 1, 1, 2, 4, 4, 5, 5, 6, 6 ]);
```

**Time Complexity:** $O(\log_2 n)$

**Space Complexity:** $O(1)$

## CREATE A JAVASCRIPT SORT COMPARATOR FUNCTION THAT WOULD SORT STRING BY LENGTH

This is fairly simple. If it is an array of strings, strings all have a property of `length`, which can be used to sort the array.

```
1    var mythical = ['dragon', 'slayer','magic','wizard of oz', 'ned stark'];
2
3    function sortComparator(a,b){
4        return a.length - b.length;
5    }
6    mythical.sort(sortComparator);
7    // ["magic", "dragon", "slayer", "ned stark", "wizard of of"]
```

### Examples

Sort string elements, putting strings with a first, as shown here:

```
1    var mythical = ['dragon', 'slayer','magic','wizard of oz', 'ned tark'];
2
3    function sortComparator(a,b){
4        return a.indexOf("a") - b.indexOf("a");
5    }
6
7    mythical.sort(sortComparator);
8    // ["magic", "dragon", "slayer", "wizard of oz", "ned stark"]
```

Sort object elements by the number of properties, as shown here:

```
1   var mythical=[{prop1:", prop2:"},{prop1:", prop2:", prop3:"},{prop1:",
    prop2:"}];
2
3   function sortComparator(a,b){
4       return Object.keys(a).length - Object.keys(b).length;
5   }
6
7   mythical.sort(sortComparator);
// [{prop1:", prop2:"},{prop1:", prop2:"},{prop1:", prop2:", prop3:"}]
```

As shown, there's a lot of flexibility with these comparators, and they can be used for sorting without needing to implement a sort yourself.

## IMPLEMENT A WORD COUNTER LIST

Create a function that generates an object of words (as keys) and the number of times the words occur in a string ordered by highest to lowest occurrences.

Here's some example input: **practice makes perfect. get perfect by practice. just practice**.

Here's the example output: `{ practice: 3, perfect: 2, makes: 1, get: 1, by: 1, just: 1 }`.

```
1    function wordCount(sentence) {
2        // period with nothing so it doesn't count as word
3        var wordsArray = sentence.replace(/[.]/g,"").split(" "),
4            occurenceList = {}, answerList = {};
5
6        for (var i=0, wordsLength=wordsArray.length; i<wordsLength;  i++) {
7            var currentWord = wordsArray[i];
8            // doesn't exist, set as 1st occurrence
9            if (!occurenceList[currentWord]) {
10               occurenceList[currentWord] = 1;
```

```
11              } else {
12                  occurenceList[currentWord]++; // add occurrences
13              }
14          }
15
16          var arrayTemp = [];
17          // push the value and key as fixed array
18          for (var prop in occurenceList) {
19              arrayTemp.push([occurenceList[prop], prop]);
20          }
21
22          function sortcomp(a, b) {
23              return b[0] - a[0]; // compare the first element of the array
24          }
25
26          arrayTemp.sort(sortcomp); //sort
27
28          for (var i = 0, arrlength = arrayTemp.length; i < arrlength; i++) {
29              var current = arrayTemp[i];
30              answerList[current[1]] = current[0]; // key value pairs
31          }
32          return answerList;
33      }
34      wordCount("practice makes perfect. get perfect by practice. just practice");
```

**Time Complexity:** $O(nlog_2(n))$

**Space Complexity:** $O(n)$

Time complexity is limited by the sorting algorithm that the JavaScript engine uses. Most use either mergesort or quicksort, which are both $O(nlog_2(n))$.

# CHAPTER 11

# Hash Tables

A *hash table* is a fixed-sized data structure in which the size is defined at the start. This chapter explains how hash tables work by focusing on hashing, the method of generating a unique key. By the end of this chapter, you will understand various hashing techniques and know how to implement a hash table from scratch.

## Introducing Hash Tables

Hash tables are excellent for quick storage and retrieval of data based on key-value pairs. In JavaScript, JavaScript objects work this way by defining a key (property) and its associated value. Figure 11-1 shows each key and its associated item.

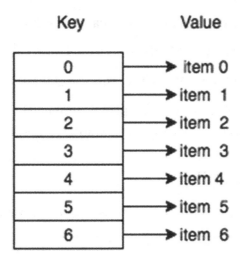

*Figure 11-1.* Simple hash table overview

© Sammie Bae 2019
S. Bae, *JavaScript Data Structures and Algorithms*, https://doi.org/10.1007/978-1-4842-3988-9_11

A hash table contains two main functions: put() and get(). put() is used for storing data into the hash table, while get() is used for retrieving data from the hash table. Both of these functions have a time complexity of O(1).

In a nutshell, a hash table is analogous to an array whose index is calculated with a hashing function to identify a space in memory uniquely.

localStorage is an example of a data structure based on a hash table. It is a native JavaScript object supported by all major browsers. It lets developers persist data inside the browser, meaning it can be accessed after a session.

```
1    localStorage.setItem("testKey","testValue");
2    location = location; // refreshes the page
3
4    //-----------------------------------
5    localStorage.getItem("testKey"); // prints "testValue"
```

# Hashing Techniques

The most important part of a hash table is the hash function. The hash function converts a specified key into an index for an array that stores all of the data. The three primary requirements for a good hash function are as follows:

- *Deterministic*: Equal keys produce equal hash values.

- *Efficiency*: It should be O(1) in time.

- *Uniform distribution*: It makes the most use of the array.

The first technique for hashing is to use prime numbers. By using the modulus operator with prime numbers, a uniform distribution of the index can be guaranteed.

## Prime Number Hashing

Prime numbers in hashing are important. This is because modulus division using prime numbers yields an array index in a distributed manner.

**Modulus number:** 11

```
      4 % 11      = 4
      7 % 11      = 7
      9 % 11      = 9
     15 % 11      = 4
```

Collisions can be seen with 15 and 4 yielding the same key; handling this collision is discussed later in this chapter. What is important here is that modulus by prime numbers guarantees the best distribution for a fixed size. Modulus by a small nonprime number such as 4 guarantees only a range from 0 to 3 and leads to a large number of collisions.

```
Modulus number: 4
        6 % 4      = 2
       10 % 4      = 2
```

This is the first hashing technique that will be observed. Take a look at Figure 11-2, which is a hash table with two arrays of size 11, and each of the 11 elements is empty. One array is for the keys, and the other is for values.

| | 0 | 1 | 2 | 3 | 4 | 5 | 6 | 7 | 8 | 9 | 10 |
|---|---|---|---|---|---|---|---|---|---|---|---|
| Keys | | | | | | | | | | | |
| Values | | | | | | | | | | | |

*Figure 11-2.* *Hash table of size 11, with all empty elements*

In this example, keys are integers, and strings are being stored as keys. Let's hash the following key-value pairs:

```
{key:7, value: "hi"}
{key:24, value: "hello"}
{key:42, value: "sunny"}
{key:34, value: "weather"}
```

```
Prime number: 11
7 % 11  = 7
24 % 11 = 2
42 % 11 = 9
34 % 11 = 1
```

After all the key-value pairs have been inserted, the resulting hash table is shown in Figure 11-3.

| 0 | 1 | 2 | 3 | 4 | 5 | 6 | 7 | 8 | 9 | 10 |
|---|---|---|---|---|---|---|---|---|---|----|
|   | 34 | 24 |   |   |   |   | 7 |   | 42 |   |
|   | weathe | hello |   |   |   |   | hi |   | sunny |   |

*Figure 11-3.* *Hash table after inserting the value pairs*

Now let's hash {key:18, value: "wow"}.

```
Prime number: 11
18 % 11  = 7
```

This is a problem because 7 already exists in the index of 7 and causes an index collision. With a perfect hashing function, there are no collisions. However, collision-free hashing is almost impossible in most cases. Therefore, strategies for handling collisions are needed for hash tables.

# Probing

To work around occurring collisions, the probing hashing technique finds the next available index in the array. The *linear probing* technique resolves conflicts by finding the next available index via incremental trials, while *quadratic probing* uses quadratic functions to generate incremental trials.

## Linear Probing

Linear probing works by finding the next available index by incrementing one index at a time. For example, in the case of 18 and 7 hashing to the same key, 18 would be hashed into key 8 because that's the next empty spot (see Figure 11-4).

| 0 | 1 | 2 | 3 | 4 | 5 | 6 | 7 | 8 | 9 | 10 |
|---|---|---|---|---|---|---|---|---|---|----|
|   | 34 | 24 |   |   |   |   | 7 | 18 | 42 |   |
|   | weathe | hello |   |   |   |   | hi | wow | sunny |   |

*Figure 11-4.* *Hash table 1 after using linear probing*

However, now when the get(key) function is used, it has to start at the original hash result (7) and then iterate until 18 is found.

The main disadvantage of linear probing is it easily creates *clusters*, which are bad because they create more data to iterate through.

## Quadratic Probing

Quadratic probing is a good technique for addressing the cluster issue. Quadratic probing uses perfect squares instead of incrementing by 1 each time, and this helps to evenly distribute across the available indices, as shown in Figure 11-5.

```
h + (1)^2, h + (2)^2, h + (3)^2, h + (4)^2
h + 1, h + 4, h + 9, h + 16
```

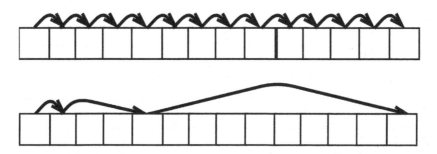

***Figure 11-5.*** *Linear probing (on top) and quadratic probing (on bottom)*

## Rehashing/Double-Hashing

Another great way to uniformly distribute the keys is by having a second hashing function that hashes the result from the original. These are the three primary requirements for a good second hash function:

- *Different*: It needs to be different to distribute it better.

- *Efficiency*: It should still be O(1) in time.

- *Nonzero*: It should never evaluate to zero. Zero gives the initial hash value.

A commonly used second hashing function is as follows:

$$hash2(x) = R - (x \% R)$$

Here, $x$ is the result from hashing the first time, and $R$ is less than the size of the hash table. Each hash collision is resolved by the following, where $i$ is the iteration trial number:

$$i * hash_2(x)$$

# Hash Table Implementation

Now that hash tables have been explained, let's implement one from scratch. In this section, you will apply three different techniques to the same example. The following are the example key-value pairs that will be used:

7, "hi"

20, "hello"

33, "sunny"

46, "weather"

59, "wow"

72, "forty"

85, "happy"

98, "sad"

## Using Linear Probing

Let's start the example with simple linear probing.

```
1   function HashTable(size) {
2       this.size = size;
3       this.keys = this.initArray(size);
4       this.values = this.initArray(size);
5       this.limit = 0;
6   }
7
8   HashTable.prototype.put = function(key, value) {
9       if (this.limit >= this.size) throw 'hash table is full'
10
```

```
11        var hashedIndex = this.hash(key);
12
13        // Linear probing
14        while (this.keys[hashedIndex] != null) {
15            hashedIndex++;
16
17            hashedIndex = hashedIndex % this.size;
18
19        }
20
21        this.keys[hashedIndex] = key;
22        this.values[hashedIndex] = value;
23        this.limit++;
24    }
25
26    HashTable.prototype.get = function(key) {
27        var hashedIndex = this.hash(key);
28
29        while (this.keys[hashedIndex] != key) {
30            hashedIndex++;
31
32            hashedIndex = hashedIndex % this.size;
33
34        }
35        return this.values[hashedIndex];
36    }
37
38    HashTable.prototype.hash = function(key) {
39        // Check if int
40        if (!Number.isInteger(key)) throw 'must be int';
41            return key % this.size;
42    }
43
44    HashTable.prototype.initArray = function(size) {
45        var array = [];
```

```
46          for (var i = 0; i < size; i++) {
47              array.push(null);
48          }
49          return array;
50      }
51
52      var exampletable = new HashTable(13);
53      exampletable.put(7, "hi");
54      exampletable.put(20, "hello");
55      exampletable.put(33, "sunny");
56      exampletable.put(46, "weather");
57      exampletable.put(59, "wow");
58      exampletable.put(72, "forty");
59      exampletable.put(85, "happy");
60      exampletable.put(98, "sad");
```

Here is the result:

```
Keys:
        [ 85, 98, null, null, null, null, null, 7, 20, 33, 46, 59, 72 ]
Values:
        [ 'happy', 'sad', null, null, null, null, null, 'hi', 'hello',
          'sunny', 'weather', 'wow', 'forty' ]
```

## Using Quadratic Probing

Now, let's change the put() and get() methods to use quadratic probing.

```
1      HashTable.prototype.put = function (key, value) {
2          if (this.limit >= this.size) throw 'hash table is full'
3
4          var hashedIndex = this.hash(key), squareIndex = 1;
5
6          // quadratic probing
7          while (this.keys[hashedIndex] != null) {
8              hashedIndex += Math.pow(squareIndex,2);
9
```

```
10              hashedIndex
11              squareIndex++;
12          }
13
14          this.keys[hashedIndex] = key;
15          this.values[hashedIndex] = value;
16          this.limit++;
17      }
18
19      HashTable.prototype.get = function (key) {
20          var hashedIndex = this.hash(key), squareIndex = 1;
21
22          while ( this.keys[hashedIndex] != key ) {
23              hashedIndex += Math.pow(squareIndex, 2);
24
25              hashedIndex = hashedIndex % this.size;
26              squareIndex++;
27          }
28
29          return this.values[hashedIndex];
30      }
```

Here is the result:

Keys:
```
    [ null, null, null, 85, 72, null, 98, 7, 20, null, 59, 46, 33 ]
```
Values:
```
    [ null, null,  null, 'happy', 'forty', null, 'sad', 'hi', 'hello',
      null, 'wow', 'weather',  'sunny' ]
```

This result is more uniformly distributed than the result from linear probing. It would be easier to see with a bigger array size and more elements.

# Using Double-Hashing with Linear Probing

Finally, let's combine double-hashing and linear probing. Recall the common second hash function, $hash_2(x) = R - (x \% R)$, where $x$ is the result from hashing the first time, and $R$ is less than the size of the hash table.

```
1    HashTable.prototype.put = function(key, value) {
2        if (this.limit >= this.size) throw 'hash table is full'
3
4        var hashedIndex = this.hash(key);
5
6        while (this.keys[hashedIndex] != null) {
7            hashedIndex++;
8
9            hashedIndex = hashedIndex % this.size;
10
11       }
12       this.keys[hashedIndex] = key;
13       this.values[hashedIndex] = value;
14       this.limit++;
15   }
16
17   HashTable.prototype.get = function(key) {
18       var hashedIndex = this.hash(key);
19
20       while (this.keys[hashedIndex] != key) {
21           hashedIndex++;
22
23           hashedIndex = hashedIndex % this.size;
24
25       }
26       return this.values[hashedIndex];
27   }
28
29   HashTable.prototype.hash = function(key) {
30       if (!Number.isInteger(key)) throw 'must be int'; // check if int
```

```
31          return this.secondHash(key % this.size);
32      }
33
34      HashTable.prototype.secondHash = function(hashedKey) {
35          var R = this.size - 2;
36          return R - hashedKey % R;
37      }
```

Here is the result:

```
Keys:
        [ null, 59, 20, 85, 98, 72, null, 7, null, 46, null, 33, null ]
Values:
        [ null, 'wow', 'hello', 'happy', 'sad', 'forty', null, 'hi', null,
          'weather', null, 'sunny', null ]
```

Again, double-hashing results in a more uniformly distributed array than the result from linear probing. Both quadratic probing and double-hashing are great techniques to reduce the number of collisions in a hash table. There are collision resolution algorithms far more advanced than these techniques, but they are beyond the scope of this book.

# Summary

A hash table is a fixed-sized data structure in which the size is defined at the start. Hash tables are implemented using a hash function to generate an index for the array. A good hash function is deterministic, efficient, and uniformly distributive. Hash collisions should be minimized with a good uniformly distributive hash function, but having some collisions is unavoidable. Hash collision-handling techniques include but are not limited to linear probing (incrementing the index by 1), quadratic probing (using a quadratic function to increment the index), and double-hashing (using multiple hash functions).

The next chapter explores stacks and queues, which are dynamically sized data structures.

# CHAPTER 12

# Stacks and Queues

This chapter covers stacks and queues; both are versatile data structures commonly used in the implementation of other, more complex data structures. You will learn what stacks and queues are, how and when they are used, and how to implement them. Finally, the exercises will help you to understand these concepts as well as when to apply stacks and queues to an algorithmic problem.

## Stacks

A *stack* is a data structure in which only the last inserted element can be removed and accessed (see Figure 12-1). Think about stacking plates on a table. To get to the bottom one, you must remove all the other ones on the top. This is a principle known as *last in, first out* (LIFO). A stack is great because it is fast. Since it is known that the last element is to be removed, the lookup and insertion happen in a constant time of $O(1)$. Stacks should be used over arrays when you need to work with data in the LIFO form where the algorithm needs to access only the last-added element. The limitation of stacks is that they cannot access the non-last-added element directly like arrays can; in addition, accessing deeper elements requires you to remove the elements from the data structure.

163

© Sammie Bae 2019
S. Bae, *JavaScript Data Structures and Algorithms*, https://doi.org/10.1007/978-1-4842-3988-9_12

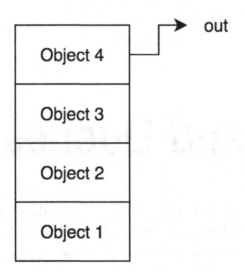

***Figure 12-1.*** *Stack, LIFO*

In JavaScript, arrays have methods that define the stack class: pop and push (as discussed in Chapter 5). With this, a stack can be easily implemented.

Here is some skeleton code to start. You can find the code on GitHub.[1]

```
1    function Stack(array){
2         this.array = [];
3         if(array) this.array = array;
4    }
5
6    Stack.prototype.getBuffer = function(){
7         return this.array.slice();
8    }
9
10   Stack.prototype.isEmpty = function(){
11        return this.array.length == 0;
12   }
13
```

---

[1]https://github.com/Apress/js-data-structures-and-algorithms

```
14   //instance of the stack class
15   var stack1 = new Stack();
16
17   console.log(stack1); // {array: []}
```

Let's first consider "peeking" at the most recently added element. This can be done simply by using the largest index of the array.

# Peek

*Peeking* at the last added element of the stack means returning the last-added element without removing it from the data structure. Peeking is often used to compare the last-added element to some other variable and to evaluate whether the last-added element should be removed from the data structure.

```
1   Stack.prototype.peek = function(){
2       return this.array[this.array.length-1];
3   }
4   stack1.push(10);
5   console.log(stack1.peek()); // 10
6   stack1.push(5);
7   console.log(stack1.peek()); // 5
```

**Time Complexity:** O(1)

# Insertion

Inserting into a stack can be done via the push function natively supported with JavaScript arrays.

```
1   Stack.prototype.push = function(value){
2       this.array.push(value);
3   }
4
5   stack1.push(1);
6   stack1.push(2);
7   stack1.push(3);
8   console.log(stack1); // {array: [1,2,3]}
```

**Time Complexity:** O(1)

# Deletion

Deletion can also be implemented using a native JavaScript array method, called pop.

```
1    Stack.prototype.pop = function() {
2        return this.array.pop();
3    };
4
5    stack1.pop(1);
6    stack1.pop(2);
7    stack1.pop(3);
8
9    console.log(stack1); // {array: []}
```

**Time Complexity:** O(1)

# Access

Accessing specific elements in a data structure is important. Here, let's take a look at how to access an element based on order.

To access the *n*th node from the top, you need to call pop *n* number of times.

```
1    function stackAccessNthTopNode(stack, n){
2        var bufferArray = stack.getBuffer();
3        if(n<=0) throw 'error'
4
5        var bufferStack = new Stack(bufferArray);
6
7        while(--n!==0){
8            bufferStack.pop();
9        }
10       return bufferStack.pop();
11   }
12
13   var stack2 = new Stack();
14   stack2.push(1);
```

```
15    stack2.push(2);
16    stack2.push(3);
17    stackAccessNthTopNode(stack2,2); // 2
```

**Time Complexity:** O($n$)

Search will be implemented in a similar way.

# Search

Searching the stack data structure for a specific element is a critical operation. To do this, you must first create a buffer stack so that pop can be called on that buffer stack. This way, the original stack is not mutated, and nothing is removed from it.

```
1     function stackSearch(stack, element) {
2     var bufferArray = stack.getBuffer();
3
4     var bufferStack = new Stack(bufferArray); // copy into  buffer
5
6     while(!bufferStack.isEmpty()){
7         if(bufferStack.pop()==element){
8             return true;
9         }
10    }
11    return false;
12    }
```

**Time Complexity:** O($n$)

# Queues

A queue is also a data structure, but you can remove only the first added element (see Figure 12-2). This is a principle known as *first in, first out* (FIFO). A queue is also great because of the constant time in its operations. Similar to a stack, it has limitations because only one item can be accessed at a time. Queues should be used over arrays when you need to work with data in the FIFO form where the algorithm only needs to access the first added element.

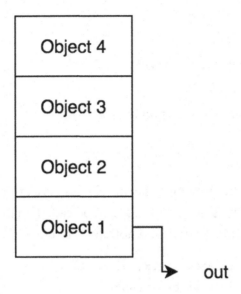

***Figure 12-2.*** *Queue, FIFO*

In JavaScript, arrays have methods that define the queue class: shift() and push() (as discussed in Chapter 5). Recall that the shift() method on an array in JavaScript removes and returns the first element of the array. Adding to a queue is commonly known as *enqueuing,* and removing from a queue is known as *dequeuing.* shift() can be used for the dequeue, and .push() can be used for the enqueue.

Here is some skeleton code to start. You can find the code on GitHub.[2]

```
1   function Queue(array){
2       this.array = [];
3       if(array) this.array = array;
4   }
5
6   Queue.prototype.getBuffer = function(){
7       return this.array.slice();
8   }
9
10  Queue.prototype.isEmpty = function(){
```

²https://github.com/Apress/js-data-structures-and-algorithms

```
11        return this.array.length == 0;
12    }
13
14    //instance of the queue class
15    var queue1 = new Queue();
16
17    console.log(queue1); // { array: [] }
```

## Peek

The peek function looks at the first item without popping it from the queue. In the stack implementation, the last element in the array was returned, but a queue returns the first element in the array because of FIFO.

```
1    Queue.prototype.peek = function(){
2         return this.array[0];
3    }
```

## Insertion

As mentioned, insertion for a queue is known as *enqueue*. Since an array is used to hold the stack data, the push() method can be used to implement enqueue.

```
1    Queue.prototype.enqueue = function(value){
2         return this.array.push(value);
3    }
```

   **Time Complexity:** O(1)

## Deletion

As mentioned, deletion for a queue also is known as *dequeue*. Since an array is used to hold the stack data, the shift() method can be used to remove and return the first element in the queue.

```
1    Queue.prototype.dequeue = function() {
2         return this.array.shift();
```

```
3    };
4
5    var queue1 = new Queue();
6
7    queue1.enqueue(1);
8    queue1.enqueue(2);
9    queue1.enqueue(3);
10
11   console.log(queue1); // {array: [1,2,3]}
12
13   queue1.dequeue();
14   console.log(queue1); // {array: [2,3]}
15
16   queue1.dequeue();
17   console.log(queue1); // {array: [3]}
```

**Time Complexity:** O(n)

Because the shift() implementation removes the element at zero indexes and then shifts remaining indexes down consecutively, all other elements in the array need to have their indexes altered, and this takes $O(n)$. With a linked-list implementation, as covered in Chapter 13, this can be reduced to O(1).

## Access

Unlike an array, items in a queue cannot be accessed via index. To access the nth last-added node, you need to call dequeue n number of times. A buffer is needed to prevent modification to the original queue.

```
1    function queueAccessNthTopNode(queue, n){
2        var bufferArray = queue.getBuffer();
3        if(n<=0) throw 'error'
4
5        var bufferQueue = new Queue(bufferArray);
6
7        while(--n!==0){
8            bufferQueue.dequeue();
```

```
 9          }
10          return bufferQueue.dequeue();
11    }
```

**Time Complexity:** O(*n*)

# Search

You might need to search a queue to check whether an element exists within a queue. Again, this involves creating a buffer queue first to avoid modifications to the original queue.

```
 1    function queueSearch(queue, element){
 2        var bufferArray = queue.getBuffer();
 3
 4        var bufferQueue = new Queue(bufferArray);
 5
 6        while(!bufferQueue.isEmpty()){
 7            if(bufferQueue.dequeue()==element){
 8                return true;
 9            }
10        }
11        return false;
12    }
```

**Time Complexity:** O(*n*)

# Summary

Both stacks and queues support peek, insertion, and deletion in O(1). The most important distinction between a stack and a queue is that a stack is LIFO and a queue is FIFO. Table 12-1 summarizes the time complexity.

***Table 12-1.*** *Queue and Stack Time Complexity Summary*

|         | Access | Search | Peek | Insertion | Deletion |
|---------|--------|--------|------|-----------|----------|
| Queue   | O(n)   | O(n)   | O(1) | O(1)      | $O(n)^3$ |
| Stack   | O(n)   | O(n)   | O(1) | O(1)      | O(1)     |

# Exercises

All the code for the exercises can be found on GitHub.[4]

---

| DESIGN A STACK USING ONLY QUEUES AND THEN DESIGN A QUEUE USING ONLY STACKS |

### <u>Stack Using Queues</u>

A queue can be made with two stacks. A queue is a data structure that returns the first-added element with the dequeue() method. A stack is a data structure that returns the last-added element via pop. In other words, a queue removes elements in the reverse direction of a stack.

For example, examine a stack array with [1,2,3,4,5].

To reverse the order, all of the elements could be pushed onto a second stack and pop that second stack. So, the second stack array will look like this: [5,4,3,2,1].

When this is popped off, the last element is removed, which is 1. So, 1 is originally the first element. Hence, a queue was implemented using only two stacks.

```
1    function TwoStackQueue(){
2        this.inbox = new Stack();
3        this.outbox= new Stack();
4    }
5
6    TwoStackQueue.prototype.enqueue = function(val) {
7        this.inbox.push(val);
```

---

[3]This could be improved to O(1) with a linked-list implementation.
[4]https://github.com/Apress/js-data-structures-and-algorithms

```
8    }
9
10   TwoStackQueue.prototype.dequeue = function() {
11       if(this.outbox.isEmpty()){
12           while(!this.inbox.isEmpty()){
13               this.outbox.push(this.inbox.pop());
14           }
15       }
16       return this.outbox.pop();
17   };
18   var queue = new TwoStackQueue();
19   queue.enqueue(1);
20   queue.enqueue(2);
21   queue.enqueue(3);
22   queue.dequeue(); // 1
23   queue.dequeue(); // 2
24   queue.dequeue(); // 3
```

## Queue Using Stacks

A stack can be made with two queues. A stack is a data structure that returns the last element. To implement this using a queue, simply enqueue all the elements inside the main queue except for the last element. Then return that last element.

```
1    function QueueStack(){
2        this.inbox = new Queue(); // first stack
3    }
4
5    QueueStack.prototype.push = function(val) {
6        this.inbox.enqueue(val);
7    };
8
9    QueueStack.prototype.pop = function() {
10       var size = this.inbox.array.length-1;
11       var counter =0;
12       var bufferQueue = new Queue();
13
14       while(++counter<=size){
15           bufferQueue.enqueue(this.inbox.dequeue());
```

```
16          }
17          var popped = this.inbox.dequeue();
18          this.inbox = bufferQueue;
19          return popped
20     };
21
22     var stack = new QueueStack();
23
24     stack.push(1);
25     stack.push(2);
26     stack.push(3);
27     stack.push(4);
28     stack.push(5);
29
30     console.log(stack.pop()); // 5
31     console.log(stack.pop()); // 4
32     console.log(stack.pop()); // 3
33     console.log(stack.pop()); // 2
34     console.log(stack.pop()); // 1
```

## DESIGN A CASHIER CLASS THAT TAKES IN A CUSTOMER OBJECT AND HANDLES FOOD ORDERING ON A FIRST-COME, FIRST-SERVED BASIS

Here are the requirements:

1.  The cashier requires a customer name and order item for the order.

2.  The customer who was served first is processed first.

Here are the required implementations:

- addOrder(customer): Enqueues a customer object to be processed by deliverOrder()

- deliverOrder(): Prints the name and order for the next customer to be processed

For this exercise, the `Cashier` class should enqueue customer class objects with a queue and dequeue them when finished.

```
1    function Customer(name, order){
2        this.name = name;
3        this.order = order;
4    }
5
6    function Cashier(){
7        this.customers = new Queue();
8    }
9
10   Cashier.prototype.addOrder = function (customer){
11       this.customers.enqueue(customer);
12   }
13
14   Cashier.prototype.deliverOrder = function(){
15       var finishedCustomer = this.customers.dequeue();
16
17       console.log(finishedCustomer.name+", your "+finishedCustomer.order+"
         is ready!");
18   }
19
20   var cashier = new Cashier();
21   var customer1 = new Customer('Jim',"Fries");
22   var customer2 = new Customer('Sammie',"Burger");
23   var customer3 = new Customer('Peter',"Drink");
24
25   cashier.addOrder(customer1);
26   cashier.addOrder(customer2);
27   cashier.addOrder(customer3);
28
29   cashier.deliverOrder(); // Jim, your Fries is ready!
30   cashier.deliverOrder(); // Sammie, your Burger is ready!
31   cashier.deliverOrder(); // Peter, your Drink is ready!
```

## DESIGN A PARENTHESIS VALIDATION CHECKER USING A STACK

((())) is a valid parentheses set, while ((() and ))) are not. A stack can be used to check the validity of parentheses by storing the left parenthesis and using push and triggering pop when the right parenthesis is seen.

If there is anything left in the stack afterward, it is not a valid parentheses set. Also, it is not a valid parentheses set if more right parentheses are seen than left ones. Using these rules, use a stack to store the most recent parenthesis.

```
1   function isParenthesisValid(validationString){
2       var stack = new Stack();
3       for(var pos=0;pos<validationString.length;pos++){
4           var currentChar = validationString.charAt(pos);
5           if(currentChar=="("){
6               stack.push(currentChar);
7           }else if(currentChar==")"){
8
9               if(stack.isEmpty())
10                  return false;
11
12              stack.pop();
13          }
14      }
15      return stack.isEmpty();
16  }
17  isParenthesisValid("((()"); // false;
18  isParenthesisValid("(((("); // false;
19  isParenthesisValid("()()"); // true;
```

**Time Complexity:** O(*n*)

This algorithm processes a string character by character. Hence, its time complexity is O(*n*), where *n* is the length of the string.

## DESIGN A SORTABLE STACK

The idea is to have two stacks, one that is sorted and one that is nonsorted. When sorting, pop from the unsorted stack, and when any number smaller (if descending order) or bigger (if ascending order) on the sorted stack is on top, that sorted stack element should move back to unsorted because it is out of order. Run a loop until the stack is all sorted.

```
1   function sortableStack(size){
2       this.size = size;
3
4       this.mainStack = new Stack();
5       this.sortedStack = new Stack();
6
7       // let's initialize it with some random ints
8       for(var i=0;i<this.size;i++){
9           this.mainStack.push(Math.floor(Math.random()*11));
10      }
11  }
12
13  sortableStack.prototype.sortStackDescending = function(){
14      while(!this.mainStack.isEmpty()){
15          var temp = this.mainStack.pop();
16          while(!this.sortedStack.isEmpty() && this.sortedStack.peek()< temp){
17              this.mainStack.push(this.sortedStack.pop());
18          }
19          this.sortedStack.push(temp);
20      }
21  }
22
23  var ss = new sortableStack(10);
24  console.log(ss);      // [ 8, 3, 4, 4, 1, 2, 0, 9, 7, 8 ]
25  ss.sortStackDescending();
26  console.log(ss.sortedStack);   // [ 9, 8, 8, 7, 4, 4, 3, 2, 1, 0 ]
```

**Time Complexity:** $O(n^2)$

This algorithm involves a reshuffling of the elements between two stacks, which in the worst possible case takes $O(n^2)$, where $n$ is the number of elements to be sorted.

# CHAPTER 13

# Linked Lists

This chapter will cover linked lists. A *linked list* is a data structure in which each node points to another node. Unlike arrays, which have a fixed size, a linked list is a dynamic data structure that can allocate and deallocate memory at runtime. By the end of this chapter, you will understand how to implement and work with linked lists.

There are two types of linked lists discussed in this chapter: *singly* and *doubly* linked lists. Let's examine the singly linked list first.

## Singly Linked Lists

The linked list data structure is one where each *node* (element) has reference to the next node (see Figure 13-1).

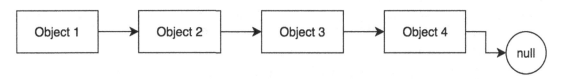

*Figure 13-1.* *Singly linked list*

A node in a singly linked list has the following properties: data and next. data is the value for the linked list node, and next is a pointer to another instance of SinglyLinkedListNode.

```
1    function SinglyLinkedListNode(data) {
2        this.data = data;
3        this.next = null;
4    }
```

© Sammie Bae 2019
S. Bae, *JavaScript Data Structures and Algorithms*, https://doi.org/10.1007/978-1-4842-3988-9_13

The following code is the base for the singly linked list example. You can find the code on GitHub.[1] The code block has a helper function to check whether the singly linked list is empty.

```
1   function SinglyLinkedList(){
2           this.head = null;
3           this.size = 0;
4   }
5
6   SinglyLinkedList.prototype.isEmpty = function(){
7           return this.size == 0;
8   }
```

The start of the linked list is referred to as the *head*. This property defaults to null before inserting any element into the linked list.

## Insertion

The following code block shows how to insert into a singly linked list. If the head of the linked list is empty, the head is set to the new node. Otherwise, the old heap is saved in temp, and the new head becomes the newly added node. Finally, the new head's next points to the temp (the old head).

```
1   SinglyLinkedList.prototype.insert = function(value) {
2       if (this.head === null) { //If first node
3           this.head = new SinglyLinkedListNode(value);
4       } else {
5           var temp = this.head;
6           this.head = new SinglyLinkedListNode(value);
7           this.head.next = temp;
8       }
9       this.size++;
10  }
11  var sll1 = new SinglyLinkedList();
12  sll1.insert(1); // linked list is now: 1 -> null
```

---

[1]https://github.com/Apress/js-data-structures-and-algorithms

```
13   sll1.insert(12); // linked list is now: 12 -> 1 -> null
14   sll1.insert(20); // linked list is now: 20 -> 12 -> 1 -> null
```

**Time Complexity:** O(*1*)

This is a constant time operation; no loops or traversal is required.

# Deletion by Value

The deletion of a node in a singly linked list is implemented by removing the reference of that node. If the node is in the "middle" of the linked list, this is achieved by having the node with the next pointer to that node point to that node's own next node instead, as shown in Figure 13-2.

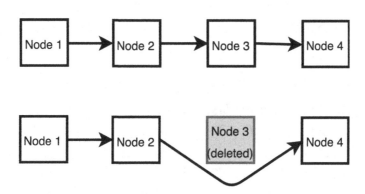

***Figure 13-2.*** *Interior node removal from a singly linked list*

If the node is at the end of the linked list, then the second-to-last element can dereference the node by setting its next to null.

```
1    SinglyLinkedList.prototype.remove = function(value) {
2        var currentHead = this.head;
3        if (currentHead.data == value) {
4            // just shift the head over. Head is now this new value
5            this.head = currentHead.next;
6            this.size--;
7        } else {
8            var prev = currentHead;
9            while (currentHead.next) {
10               if (currentHead.data == value) {
```

```
11                    // remove by skipping
12                    prev.next = currentHead.next;
13                    prev = currentHead;
14                    currentHead = currentHead.next;
15                    break; // break out of the loop
16                }
17                prev = currentHead;
18                currentHead = currentHead.next;
19            }
20            //if wasn't found in the middle or head, must be tail
21            if (currentHead.data == value) {
22                prev.next = null;
23            }
24            this.size--;
25        }
26    }
27    var sll1 = new SinglyLinkedList();
28    sll1.insert(1); // linked list is now:  1 -> null
29    sll1.insert(12); // linked list is now: 12 -> 1 -> null
30    sll1.insert(20); // linked list is now: 20 -> 12 -> 1 -> null
31    sll1.remove(12); // linked list is now: 20 -> 1 -> null
32    sll1.remove(20); // linked list is now: 1 -> null
```

**Time Complexity:** $O(n)$

In the worst case, the entire linked list must be traversed.

## Deletion at the Head

Deleting an element at the head of the linked list is possible in $O(1)$. When a node is deleted from the head, no traversal is required. The implementation of this deletion is shown in the following code block. This allows the linked list to implement a stack. The last-added item (to the head) can be removed in $O(1)$.

```
1    DoublyLinkedList.prototype.deleteAtHead = function() {
2        var toReturn = null;
3
4        if (this.head !== null) {
```

```
5              toReturn = this.head.data;

6

7              if (this.tail === this.head) {
8                  this.head = null;
9                  this.tail = null;
10             } else {
11                 this.head = this.head.next;
12                 this.head.prev = null;
13             }
14         }
15         this.size--;
16         return toReturn;
17     }
18     var sll1 = new SinglyLinkedList();
19     sll1.insert(1); // linked list is now:  1 -> null
20     sll1.insert(12); // linked list is now: 12 -> 1 -> null
21     sll1.insert(20); // linked list is now: 20 -> 12 -> 1 -> null
22     sll1.deleteAtHead(); // linked list is now:  12 -> 1 -> null
```

# Search

To find out whether a value exists in a singly linked list, simple iteration through all its next pointers is needed.

```
1     SinglyLinkedList.prototype.find = function(value) {
2         var currentHead = this.head;
3         while (currentHead.next) {
4             if (currentHead.data == value) {
5                 return true;
6             }
7             currentHead = currentHead.next;
8         }
9         return false;
10    }
```

**Time Complexity:** $O(n)$

Like with the deletion operation, in the worst case, the entire linked list must be traversed.

# Doubly Linked Lists

A doubly linked list can be thought of as a bidirectional singly linked list. Each node in the doubly linked list has both a next pointer and a prev pointer. The following code block implements the doubly linked list node:

```
1   function DoublyLinkedListNode(data) {
2         this.data = data;
3         this.next = null;
4         this.prev = null;
5   }
```

In addition, a doubly linked list has a head pointer as well as a tail pointer. The head refers to the beginning of the doubly linked list, and the tail refers to the end of the doubly linked list. This is implemented in the following code along with a helper function to check whether the doubly linked list is empty:

```
1   function DoublyLinkedList (){
2           this.head = null;
3           this.tail = null;
4           this.size = 0;
5   }
6   DoublyLinkedList.prototype.isEmpty = function(){
7           return this.size == 0;
8   }
```

Each node in a doubly linked list has next and prev properties. Deletion, insertion, and search implementations in a doubly linked list are similar to that of the singly linked list. However, for both insertion and deletion, both next and prev properties must be updated. Figure 13-3 shows an example of a doubly linked list.

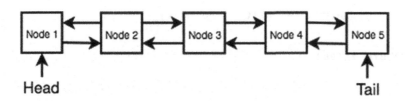

*Figure 13-3.* Doubly linked list example with five nodes

# Insertion at the Head

Inserting into the head of the doubly linked list is the same as the insertion for the singly linked list except that it has to update the prev pointer as well. The following code block shows how to insert into the doubly linked list. If the head of the linked list is empty, the head and the tail are set to the new node. This is because when there is only one element, that element is both the head and the tail. Otherwise, the temp variable is used to store the new node. The new node's next points to the current head, and then the current head's prev points to the new node. Finally, the head pointer is updated to the new node.

```
1   DoublyLinkedList.prototype.addAtFront = function(value) {
2       if (this.head === null) { //If first node
3           this.head = new DoublyLinkedListNode(value);
4           this.tail = this.head;
5       } else {
7           var temp = new DoublyLinkedListNode(value);
8           temp.next = this.head;
9           this.head.prev = temp;
10          this.head = temp;
11      }
12      this.size++;
13  }
14  var dll1 = new DoublyLinkedList();
15  dll1.insertAtHead(10); // ddl1's structure: tail: 10   head: 10
16  dll1.insertAtHead(12); // ddl1's structure: tail: 10   head: 12
17  dll1.insertAtHead(20); // ddl1's structure: tail: 10   head: 20
```

**Time Complexity:** $O(1)$

# Insertion at the Tail

Similarly, a new node can be added to the tail of a doubly linked list, as implemented in the following code block:

```
1   DoublyLinkedList.prototype.insertAtTail = function(value) {
2       if (this.tail === null) { //If first node
3           this.tail = new DoublyLinkedListNode(value);
```

```
4              this.head = this.tail;
5          } else {
6              var temp = new DoublyLinkedListNode(value);
7              temp.prev = this.tail;
8              this.tail.next = temp;
9              this.tail = temp;
10         }
11         this.size++;
12     }
13
14     var dll1 = new DoublyLinkedList();
15     dll1.insertAtHead(10); // ddl1's structure: tail: 10   head: 10
16     dll1.insertAtHead(12); // ddl1's structure: tail: 10   head: 12
17     dll1.insertAtHead(20); // ddl1's structure: tail: 10   head: 20
18     dll1.insertAtTail(30); // ddl1's structure: tail: 30   head: 20
```

**Time Complexity:** O(1)

# Deletion at the Head

Removing a node at the head from a doubly linked list can be done in O(1) time. If there is only one item in the case that the head and the tail are the same, both the head and the tail are set to null. Otherwise, the head is set to the head's next pointer. Finally, the new head's prev is set to null to remove the reference of the old head. This is implemented in the following code block. This is great because it can be used like a dequeue function from the queue data structure.

```
1     DoublyLinkedList.prototype.deleteAtHead = function() {
2         var toReturn = null;
3
4         if (this.head !== null) {
5             toReturn = this.head.data;
6
7             if (this.tail === this.head) {
8                 this.head = null;
9                 this.tail = null;
10            } else {
```

```
11              this.head = this.head.next;
12              this.head.prev = null;
13          }
14      }
15      this.size--;
16      return toReturn;
17  }
```

**Time Complexity:** O(1)

# Deletion at the Tail

Similarly to removing the node at the head, the tail node can be removed and returned in O(1) time, as shown in the following code block. By having the ability to remove at the tail as well, the doubly linked list can also be thought of as a bidirectional queue data structure. A queue can dequeue the first-added item, but a doubly linked list can dequeue either the item at the tail or the item at the head in O(1) time.

```
1   DoublyLinkedList.prototype.deleteAtTail = function() {
2       var toReturn = null;
3
4       if (this.tail !== null) {
5           toReturn = this.tail.data;
6
7           if (this.tail === this.head) {
8               this.head = null;
9               this.tail = null;
10          } else {
11              this.tail = this.tail.prev;
12              this.tail.next = null;
13          }
14      }
15      this.size--;
16      return toReturn;
17  }
18  var dll1 = new DoublyLinkedList();
```

```
19    dll1.insertAtHead(10); // ddl1's structure: tail: 10   head: 10
20    dll1.insertAtHead(12); // ddl1's structure: tail: 10   head: 12
21    dll1.insertAtHead(20); // ddl1's structure: tail: 10   head: 20
22    dll1.insertAtTail(30); // ddl1's structure: tail: 30   head: 20
23    dll1.deleteAtTail();
24    // ddl1's structure: tail: 10   head: 20
```

**Time Complexity:** O(1)

# Search

To find out whether a value exists in a doubly linked list, you can start at the head and use the next pointer or start at the tail and use the prev pointer. The following code block is the same implementation as the singly linked list search implementation, which starts at the head and looks for the item:

```
1    DoublyLinkedList.prototype.findStartingHead = function(value) {
2        var currentHead = this.head;
3        while(currentHead.next){
4            if(currentHead.data == value){
5                return true;
6            }
7            currentHead = currentHead.next;
8        }
9        return false;
10   }
11   var dll1 = new DoublyLinkedList();
12   dll1.insertAtHead(10); // ddl1's structure: tail: 10   head: 10
13   dll1.insertAtHead(12); // ddl1's structure: tail: 10   head: 12
14   dll1.insertAtHead(20); // ddl1's structure: tail: 10   head: 20
15   dll1.insertAtTail(30); // ddl1's structure: tail: 30   head: 20
16   dll1.findStartingHead(10); // true
17   dll1.findStartingHead(100); // false
```

**Time Complexity:** O($n$)

The following code traverses the doubly linked list starting with the tail using prev pointers:

```
1    DoublyLinkedList.prototype.findStartingTail = function(value) {
2        var currentTail = this.tail;
3        while (currentTail.prev){
4            if(currentTail.data == value){
5                return true;
6            }
7            currentTail = currentTail.prev;
8        }
9        return false;
10   }
11
12   var dll1 = new DoublyLinkedList();
13   dll1.insertAtHead(10); // ddl1's structure: tail: 10   head: 10
14   dll1.insertAtHead(12); // ddl1's structure: tail: 10   head: 12
15   dll1.insertAtHead(20); // ddl1's structure: tail: 10   head: 20
16   dll1.insertAtTail(30); // ddl1's structure: tail: 30   head: 20
17   dll1.findStartingTail(10); // true
18   dll1.findStartingTail(100); // false
```

**Time Complexity:** $O(n)$

Although the time complexity for search is the same as the singly linked list's search, only the doubly linked list can search bidirectionally (using prev or next). This means that if given a reference to a doubly linked list node, doubly linked lists can perform a full search, but a singly linked list is limited to only its next pointers.

# Summary

The linked list data structure works by each node having a next pointer (and previous, or prev, pointer if doubly linked) to a different node. Insertion for both singly and doubly linked lists has a constant time complexity of $O(1)$. The time complexity of deleting from the head of the singly and doubly linked lists is $O(1)$ as well. However, searching for an item in both singly and doubly linked list takes $O(n)$ time. Doubly linked lists should be used over singly linked lists when bidirectional traversal/search is required. Furthermore, doubly linked lists allow you to pop from either the tail or the head of the linked list for a flexible and fast $O(1)$ operation.

# Exercises

You can find all the code for the exercises on GitHub.[2]

---

## REVERSE A SINGLY LINKED LIST

To reverse a singly linked list, simply iterate through each node and set the `next` property on the current node to the previous node.

```
1    function reverseSingleLinkedList(sll){
2            var node = sll.head;
3            var prev = null;
4            while(node){
5                    var temp = node.next;
6                    node.next = prev;
7                    prev = node;
8                    if(!temp)
9                            break;
10                   node = temp;
11           }
12           return node;
13   }
```

**Time Complexity:** $O(n)$

**Space Complexity:** $O(1)$

To fully reverse a linked list, the entire N elements of the linked list must be traversed.

---

## DELETE DUPLICATES IN A LINKED LIST

Deleting an item in a linked list is simple. Simply iterate and store visited nodes inside an array. Delete the current element if the current element has already been seen previously.

```
1    // delete duplicates in unsorted linkedlist
2    function deleteDuplicateInUnsortedSll(sll1) {
```

---

[2]https://github.com/Apress/js-data-structures-and-algorithms

```
3        var track = [];
4
5        var temp = sll1.head;
6        var prev = null;
7        while (temp) {
8            if (track.indexOf(temp.data) >= 0) {
9                prev.next = temp.next;
10               sll1.size--;
11           } else {
12               track.push(temp.data);
13               prev = temp;
14           }
15           temp = temp.next;
16       }
17       console.log(temp);
18   }
```

**Time Complexity:** $O(n^2)$

**Space Complexity:** $O(n)$

However, this algorithm must iterate over the array with the `.indexOf()` method, which is $O(n)$ as well as iterating $n$ times. Hence, it is $O(n^2)$ in time complexity. In addition, the `track` array grows to size of $N$, and this causes the space complexity to be $O(n)$. Let's cut the time complexity down to $O(n)$.

```
1    //delete duplicates in unsorted linkedlist
2    function deleteDuplicateInUnsortedSllBest(sll1) {
3        var track = {};
4
5        var temp = sll1.head;
6        var prev = null;
7        while (temp) {
8            if (track[temp.data]) {
9                prev.next = temp.next;
10               sll1.size--;
11           } else {
12               track[temp.data] = true;
13               prev = temp;
14           }
```

```
15                temp = temp.next;
16          }
17          console.log(temp);
18    }
```

**Time Complexity:** O(*n*)

**Space Complexity:** O(*n*)

Use of the JavaScript Object as a hash table to store and check for seen elements cuts it down to O(*n*) but O(*n*) in space as extra memory is required for the hash table.

# CHAPTER 14

# Caching

*Caching* is the process of storing data into temporary memory so that it can be easily retrieved for later use if it is required again. As an example, a database system keeps data cached to avoid rereading the hard drive, and a web browser caches web pages (images and assets) to avoid redownloading the contents. Put simply, in caching, the goal is to maximize hits (an item is in the cache when requested) and minimize misses (an item is not in the cache when requested).

In this chapter, two caching techniques will be discussed: least frequently used (LFU) and least recently used (LRU) caching.

---

**Note**   The concept of caching comes from the world of operating systems. You can read more about it in a lecture presentation[1] by Jeff Zarnett from the University of Waterloo.

---

## Understanding Caching

Cache design generally considers these two factors:

- *Temporal locality*: A memory location that has been recently accessed is likely to be accessed again.

- *Spatial locality*: A memory location near one that has recently been accessed is likely to be accessed again.

---

[1]https://github.com/jzarnett/ece254/blob/master/lectures/L21-slides-Memory_
Segmentation_Paging.pdf

© Sammie Bae 2019
S. Bae, *JavaScript Data Structures and Algorithms*, https://doi.org/10.1007/978-1-4842-3988-9_14

The optimal caching algorithm would be able to replace the part of the cache that will be used most distantly in the future with the new element to be inserted. This will require, for each item, calculating how many time in the future that item will be accessed. It should be obvious to you that this is impossible to implement because it requires looking into the future.

# Least Frequently Used Caching

*Least frequently used* (LFU) caching is a caching algorithm used by the operating system to manage memory. The system tracks the number of times a block is referenced in memory. By design, when the cache exceeds its limit, the system deletes the item with the lowest reference frequency. The easiest implementation of the LFU cache is assigning a counter to every block loaded into the cache and incrementing a counter every time a reference is made to that block. When the cache exceeds its limit, the system searches for the block with the lowest counter and removes it from the cache.

Although LFU caching seems like an intuitive approach, it is not ideal when an item in memory is referenced repeatedly for a short amount of time and not accessed again. The frequency for that block is high because of its repeated reference, but this forces the system to delete other blocks that may be used more frequently outside the short block of time. In addition, new items in the system are susceptible to being deleted quickly because of their lower frequency of being accessed. Because of these issues, LFU is uncommon, but some hybrid systems utilize the core LFU concept. Examples of a such system are mobile keyboard apps. Suggested words appear on the keyboard apps, and it makes sense to implement this using LFU caching since the user likely uses the same words often. The frequency of a word would a great metric to see whether the word should exist in the cache.

The LFU cache uses a doubly linked list to remove elements in O(1) time. The doubly linked node in LFUs also has the freqCount property, which represents how frequently it has been accessed/set after being inserted for the first time.

```
1    function LFUNode(key, value) {
2        this.prev = null;
3        this.next = null;
4        this.key = key;
```

```
5      this.data = value;
6      this.freqCount = 1;
7   }
```

The LFU cache has two hash tables: keys and freq. freq has keys of frequency (1 to *n*, where *n* is the top frequency for element access), and each item is an instance of a doubly linked list class. keys stores each doubly linked list node for O(1) retrieval. The classes for a doubly linked list and the LFU cache are defined here:

```
1   function LFUDoublyLinkedList(){
2       this.head = new LFUNode('buffer head',null);
3       this.tail = new LFUNode('buffer tail',null);
4       this.head.next = this.tail;
5       this.tail.prev = this.head;
6       this.size = 0;
7   }
8
9   function LFUCache(capacity){
10      this.keys = {}; // stores LFUNode
11      this.freq = {}; // stores LFUDoublyLinkedList
12      this.capacity = capacity;
13      this.minFreq = 0;
14      this.size =0;
15  }
```

The LFUDoublyLinkedList class also requires the doubly linked list implementation for insertion and removal. However, only the insertion at the head and the removal at the tail is needed. This implementation is the same as the implementation from the doubly linked list class shown in Chapter 13 (Linked Lists).

```
1   LFUDoublyLinkedList.prototype.insertAtHead = function(node) {
2       node.next = this.head.next;
3       this.head.next.prev = node;
4       this.head.next = node;
5       node.prev = this.head;
6       this.size++;
7   }
8
```

```
9    LFUDoublyLinkedList.prototype.removeAtTail = function() {
10       var oldTail = this.tail.prev;
11       var prev = this.tail.prev;
12       prev.prev.next = this.tail;
13       this.tail.prev = prev.prev;
14       this.size--;
15       return oldTail;
16   }
17
18   LFUDoublyLinkedList.prototype.removeNode = function(node) {
19       node.prev.next = node.next
20       node.next.prev = node.prev
21       this.size--;
22   }
```

Implementing set for the LFU has a few steps. There are two cases: insert the new item and replace an old item. When inserting a new item, a new node is created. If the cache is not full, it can be inserted into the freq's doubly linked list of frequency 1. If the capacity is full, the tail item in the doubly linked list of frequency is deleted, and then the new node is inserted.

If the element already exists and needs to be replaced, the node is brought to the head of its corresponding frequency doubly linked list. Finally, the minimum frequency variable, minFreq, is incremented accordingly to compute which item should be evicted in the future.

```
1    LFUCache.prototype.set = function(key, value) {
2        var node = this.keys[key];
3
4        if (node == undefined) {
5            node = new LFUNode(key, value);
6
7            this.keys[key] = node;
8
9            if (this.size != this.capacity) {
10               // insert without deleting
11               if (this.freq[1] === undefined){
```

```
12                    this.freq[1] = new LFUDoublyLinkedList();
13                }
14              this.freq[1].insertAtHead(node);
15              this.size++;
16          } else {
17              // delete and insert
18              var oldTail = this.freq[this.minFreq].removeAtTail();
19              delete this.keys[oldTail.key];
20
21              if (this.freq[1] === undefined){
22                  this.freq[1] = new LFUDoublyLinkedList();
23              }
24
25              this.freq[1].insertAtHead(node);
26          }
27          this.minFreq = 1;
28      } else {
29          var oldFreqCount = node.freqCount;
30          node.data = value;
31          node.freqCount++;
32
33          this.freq[oldFreqCount].removeNode(node);
34
35          if (this.freq[node.freqCount] === undefined){
36              this.freq[node.freqCount] = new LFUDoublyLinkedList();
37          }
38
39          this.freq[node.freqCount].insertAtHead(node);
40
41          if (oldFreqCount == this.minFreq && Object.keys(this.
            freq[oldFreqCount]).size == 0) {
42              this.minFreq++;
43          }
44
45      }
46  }
```

To implement get, the cache needs to return existing nodes in O(1) time and increment the counter for accessing. If the element does not exist in the cache, it is forced to return a null element. Otherwise, the frequency for the element is increased, the item is brought to the head of the doubly linked list, and the minimum frequency variable, minFreq, is adjusted accordingly.

```
1    LFUCache.prototype.get = function(key) {
2        var node = this.keys[key];
3
4        if (node == undefined) {
5            return null;
6        } else {
7
8            var oldFreqCount = node.freqCount;
9            node.freqCount++;
10
11           this.freq[oldFreqCount].removeNode(node);
12
13           if (this.freq[node.freqCount] === undefined){
14               this.freq[node.freqCount] = new LFUDoublyLinkedList();
15           }
16
17           this.freq[node.freqCount].insertAtHead(node);
18
19           if (oldFreqCount == this.minFreq && Object.keys(this.
             freq[oldFreqCount]).length == 0) {
20               this.minFreq++;
21           }
22           return node.data;
23       }
24   }
```

With all the functions defined, the following code shows an example of this LFU usage:

```
1   var myLFU = new LFUCache(5);
2   myLFU.set(1, 1); // state of myLFU.freq: {1: 1}
3   myLFU.set(2, 2); // state of myLFU.freq: {1: 2<->1}
4   myLFU.set(3, 3); // state of myLFU.freq: {1: 3<->2<->1}
5   myLFU.set(4, 4); // state of myLFU.freq: {1: 4<->3<->2<->1}
6   myLFU.set(5, 5); // state of myLFU.freq: {1: 5<->4<->3<->2<->1}
7   myLFU.get(1); // returns 1, state of myLFU.freq: {1: 5<->4<->3<->2, 2: 1}
8   myLFU.get(1); // returns 1, state of myLFU.freq: {1: 5<->4<->3<->2, 3: 1}
9   myLFU.get(1); // returns 1, state of myLFU.freq: {1: 5<->4<->3<->2, 4: 1}
10  myLFU.set(6, 6); // state of myLFU.freq: {1: 6<->5<->4<->3, 4: 1}
11  myLFU.get(6); // state of myLFU.freq: {1: 5<->4<->3, 4: 1, 2: 6}
```

# Least Recently Used Caching

*Least recently used* (LRU) caching is a caching algorithm that removes the oldest (least recently used) items first, so the item replaced is the oldest accessed item. When an item in the cache is accessed, that item moves to the back (newest in the order) of the list. When a page not found in the cache is accessed, the front item (or oldest in the order) is removed, and the new item is put at the back (newest in the order) of the list.

The implementation of this algorithm requires keeping track of which node was used when. To accomplish this, the LRU cache is implemented using a doubly linked list and hash table.

A doubly linked list is needed to keep track of the head (the oldest data). A doubly linked list is required because of the most recently used requirement. Each time new data is inserted, the head moves up until the size is exceeded. Then the oldest data is evicted.

Figure 14-1 shows a diagram of an LRU cache with a size of 5.

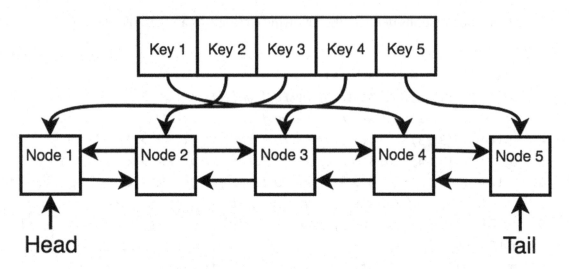

*Figure 14-1.* *LRU cache*

To implement the LRU cache, the node is defined similarly to the doubly linked list node in Chapter 13. This node also has a key property, and its implementation is shown in the following code block:

```
1   function DLLNode(key, data) {
2       this.key = key;
3       this.data = data;
4       this.next = null;
5       this.prev = null;
6   }
```

The LRU cache can be initialized by passing the capacity parameter. capacity defines how many nodes are allowed to be in the cache.

```
1   function LRUCache(capacity) {
2       this.keys = {};
3       this.capacity = capacity;
4       this.head = new DLLNode(", null);
5       this.tail = new DLLNode(", null);
6       this.head.next = this.tail;
7       this.tail.prev = this.head;
8   }
```

Since the LRU cache uses a doubly linked list, two functions for removing a node and adding a node to the tail will be defined here:

```
1   LRUCache.prototype.removeNode = function(node) {
2       var prev = node.prev,
3           next = node.next;
4       prev.next = next;
5       next.prev = prev;
6   }
7
8   LRUCache.prototype.addNode = function(node) {
9       var realTail = this.tail.prev;
10      realTail.next = node;
11
12      this.tail.prev = node;
13      node.prev = realTail;
14      node.next = this.tail;
15  }
```

Two more functions need to be defined: get and set. Whenever get is called, the LRU caching scheme brings that node to the head of the doubly linked list since it was the most recently used node. This is the same as deleting and adding the node. For setting nodes via set, the keys property on the LRU cache is used to store the node to keep retrieval in O(1) time in get. However, if the cache is at full capacity, it evicts the farthest node from the tail.

```
1   LRUCache.prototype.get = function(key) {
2       var node = this.keys[key];
3       if (node == undefined) {
4           return null;
5       } else {
6           this.removeNode(node);
7           this.addNode(node);
8           return node.data;
9       }
10  }
11
```

```
12    LRUCache.prototype.set = function(key, value) {
13        var node = this.keys[key];
14        if (node) {
15            this.removeNode(node);
16        }
17
18        var newNode = new DLLNode(key, value);
19
20        this.addNode(newNode);
21        this.keys[key] = newNode;
22
23        // evict a node
24        if (Object.keys(this.keys).length > this.capacity) {
25            var realHead = this.head.next;
26            this.removeNode(realHead);
27            delete this.keys[realHead.key];
28        }
29    }
```

Finally, the following is an example of an LRU cache of size 5:

```
1    var myLRU = new LRUCache(5);
2
3    myLRU.set(1, 1); // 1
4    myLRU.set(2, 2); // 1 <-> 2
5    myLRU.set(3, 3); // 1 <-> 2 <-> 3
6    myLRU.set(4, 4); // 1 <-> 2 <-> 3 <-> 4
7    myLRU.set(5, 5); // 1 <-> 2 <-> 3 <-> 4 <-> 5
8
9
10   myLRU.get(1);    // 2 <-> 3 <-> 4 <-> 5 <-> 1
11   myLRU.get(2);    // 3 <-> 4 <-> 5 <-> 1 <-> 2
12
13   myLRU.set(6, 6);// 4 <-> 5 <-> 1 <-> 2 <-> 6
14   myLRU.set(7, 7);// 5 <-> 1 <-> 2 <-> 6 <-> 7
15   myLRU.set(8, 8);// 1 <-> 2 <-> 6 <-> 7 <-> 8
```

# Summary

This chapter covered two main caching ideas: least frequently used and least recently used. The chapter talked about the concept of an optimal caching algorithm, which is impossible to implement but provides an idea of what you would want to approximate. LFU caching sounds great because it uses frequency to determine what node should be evicted, but LFU is inferior to the LRU in most cases because it does not account for temporal locality. There are other caching algorithms, but most of those algorithms are worse in general cases, such as the not recently used and first in, first out algorithms. Finally, it should be noted that given the many known data of real-life system behavior workloads, LRU is the most effective algorithm in most cases. Table 14-1 summarizes the caching algorithms.

*Table 14-1.* *Caching Summary*

| Algorithm | Comment |
| --- | --- |
| Optimal | Impossible to implement |
| Least frequently used | Bad for temporal locality |
| Least recently used | Uses doubly-linked + hashmap |

# CHAPTER 15

# Trees

A general tree data structure is composed of nodes with children nodes. The first/top node is called the *root node*. This chapter will explore many different types of trees such as binary trees, binary search trees, and self-balancing binary search trees. First, this chapter will cover what trees are and how they are structured. Then, it will cover methods of traversing the tree data structure in detail. Finally, you will learn about binary search trees and self-balancing binary search trees to understand how to store easily searchable data.

## General Tree Structure

A general tree data structure looks like Figure 15-1 when it can have any number of children.

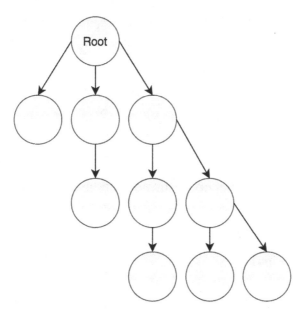

***Figure 15-1.*** *Generalized tree with any number of children*

© Sammie Bae 2019
S. Bae, *JavaScript Data Structures and Algorithms*, https://doi.org/10.1007/978-1-4842-3988-9_15

The code block for the node in the Figure 15-1 tree is as follows:

```
1    function TreeNode(value){
2         this.value = value;
3         this.children = [];
4    }
```

# Binary Trees

A *binary tree* is a type of tree that has only two children nodes: left and right. See the following code and Figure 15-2:

```
1    function BinaryTreeNode(value) {
2         this.value = value;
3         this.left = null;
4         this.right = null;
5    }
```

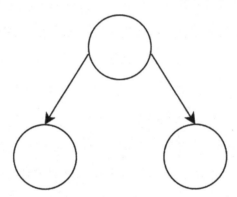

***Figure 15-2.*** *Binary tree*

A binary tree always has a root node (the node at the top), which is initialized to null before any element is inserted.

```
1    function BinaryTree(){
2         this._root = null;
3    }
```

# Tree Traversal

Traversal through an array is simple: you access the tree using the index and increment the index until the index reaches the size limit. With trees, the left and right pointers have to be followed in order to go through every element in the tree. There are various ways to do this, of course; the most popular traversal techniques are pre-order traversal, post-order traversal, in-order traversal, and level-order traversal.

All the code for tree traversals is available on GitHub.[1]

## Pre-order Traversal

*Pre-order traversal* visits nodes in the following order: root (the current node), left, right. In Figure 15-3, you can see that 42 is the root, so it's visited first. Then it goes left; at this point, the left of the parent (41) is now considered the new root. This new root (41) is printed; then it goes left again to 10. So, 10 is set to the new root but cannot continue without a child. Then 40 is visited because that is the right of the previous parent (41). This process continues, and the whole order is denoted by the gray squares in Figure 15-3.

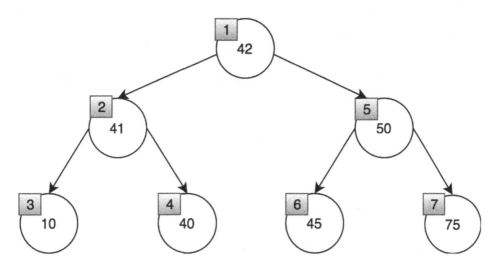

**Figure 15-3.**  *Pre-order traversal*

---

[1]https://github.com/Apress/js-data-structures-and-algorithms

Recursively, this is implemented easily. The base case terminates when the node is null. Otherwise, it prints the node value and then calls the recursive function on its left child and then its right child.

```
1    BinaryTree.prototype.traversePreOrder = function() {
2        traversePreOrderHelper(this._root);
3
4        function traversePreOrderHelper(node) {
5            if (!node)
6                return;
7            console.log(node.value);
8            traversePreOrderHelper(node.left);
9            traversePreOrderHelper(node.right);
10       }
11   }
```

This can also be done iteratively, but it is harder to implement.

```
1    BinaryTree.prototype.traversePreOrderIterative = function() {
2        //create an empty stack and push root to it
3        var nodeStack = [];
4        nodeStack.push(this._root);
5
6        // Pop all items one by one. Do following for every popped item
7        //   a) print it
8        //   b) push its right child
9        //   c) push its left child
10       // Note that right child is pushed first so that left
11       // is processed first */
12       while (nodeStack.length) {
13           //# Pop the top item from stack and print it
14           var node = nodeStack.pop();
15           console.log(node.value);
16
17           //# Push right and left children of the popped node to stack
```

```
18              if (node.right)
19                  nodeStack.push(node.right);
20              if (node.left)
21                  nodeStack.push(node.left);
22          }
23      }
```

Here is the result: [42, 41, 10, 40, 50, 45, 75].

## In-Order Traversal

In-order traversal visits nodes in the following order: left, root (current node), right. For the tree shown in Figure 15-4, the gray squares indicate the in-order traversal order. As you can see, 10 (the leftmost node) is printed first, and 7 (the rightmost node) is printed last.

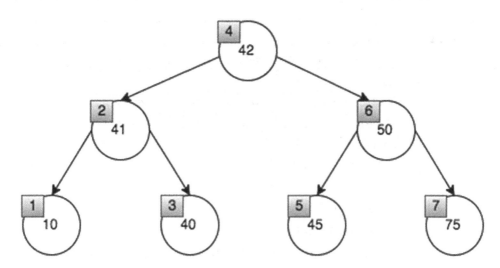

**Figure 15-4.** *In-order traversal*

In-order traversal is also implemented easily with recursion. The base case is when a node is null. In the nonbase case, it calls the recursive function on the left child, prints the current node, and then calls the recursive function on the right child.

```
1    BinaryTree.prototype.traverseInOrder = function() {
2        traverseInOrderHelper(this._root);
3
4        function traverseInOrderHelper(node) {
5            if (!node)
6                return;
7            traverseInOrderHelper(node.left);
8            console.log(node.value);
9            traverseInOrderHelper(node.right);
10        }
11   }
12
13   BinaryTree.prototype.traverseInOrderIterative = function() {
14       var current = this._root,
15           s = [],
16           done = false;
17
18       while (!done) {
19           // Reach the left most Node of the current Node
20           if (current != null) {
21               // Place pointer to a tree node on the stack
22               // before traversing the node's left subtree
23               s.push(current);
24               current = current.left;
25           } else {
26               if (s.length) {
27                   current = s.pop();
28                   console.log(current.value);
29                   current = current.right;
30               } else {
31                   done = true;
32               }
33           }
34       }
35   }
```

Here is the result of this traversal: [10, 41, 40, 42, 45, 50, 75].

# Post-order Traversal

*Post-order traversal* visits nodes in the following order: left, right, root (the current node). For the tree shown in Figure 15-5, the gray squares indicate the in-order traversal order. As you can see, 10 (the leftmost node) is printed first, and 42 (the root node) is printed last.

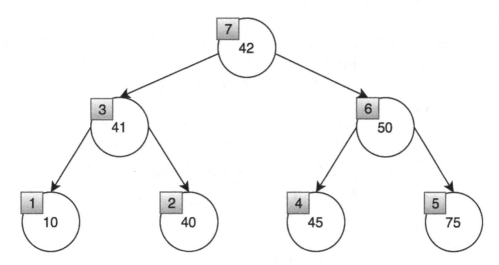

***Figure 15-5.*** *Post-order traversal*

Here's the code:

```
1  BinaryTree.prototype.traversePostOrder = function() {
2      traversePostOrderHelper(this._root);
3
4      function traversePostOrderHelper(node) {
5          if (node.left)
6              traversePostOrderHelper(node.left);
7          if (node.right)
8              traversePostOrderHelper(node.right);
9          console.log(node.value);
10     }
11 }
12
```

```
13    BinaryTree.prototype.traversePostOrderIterative = function() {
14        // Create two stacks
15        var s1 = [],
16            s2 = [];
17
18        // Push root to first stack
19            s1.push(this._root);
20
21        //# Run while first stack is not empty
22        while (s1.length) {
23            // Pop an item from s1 and append it to s2
24            var node = s1.pop();
25            s2.push(node);
26
27            // Push left and right children of removed item to s1
28            if (node.left)
29                s1.push(node.left);
30            if (node.right)
31                s1.push(node.right);
32        }
33        // Print all elements of second stack
34        while (s2.length) {
35            var node = s2.pop();
36            console.log(node.value);
37        }
38    }
```

Here is the result: [10, 40, 41, 45, 75, 50, 42].

## Level-Order Traversal

*Level-order traversal,* illustrated in Figure 15-6, is also known as *breadth first search* (BFS).

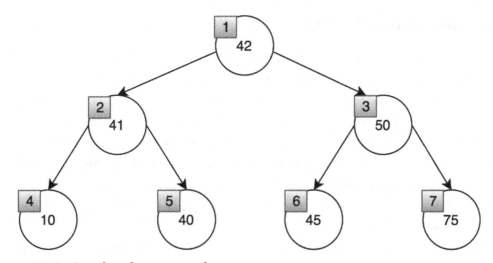

**Figure 15-6.** *Level-order traversal*

More of this will be covered in Chapter 17, but this method essentially visits each node level by level instead of going deep into the left or right.

```
1    BinaryTree.prototype.traverseLevelOrder = function() {
2        // Breath first search
3        var root = this._root,
4            queue = [];
5
6        if (!root)
7            return;
8        queue.push(root);
9
10       while (queue.length) {
11           var temp = queue.shift();
12           console.log(temp.value);
13           if (temp.left)
14               queue.push(temp.left);
15           if (temp.right)
16               queue.push(temp.right);
17       }
18   }
```

Here is the result: [42, 41, 50, 10, 40, 45, 75].

# Tree Traversal Summary

If you know you need to explore the roots before inspecting any leaves, choose pre-order traversal because you will encounter all the roots before all of the leaves.

If you know you need to explore all the leaves before any nodes, choose post-order traversal because you don't waste any time inspecting roots when searching for leaves.

If you know that the tree has an inherent sequence in the nodes and you want to flatten the tree into its original sequence, then you should use an in-order traversal. The tree would be flattened in the same way it was created. A pre-order or post-order traversal might not unwind the tree back into the sequence that was used to create it.

**Time Complexity:** $O(n)$

The time complexity of any of these traversals is the same because each traversal requires that all nodes are visited.

# Binary Search Trees

Binary search trees (BSTs) also have two children, left and right. However, in a binary search tree, the left child is smaller than the parent, and the right child is bigger than the parent. BSTs have this structure because this property enables for searching, inserting, and removing specific values with $O(\log_2(n))$ time complexity.

Figure 15-7 shows the BST property. 1 is smaller than 2, so it is the left child of 2, and since 3 is bigger than 3, it is the right child of 2.

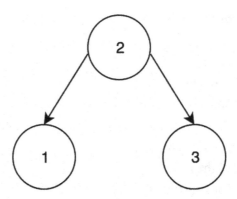

**Figure 15-7.** *Binary search tree*

Binary search trees have a root node (the topmost node), which is originally initialized null (before any item is inserted).

```
1   function BinarySearchTree(){
2       this._root = null;
3   }
```

Figure 15-7 also shows a balanced binary search tree where the height is minimized by having children on both the left and right sides. However, Figure 15-8 shows an unbalanced tree where children are only to the right of the parent. This has significant impact on the data structure and increases the time complexity of insertion, deletion, and search from $O(\log_2(n))$ to $O(n)$. The height of a perfect balanced tree is $\log_2(n)$, while an unbalanced tree can be $n$ in the worst case.

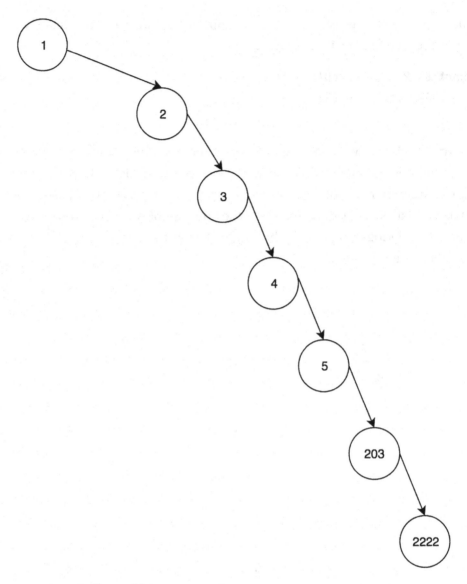

**Figure 15-8.** *Unbalanced binary search tree*

## Insertion

Inserting into the BST requires a couple of steps. First, if the root is empty, the root becomes the new node. Otherwise, a while loop is used to traverse the BST until the right condition is met. At each loop iteration, it is checked whether the new node is greater or smaller than the currentRoot.

```
1   BinarySearchTree.prototype.insert =  function(value) {
2       var thisNode = {left: null, right: null, value: value};
3       if(!this._root){
4           //if there is no root value yet
5           this._root = thisNode;
6       }else{
7           //loop traverse until
8           var currentRoot = this._root;
9           while(true){
10              if(currentRoot.value>value){
11                  //let's increment if it's not a null and insert if it
                    is a null
12                  if(currentRoot.left!=null){
13                      currentRoot = currentRoot.left;
14                  }else{
15                      currentRoot.left = thisNode;
16                      break;
17                  }
18              } else if (currentRoot.value<value){
19                  //if bigger than current, put it on the right
20                  //let's increment if it's not a null and insert if it
                    is a null
21                  if(currentRoot.right!=null){
22                      currentRoot = currentRoot.right;
23                  }else{
24                      currentRoot.right = thisNode;
25                      break;
26                  }
27              } else {
28                  //case that both are the same
29                  break;
30              }
31          }
32      }
33  }
```

**Time Complexity (for balanced trees):** $O(log_2(n))$

**Time Complexity (for unbalanced trees):** $O(n)$

Time complexity is dependent on the height of the binary search tree.

# Deletion

This algorithm works by first traversing down the tree looking specifically for the node with the specified value. When the node is found, there are three possible cases:

- **Case 1: The node has no children.**

  This is the simplest case. If the node has no child, return null. That node has been deleted now.

- **Case 2: The node has one child.**

  If the node has one child, simply return the existing child. That child has now bubbled up and replaced the parent.

- **Case 3: The node has two children.**

  If the node has two children, either find the maximum of the left subtree or find the minimum of the right subtree to replace that node.

The following code implements the described three cases. First, it traverses recursively until one of those cases is met, and then the node is removed.

```
1    BinarySearchTree.prototype.remove = function(value) {
2
3        return deleteRecursively(this._root, value);
4
5        function deleteRecursively(root, value) {
6            if (!root) {
7                return null;
8            } else if (value < root.value) {
9                root.left = deleteRecursively(root.left, value);
10           } else if (value > root.value) {
11               root.right = deleteRecursively(root.right, value);
```

```
12              } else {
13                  //no child
14                  if (!root.left && !root.right) {
15                      return null; // case 1
16                  } else if (!root.left) { // case 2
17                      root = root.right;
18                      return root;
19                  } else if (!root.right) { // case 2
20                      root = root.left;
21                      return root;
22                  } else {
23                      var temp = findMin(root.right); // case 3
24                      root.value = temp.value;
25                      root.right = deleteRecursively(root.right, temp.
                        value);
26                      return root;
27                  }
28              }
29          return root;
30      }
31
32      function findMin(root) {
33          while (root.left) {
34              root = root.left;
35          }
36          return root;
37      }
38  }
```

**Time Complexity (for balanced tree):** $O(log_2(n))$
**Time Complexity (for unbalanced trees):** $O(n)$

Time complexity for deletion is also $O(log_2(n))$ because at most that's the height that will need to be traversed to find and delete the desired node.

# Search

Search can be performed using the property that BST node's left child is always smaller than its parent and that BST node's right child is always greater than its parent. Traversing the tree can be done by checking whether currentRoot is smaller or greater than the value to be searched. If currentRoot is smaller, the right child is visited. If currentRoot is bigger, the left child is visited.

```
1    BinarySearchTree.prototype.findNode = function(value) {
2        var currentRoot = this._root,
3            found = false;
4        while (currentRoot) {
5            if (currentRoot.value > value) {
6                currentRoot = currentRoot.left;
7            } else if (currentRoot.value < value) {
8                currentRoot = currentRoot.right;
9            } else {
10               //we've found the node
11               found = true;
12               break;
13           }
14       }
15       return found;
16   }
17   var bst1 = new BinarySearchTree();
18   bst1.insert(1);
19   bst1.insert(3);
20   bst1.insert(2);
21   bst1.findNode(3); // true
22   bst1.findNode(5); // false
```

**Time Complexity (for balanced tree):** $O(log_2(n))$
**Time Complexity (for unbalanced trees):** $O(n)$

Note that all of the operations' time complexities are equal to the height of the binary tree search. With unbalanced binary search trees, the time complexity is high. To address this, there are families of binary search trees that ensure the height is balanced. One example of such self-balancing trees is an AVL tree.

# AVL Trees

AVL is a binary search tree that balances itself; it's named after the inventors Georgy Adelson-Velsky and Evgenii Landis. An AVL tree keeps the BST height to a minimum and ensures $O(log_2(n))$ time complexities for search, insertion, and deletion. In previous examples, we defined both TreeNode and a Tree class and set the root of Tree as a TreeNode class. However, for the AVL tree implementation, only the AVLTree class, which represents the node of the AVL tree, will be used for the simplification of the code.

```
1    function AVLTree (value) {
2        this.left = null;
3        this.right = null;
4        this.value = value;
5        this.depth = 1;
6    }
```

The height of the AVL tree is based on the height of the children and can be calculated using the following code block:

```
1    AVLTree.prototype.setDepthBasedOnChildren = function() {
2        if (this.node == null) {
3            this.depth = 0;
4        } else {
5            this.depth = 1;
6        }
7
8        if (this.left != null) {
9            this.depth = this.left.depth + 1;
10        }
11        if (this.right != null && this.depth <= this.right.depth) {
12            this.depth = this.right.depth + 1;
13        }
14    }
```

# Single Rotation

AVL trees rotate their children to maintain balance after insertion.

## Rotate Left

Here is an example of when a node has to rotate left. Node 40's children, the 45 and 47 nodes, cause the height to be unbalanced, as shown in Figure 15-9. The 45 becomes the parent node in Figure 15-10 to balance the BST.

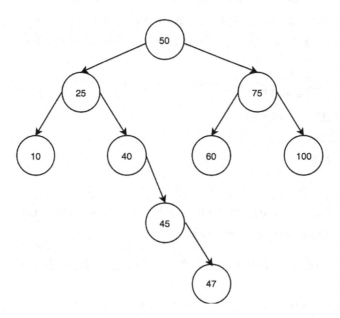

***Figure 15-9.*** *Rotate left before*

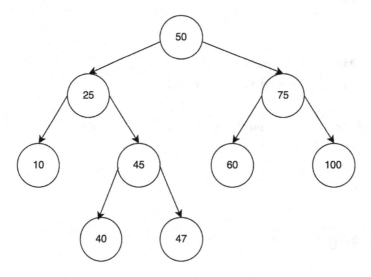

***Figure 15-10.*** *Rotate left after*

To perform a left rotation, first get the left child and store it. This is the "original" left child. The original left child is to be the parent of the node now. Set the node's left child to be the original left child's left child. Finally, set the right child of the original left child to be the node.

```
1    AVLTree.prototype.rotateLL = function() {
2
3        var valueBefore = this.value;
4        var rightBefore = this.right;
5        this.value = this.left.value;
6
7        this.right = this.left;
8        this.left = this.left.left;
9        this.right.left = this.right.right;
10       this.right.right = rightBefore;
11       this.right.value = valueBefore;
12
13       this.right.getDepthFromChildren();
14       this.getDepthFromChildren();
15   };
```

## Rotate Right

Here is an example of when a node has to rotate right. 60's children, the 55 and 52 nodes, cause the height to be unbalanced, as shown in Figure 15-11. The 55 node becomes the parent in Figure 15-12 to balance the BST.

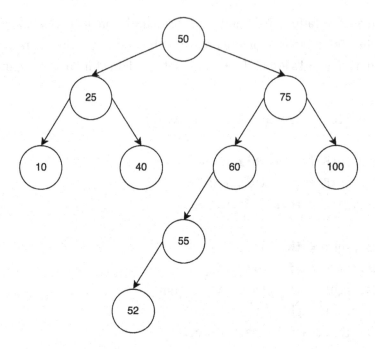

**Figure 15-11.** *Rotate right before*

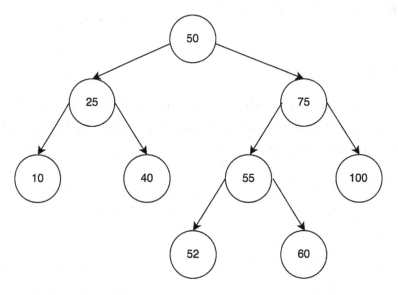

**Figure 15-12.** *Rotate right after*

To implement this previously described algorithm, first get the left child and store it. This the original left child. The original left child is to be the parent of the node now. Set the node's left child to be the original left child's left child. Finally, set the right child of the original left child to be the node.

```
1    AVLTree.prototype.rotateRR = function() {
2        // the right side is too long => rotate from the right
             (_not_ rightwards)
3        var valueBefore = this.value;
4        var leftBefore = this.left;
5        this.value = this.right.value;
6
7        this.left = this.right;
8        this.right = this.right.right;
9        this.left.right = this.left.left;
10       this.left.left = leftBefore;
11       this.left.value = valueBefore;
12
13       this.left.updateInNewLocation();
14       this.updateInNewLocation();
15   }
```

# Double Rotation

If an AVL tree is still unbalanced after one rotation, it has to rotate twice for full balance.

## Rotate Right Left (Right Then Left)

In this example, Figure 15-13 shows a BST where the height is 3. By rotating right and then left, as shown in Figure 15-14 and Figure 15-15, balance is achieved.

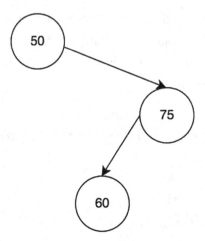

***Figure 15-13.*** *A situation where rotating right and then rotating left is appropriate*

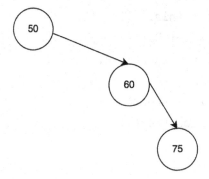

***Figure 15-14.*** *Rotate right first*

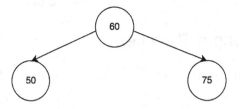

***Figure 15-15.*** *Rotate left after*

## Rotate Left Right (Left Then Right)

Similarly, in this example, Figure 15-16 shows a BST where the height is 3. By rotating left and then right, as shown in Figure 15-17 and Figure 15-18, balance is achieved.

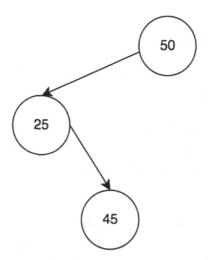

***Figure 15-16.*** *A situation where rotating left and then rotating right is appropriate*

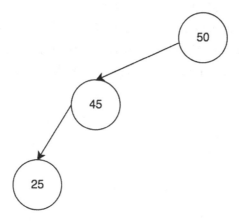

***Figure 15-17.*** *Rotate left first*

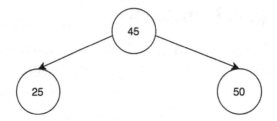

***Figure 15-18.*** *Rotate right after*

## Balancing the Tree

To check for balance of the AVL tree, it is a simple comparison of the left and right children's heights. If the heights are not balanced, rotations are needed. When left is bigger than right, left rotation is done. When right is bigger than left, right rotation is done.

```
1    AVLTree.prototype.balance = function() {
2        var ldepth = this.left == null ? 0 : this.left.depth;
3        var rdepth = this.right == null ? 0 : this.right.depth;
4
5        if (ldepth > rdepth + 1) {
6        // LR or LL rotation
7            var lldepth = this.left.left == null ? 0 : this.left.left.depth;
8            var lrdepth = this.left.right == null ? 0 : this.left.right.depth;
9
10           if (lldepth < lrdepth) {
11               // LR rotation consists of a RR rotation of the left child
12               this.left.rotateRR();
13               // plus a LL rotation of this node, which happens anyway
14           }
15           this.rotateLL();
16       } else if (ldepth + 1 < rdepth) {
17           // RR or RL rorarion
18           var rrdepth = this.right.right == null ? 0 : this.right.right.depth;
19           var rldepth = this.right.left == null ? 0 : this.right.left.depth;
20
```

```
21          if (rldepth > rrdepth) {
22              // RR rotation consists of a LL rotation of the right child
23              this.right.rotateLL();
24              // plus a RR rotation of this node, which happens anyway
25          }
26          this.rotateRR();
27      }
28  }
```

# Insertion

Insertion in AVL BST is the same as the insertion in normal BST except that, once inserted, the parent must balance its children and set the right depth.

```
1   AVLTree.prototype.insert = function(value) {
2       var childInserted = false;
3       if (value == this.value) {
4           return false; // should be all unique
5       } else if (value < this.value) {
6           if (this.left == null) {
7               this.left = new AVLTree(value);
8               childInserted = true;
9           } else {
10              childInserted = this.left.insert(value);
11              if (childInserted == true) this.balance();
12          }
13      } else if (value > this.value) {
14          if (this.right == null) {
15              this.right = new AVLTree(value);
16              childInserted = true;
17          } else {
18              childInserted = this.right.insert(value);
19
20              if (childInserted == true) this.balance();
21          }
22      }
```

```
23        if (childInserted == true) this.setDepthBasedOnChildren();
24        return childInserted;
25   }
```

**Time Complexity:** $O(nlog_2(n))$

**Space Complexity:** $O(nlog_2(n))$

Space complexity is from the recursive call stacks in memory.

## Deletion

AVL BST is a type of BST, and therefore the deletion function is the same. Adjusting the depths can be done by calling setDepthBasedOnChildren() during traversal.

```
1    AVLTree.prototype.remove = function(value) {
2        return deleteRecursively(this, value);
3
4        function deleteRecursively(root, value) {
5            if (!root) {
6                return null;
7            } else if (value < root.value) {
8                root.left = deleteRecursively(root.left, value);
9            } else if (value > root.value) {
10               root.right = deleteRecursively(root.right, value);
11           } else {
12               //no child
13               if (!root.left && !root.right) {
14                   return null; // case 1
15               } else if (!root.left) {
16                   root = root.right;
17                   return root;
18               } else if (!root.right) {
19                   root = root.left;
20                   return root;
21               } else {
22                   var temp = findMin(root.right);
23                   root.value = temp.value;
24                   root.right = deleteRecursively(root.right, temp.value);
```

```
25              return root;
26          }
27      }
28      root.updateInNewLocation(); // ONLY DIFFERENCE from the BST one
29      return root;
30  }
31  function findMin(root) {
32      while (root.left) root = root.left;
33      return root;
34  }
35  }
```

The time complexity and space complexity are both O($nlog_2(n)$) because AVL trees are balanced. The space complexity is from the recursive call stacks in memory.

## Putting It All Together: AVL Tree Example

With the AVL tree class implemented, Figure 15-19 shows an example of an AVL tree produced by the following code block:

```
1  var avlTest = new AVLTree(1,");
2  avlTest.insert(2);
3  avlTest.insert(3);
4  avlTest.insert(4);
5  avlTest.insert(5);
6  avlTest.insert(123);
7  avlTest.insert(203);
8  avlTest.insert(2222);
9  console.log(avlTest);
```

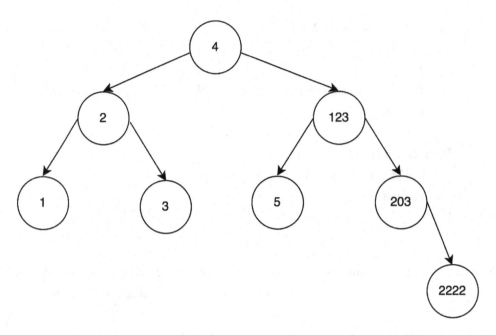

**Figure 15-19.** *AVL result*

If a plain binary search tree were used instead, Figure 15-20 shows what it would look like for the same order of insertion.

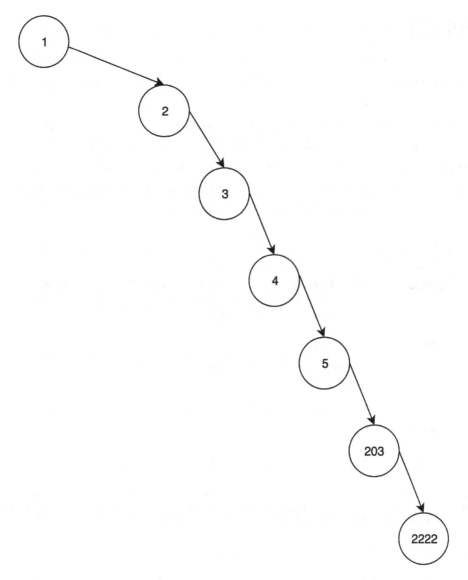

***Figure 15-20.*** *BST result*

Clearly, this is a skewed binary search tree that is completely unbalanced. At this point, it looks like a linked list. Once the tree becomes completely unbalanced like this, it has a linear time complexity for deletion, insertion, and search instead of logarithmic time.

# Summary

Table 15-1 shows the time complexity for each binary search tree operation. Compared to other data structures, the search operation is faster than linked lists, arrays, stacks, and queues. As the name implies, a binary *search* tree is great for searching elements. However, the insertion and deletion operations are slower, with a time complexity of $O(log_2(n))$ instead of $O(1)$ like a stack or a queue, for example. Furthermore, all operations become $O(n)$ as the tree becomes unbalanced. To ensure the tree stays balanced, self-balancing trees such as a red-black tree or an AVL tree should be used to ensure tree operations have logarithmic time complexity.

***Table 15-1.*** *Tree Summary*

| Operation | Best (If Balanced) | Worst (If Completely Unbalanced) |
|---|---|---|
| Deletion | $O(log_2(n))$ | $O(n)$ |
| Insertion | $O(log_2(n))$ | $O(n)$ |
| Search | $O(log_2(n))$ | $O(n)$ |

# Exercises

You can find all the code for the exercises on GitHub.[2]

## FIND THE LOWEST COMMON ANCESTOR OF TWO NODES IN A GIVEN BINARY TREE

The logic for this one is actually fairly simple but hard to notice at first.

If the maximum of the two values is smaller than the current root, go left. If the minimum of the two values is bigger than the current root, go right. Figures 15-21 and 15-22 show the two different cases of this.

---

[2]https://github.com/Apress/js-data-structures-and-algorithms

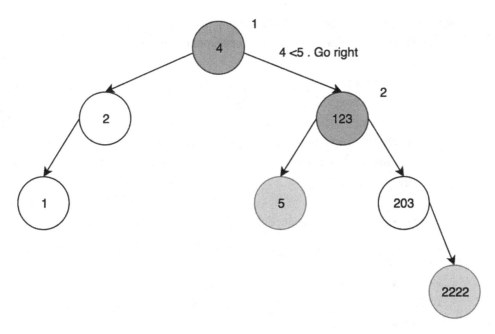

***Figure 15-21.*** *Lowest common ancestor, example 1*

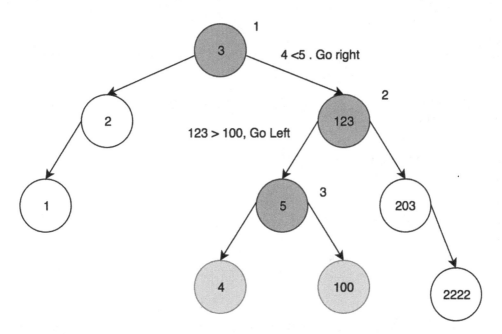

***Figure 15-22.*** *Lowest common ancestor, example 2*

```
1    function findLowestCommonAncestor(root, value1, value2) {
2        function findLowestCommonAncestorHelper(root, value1, value2) {
3            if (!root)
4                return;
5            if (Math.max(value1, value2) < root.value)
6                return findLowestCommonAncestorHelper(root.left, value1, value2);
7            if (Math.min(value1, value2) > root.value)
8                return findLowestCommonAncestorHelper(root.right, value1, value2);
9            return root.value
10       }
11       return findLowestCommonAncestorHelper(root, value1, value2);
12   }
13   var node1 = {
14       value: 1,
15       left: {
16           value: 0
17       },
18       right: {
19           value: 2
20       }
21   }
22
23   var node2 = {
24       value: 1,
25       left: {
26           value: 0,
27           left: {
28               value: -1
29           },
30           right: {
31               value: 0.5
32           }
33       },
34       right: {
35           value: 2
36       }
37   }
```

```
38    console.log(findLowestCommonAncestor(node1, 0, 2)); // 1
39    console.log(findLowestCommonAncestor(node2, 0, 2)); // 1
40    console.log(findLowestCommonAncestor(node1, 0.5, -1)); // 0
```

**Time Complexity:** $O(log_2(n))$

---

## PRINT NODES NTH DISTANCE FROM THE ROOT

For this question, traverse the BST in any way (level order was used in this example) and check the height for each BST node to see whether it should be printed.

```
1    function printKthLevels(root, k) {
2        var arrayKth = [];
3            queue = [];
4
5        if (!root) return;
6
7        // Breath first search for tree
8        queue.push([root, 0]);
9
10       while (queue.length) {
11           var tuple = queue.shift(),
12               temp = tuple[0],
13               height= tuple[1];
14
15           if (height == k) {
16               arrayKth.push(temp.value);
17           }
18           if (temp.left) {
19               queue.push([temp.left, height+1]);
20           }
21           if (temp.right) {
22               queue.push([temp.right,height+1]);
23           }
24       }
25       console.log(arrayKth);
26   }
```

```
1    var node1 = {
2        value: 1,
3        left: {
4            value: 0
5        },
6        right: {
7            value: 2
8        }
9    }
10
11   var node2 = {
12       value: 1,
13       left: {
14           value: 0,
15           left: {
16               value: -1
17           },
18           right: {
19               value: 0.5
20           }
21       },
22       right: {
23           value: 2
24       }
25   }
26
27   var node3 = {
28       value: 1,
29     left: {
30           value: 0
31       },
32       right: {
33           value: 2,
34           left: {
35               value: 1.5
36           },
37           right: {
```

```
38                value: 3,
39                left: {
40                    value: 3.25
41                }
42            }
43        }
44    }
45
46    printKthLevels(node1, 1); // 1
47    printKthLevels(node1, 2); // [0,2]
```

## CHECK WHETHER A BINARY TREE IS A SUBTREE OF ANOTHER TREE

To do this, traverse the binary tree in any way (I'm choosing to do level order) and check whether the one that it is currently on is the same as the subtree.

```
1    function isSameTree(root1, root2) {
2        if (root1 == null && root2 == null) {
3            return true;
4        }
5        if (root1 == null || root2 == null) {
6            return false;
7        }
8
9        return root1.value == root2.value &&
10            isSameTree(root1.left, root2.left) &&
11            isSameTree(root1.right, root2.right)
12    }
13
14    function checkIfSubTree(root, subtree) {
15        // Breath first search
16        var queue = [],
17            counter = 0;
18
19        // sanity check for root
20        if (!root) {
21            return;
```

```
22          }
23
24          queue.push(root);
25
26          while (queue.length) {
27              var temp = queue.shift();
28
29              if (temp.data == subtree.data == isSameTree(temp, subtree)) {
30                  return true;
31              }
32
33              if (temp.left) {
34                  queue.push(temp.left);
35              }
36              if (temp.right) {
37                  queue.push(temp.right);
38              }
39          }
40          return false;
41      }
42
43      var node1 = {
44          value: 5,
45          left: {
46              value: 3,
47              left: {
48                  value: 1
49              },
50              right: {
51                  value: 2
52              }
53          },
54          right: {
55              value: 7
56          }
57      }
58
```

```
59    var node2 = {
60        value: 3,
61        left: {
62            value: 1
63        },
64        right: {
65            value: 2
66        }
67    }
68
69
70    var node3 = {
71        value: 3,
72        left: {
73            value: 1
74        }
75    }
76
77    console.log(checkIfSubTree(node1, node2)); // true
78    console.log(checkIfSubTree(node1, node3)); // false
79    console.log(checkIfSubTree(node2, node3)); // false
```

## CHECK WHETHER A TREE IS A MIRROR OF ANOTHER TREE

Figure 15-23 shows an example.

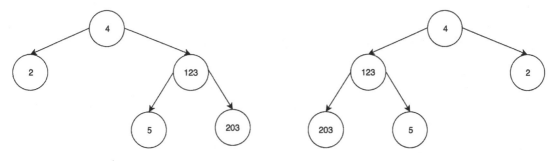

***Figure 15-23.*** *Mirror trees*

Here are three possible cases:

- Their root node's key must be the same.

- The left subtree of root of *a* and the right subtree root of *b* are mirrors.

- The right subtree of *a* and the left subtree of *b* are mirrors.

```
1    function isMirrorTrees(tree1, tree2) {
2        // Base case, both empty
3        if (!tree1 && !tree2) {
4            return true;
5        }
6
7        // One of them is empty, since only one is empty, not mirrored
8        if (!tree1 || !tree2) {
9            return false;
10       }
11
12       // Both non-empty, compare them recursively.
13       // Pass left of one and right of the other
14
15       var checkLeftwithRight = isMirrorTrees(tree1.left, tree2.right),
16           checkRightwithLeft = isMirrorTrees(tree2.right, tree1.left);
17
18       return tree1.value == tree2.value && checkLeftwithRight &&
         checkRightwithLeft;
19   }
20
21   var node1 = {
22       value: 3,
23       left: {
24           value: 1
25       },
26       right: {
27           value: 2
28       }
29   }
30
```

```
31    var node2 = {
32        value: 3,
33        left: {
34            value: 2
35        },
36        right: {
37            value: 1
38        }
39    }
40
41    var node3 = {
42        value: 3,
43        left: {
44            value: 1
45        },
46        right: {
47            value: 2,
48            left: {
49                value: 2.5
50            }
51        }
52    }
53
54    console.log(isMirrorTrees(node1, node2)); // true
55    console.log(isMirrorTrees(node2, node3)); // false
```

# CHAPTER 16

# Heaps

This chapter will introduce heaps. A heap is an important data structure that returns the highest or lowest element in O(1) time. This chapter will focus on explaining how heaps are implemented as well as how to work with them. One example is heap sort, which is a sorting algorithm based on heaps.

## Understanding Heaps

A *heap* is a type of tree-like data structure in which the parent is bigger than its children (if max-heap) or smaller than its children (if min-heap). This property of the heap makes it useful for sorting data.

Heaps, unlike other tree data structures, use an array to store data instead of having pointers to their children. A heap node's children's positions (indices) in the array can be calculated easily. This is because the parent-child relationship is easily defined with a heap.

There are many types of heaps that have different numbers of children. In this chapter, only binary heaps will be considered. Since a heap uses an array to store the data, the indices of the array define the order/height of each element. A binary heap can be built by placing the first array element as the root and then filling each left and right element in order.

For example, for the heap shown in Figure 16-1, the array would look like this: [2, 4, 23, 12, 13].

© Sammie Bae 2019
S. Bae, *JavaScript Data Structures and Algorithms*, https://doi.org/10.1007/978-1-4842-3988-9_16

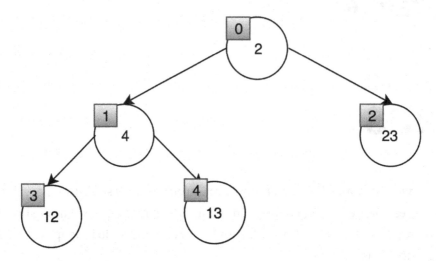

**Figure 16-1.**  *Heap indices*

There are two types of binary heaps: max-heap and min-heap. In *max-heap*, the root node has the highest value, and each node's value is greater than its children. In *min-heap*, the root node has the lowest value, and each node's value is smaller than its children.

Heaps can store any values of any type: strings, integer, and even custom classes. As covered in Chapters 3 and 4, strings and integer value comparisons are handled natively by JavaScript (e.g., 9 is greater than 1, *z* is greater than *a*). However, for custom classes, the developer needs to implement a way to compare two classes. This chapter will look at heaps that store integer values only.

## Max-Heap

A max-heap is a heap where the parent is always greater than any of its children (see Figure 16-2).

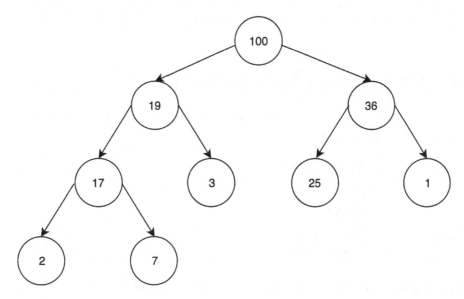

**Figure 16-2.** *Max-heap*

Here is the array for the max-heap shown in Figure 16-2: [100, 19, 36, 17, 3, 25, 1, 2, 7].

# Min-Heap

A min-heap is a heap where the parent is always smaller than any of its children (see Figure 16-3).

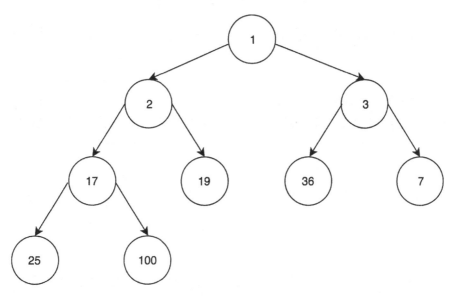

**Figure 16-3.** *Min-heap*

Here is the array for the max-heap shown in Figure 16-3: [1, 2, 3, 17, 19, 36, 7, 25, 100].

## Binary Heap Array Index Structure

For a binary heap, an array is used to represent the heap by using the following indices, where N is the index of the node:

```
Node                Index
(itself)            N
Parent              (N-1) / 2
Left Child          (N*2) + 1
Right Child         (N*2) + 2
```

Figure 16-4 illustrates this familial relationship using indices.

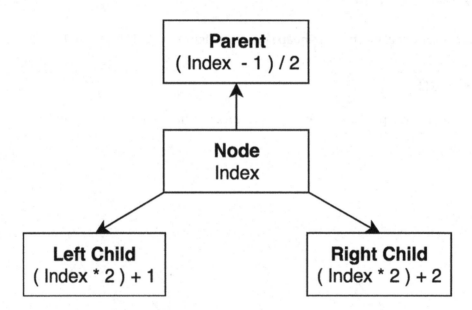

***Figure 16-4.*** *Heap relationship*

Let's first define a generic Heap class. An array will be used to store all the values using the index structure described earlier. The following heap class implements helper functions that retrieve the parent node, the left child, and the right child. The following code block has a peek function that returns the maximum value for a max-heap and the minimum value for a min-heap.

```
1   function Heap() {
2       this.items = [];
3   }
4
5   Heap.prototype.swap = function(index1, index2) {
6       var temp = this.items[index1];
7       this.items[index1] = this.items[index2];
8       this.items[index2] = temp;
9   }
10
11  Heap.prototype.parentIndex = function(index) {
12      return Math.floor((index - 1) / 2);
13  }
14
15  Heap.prototype.leftChildIndex = function(index) {
16      return index * 2 + 1;
17  }
18
19  Heap.prototype.rightChildrenIndex = function(index) {
20      return index * 2 + 2;
21  }
22
23  Heap.prototype.parent = function(index) {
24      return this.items[this.parentIndex(index)];
25  }
26
27  Heap.prototype.leftChild = function(index) {
28      return this.items[this.leftChildIndex(index)];
29  }
30
```

```
31   Heap.prototype.rightChild = function(index) {
32       return this.items[this.rightChildrenIndex(index)];
33   }
34
35   Heap.prototype.peek = function(item) {
36       return this.items[0];
37   }
38   Heap.prototype.size = function() {
39       return this.items.length;
40   }
```

The size function is another helper that returns the size (number of elements) of the heap.

## Percolation: Bubbling Up and Down

When elements are added or removed, the structure of the heap must remain (the node being greater than its children for a max-heap or smaller than its children for a min-heap).

This requires items to swap and "bubble up" to the top of the heap. Similar to bubbling up, some items need to "bubble down" to their rightful position in order to keep the structure of the heap. Percolation takes $O(log_2(n))$ in time.

Let's step through a min-heap example and insert the following values into the min-heap in this order: 12, 2, 23, 4, 13. Here are the steps:

1.  Insert 12 as the first node (Figure 16-5).

**Figure 16-5.**  *The min-heap root node*

2. Insert a new 2 node (Figure 16-6).

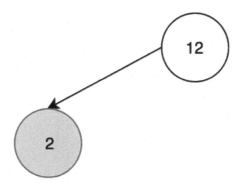

***Figure 16-6.*** *The newest node is smaller than the parent*

3. The 2 node bubbles up because it is smaller than 12 and hence should be on the top of the min-heap (Figure 16-7).

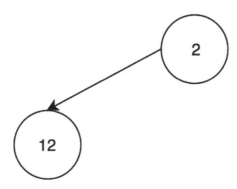

***Figure 16-7.*** *The smaller node has bubbled up to the parent position*

4. Insert a new 23 node in the second child position (Figure 16-8).

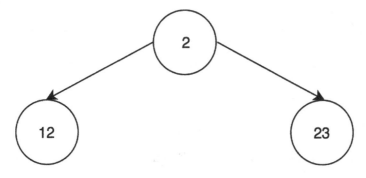

***Figure 16-8.*** *The larger 23 node remains in place in the min-heap structure*

5.  Insert 4 in the heap, as in Figure 16-9.

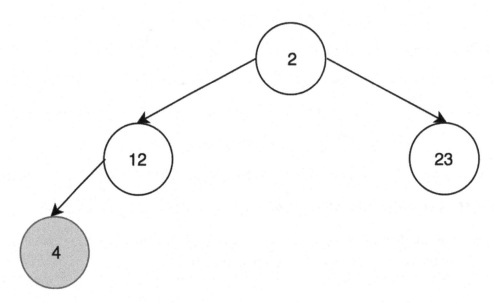

***Figure 16-9.*** *The new node in the min-heap is smaller than the one above it*

6.  12 is swapped with 4 to maintain the min-heap structure (Figure 16-10).

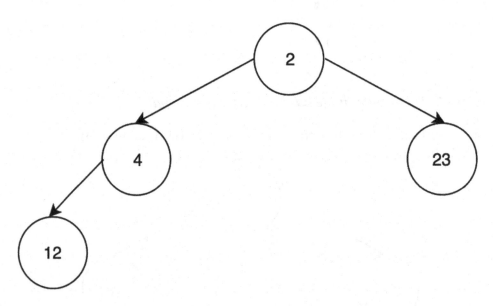

***Figure 16-10.*** *The smaller 4 node has bubbled up to maintain the min-heap structure*

7.    Insert 13, as in Figure 16-11.

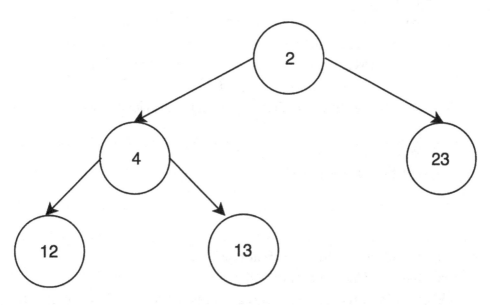

**Figure 16-11.**  *The newest and larger 13 node remains in place*

Here is the array content for this heap: [2, 4, 23, 12, 13].

# Implementing Percolation

To implement the "bubbling up and down" of percolation, swap until the min-heap structure is formed with the minimum element on the top. For bubbling down, swap the top element (first in the array) with one of its children if that child is smaller. Likewise, for bubbling up, swap the new element with its parent if the parent is greater than the new element.

```
1    function MinHeap() {
2        this.items = [];
3    }
4    MinHeap.prototype = Object.create(Heap.prototype);
     // inherit helpers from heap by copying prototype
5    MinHeap.prototype.bubbleDown = function() {
6        var index = 0;
```

```
7        while (this.leftChild(index) && this.leftChild(index) < this.
         items[index]) {
8            var smallerIndex = this.leftChildIndex(index);
9            if (this.rightChild(index)
10               && this.rightChild(index) < this.items[smallerIndex]) {
11               // if right is smaller, right swaps
12               smallerIndex = this.rightChildrenIndex(index);
13           }
14           this.swap(smallerIndex, index);
15           index = smallerIndex;
16       }
17   }
18
19   MinHeap.prototype.bubbleUp = function() {
20       var index = this.items.length - 1;
21       while (this.parent(index) && this.parent(index) > this.items[index]) {
22           this.swap(this.parentIndex(index), index);
23           index = this.parentIndex(index);
24       }
25   }
```

A max-heap implementation differs only in the comparators. For bubbling down, the max-heap node swaps with one of its children if the child is greater. Likewise, for bubbling up, the newest node swaps with its parent if its parent is smaller than the new node.

## Max-Heap Example

Let's build a max-heap now with the same values as the one used in the previous min-heap example by inserting the following values in the order: 12, 2, 23, 4, 13.

1.  Insert the first node, which is 12 (Figure 16-12).

**Figure 16-12.**  *The first max-heap node*

2. Insert a new 2 node (Figure 16-13).

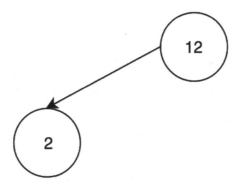

***Figure 16-13.*** *The new smaller node remains in place in the max-heap structure*

3. Insert 23, as in Figure 16-14.

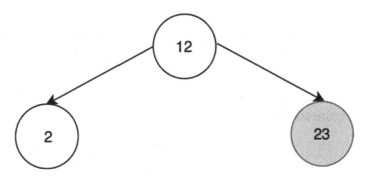

***Figure 16-14.*** *The new child node is larger than the parent*

4. The 23 node "bubbles" to the top to maintain max-heap structure (Figure 16-15).

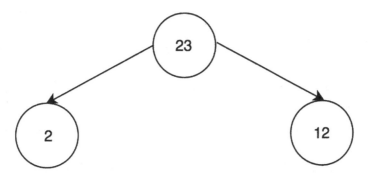

***Figure 16-15.*** *The new larger node is swapped with the smaller 12*

5. Insert 4, as in Figure 16-16.

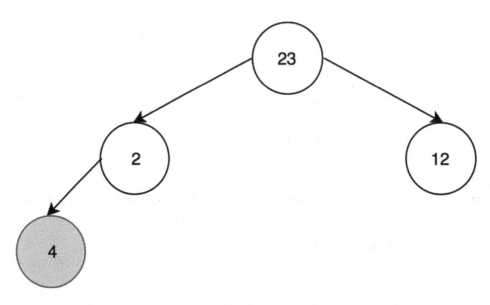

***Figure 16-16.*** *The new node is larger than the one above it*

6. To maintain the max-heap structure, 4 bubbles up, and 2 bubbles down (Figure 16-17).

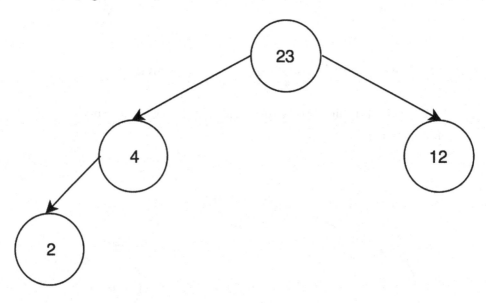

***Figure 16-17.*** *The 4 and 2 nodes swap places*

7. Insert 13, as in Figure 16-18.

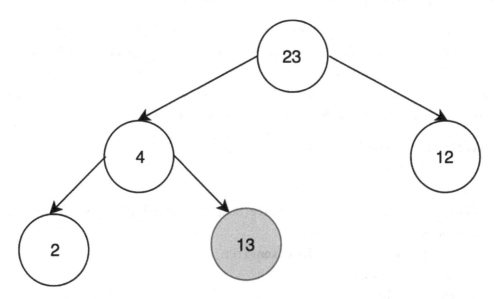

***Figure 16-18.***  *The new node is larger than the one above it*

8. Because of the max-heap structure, 13 and 4 swap positions (Figure 16-19).

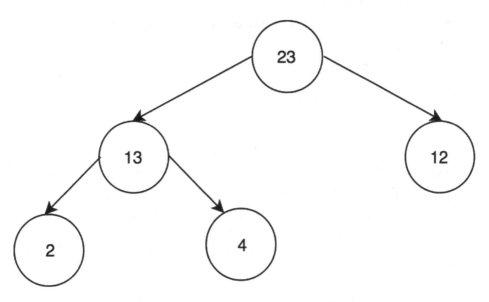

***Figure 16-19.***  *Percolation restores the max-heap structure*

Here is the array content for this heap: [23, 13, 12, 2, 4].

# Min-Heap Complete Implementation

Putting all the functions defined together and inheriting Heap's functions, the complete implementation and example of min-heap is shown next. The add and poll functions were added. add simply adds a new element to the heap, but bubbleUp ensures that this element in the min-heap satisfies the order. poll removes the minimum element (the root) from the heap and calls bubbleDown to keep the min-heap order.

```
1    function MinHeap() {
2        this.items = [];
3    }
4    MinHeap.prototype = Object.create(Heap.prototype); // inherit helpers
     from heap by copying prototype
5    MinHeap.prototype.add = function(item) {
6        this.items[this.items.length] = item;
7        this.bubbleUp();
8    }
9
10   MinHeap.prototype.poll = function() {
11       var item = this.items[0];
12       this.items[0] = this.items[this.items.length - 1];
13       this.items.pop();
14       this.bubbleDown();
15       return item;
16   }
17
18   MinHeap.prototype.bubbleDown = function() {
19       var index = 0;
20       while (this.leftChild(index) && (this.leftChild(index) < this.
         items[index] || this.rightChild(index) < this.items[index]) ) {
21           var smallerIndex = this.leftChildIndex(index);
22           if (this.rightChild(index) && this.rightChild(index) < this.
             items[smallerIndex]) {
23               smallerIndex = this.rightChildrenIndex(index);
24           }
25           this.swap(smallerIndex, index);
```

```
26              index = smallerIndex;
27          }
28      }
29
30      MinHeap.prototype.bubbleUp = function() {
31          var index = this.items.length - 1;
32          while (this.parent(index) && this.parent(index) > this.
            items[index]) {
33              this.swap(this.parentIndex(index), index);
34              index = this.parentIndex(index);
35          }
36      }
37
38      var mh1 = new MinHeap();
39      mh1.add(1);
40      mh1.add(10);
41      mh1.add(5);
42      mh1.add(100);
43      mh1.add(8);
44
45      console.log(mh1.poll()); // 1
46      console.log(mh1.poll()); // 5
47      console.log(mh1.poll()); // 8
48      console.log(mh1.poll()); // 10
49      console.log(mh1.poll()); // 100
```

# Max-Heap Complete Implementation

As previously discussed, the only difference between the min-heap and max-heap
implementations is the comparator in bubbleDown and bubbleUp. With the same
elements added as the previous example, meaning (1, 10, 5, 100, 8), the max-heap
returns the highest elements when poll is called.

```
1       function MaxHeap() {
2           this.items = [];
3       }
```

```
4    MaxHeap.prototype = Object.create(Heap.prototype);
     // inherit helpers from heap by copying prototype
5    MaxHeap.prototype.poll = function() {
6        var item = this.items[0];
7        this.items[0] = this.items[this.items.length - 1];
8        this.items.pop();
9        this.bubbleDown();
10       return item;
11   }
12
13   MaxHeap.prototype.bubbleDown = function() {
14       var index = 0;
15       while (this.leftChild(index) && (this.leftChild(index) > this.
         items[index] || this.rightChild(index) > this.items[index] ) ) {
16           var biggerIndex = this.leftChildIndex(index);
17           if (this.rightChild(index) && this.rightChild(index) > this.
             items[bigger\Index])
18           {
19               biggerIndex = this.rightChildrenIndex(index);
20           }
21           this.swap(biggerIndex, index);
22           index = biggerIndex;
23       }
24   }
25
26   MaxHeap.prototype.bubbleUp = function() {
27       var index = this.items.length - 1;
28       while (this.parent(index) && this.parent(index) < this.
         items[index]) {
29           this.swap(this.parentIndex(index), index);
30           index = this.parentIndex(index);
31       }
32   }
33
```

```
34    var mh2 = new MaxHeap();
35    mh2.add(1);
36    mh2.add(10);
37    mh2.add(5);
38    mh2.add(100);
39    mh2.add(8);
40
41    console.log(mh2.poll()); // 100
42    console.log(mh2.poll()); // 10
43    console.log(mh2.poll()); // 8
44    console.log(mh2.poll()); // 5
45    console.log(mh2.poll()); // 1
```

# Heap Sort

Now that heap classes have been created, sorting with a heap is fairly straightforward. To get a sorted array, simply call .pop() on the heap until it is empty and store the stored popped objects. This is as known as a *heap sort*. Since percolation takes $O(log_2(n))$, and sorting must pop *n* number of elements, the time complexity for a heap sort is $O(nlog_2(n))$, like quicksort and mergesort.

In this section, we will first do an ascending sort implemented using a min-heap and then a descending sort implemented using a max-heap.

## Ascending-Order Sort (Min-Heap)

Figure 16-20 shows the min-heap when all the items have been added to the min-heap, and Figures 16-21 to 16-23 show the heap restructuring as items are popped. Finally, when it is empty, the sort is complete.

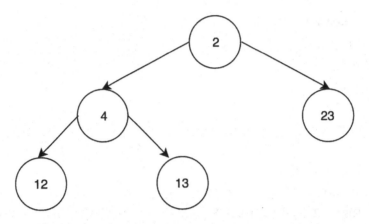

***Figure 16-20.*** *Min-heap sort after all items added*

```
1    var minHeapExample = new MinHeap();
2    minHeapExample.add(12);
3    minHeapExample.add(2);
4    minHeapExample.add(23);
5    minHeapExample.add(4);
6    minHeapExample.add(13);
7    minHeapExample.items; // [2, 4, 23, 12, 13]
8
9    console.log(minHeapExample.poll()); // 2
10   console.log(minHeapExample.poll()); // 4
11   console.log(minHeapExample.poll()); // 12
12   console.log(minHeapExample.poll()); // 13
13   console.log(minHeapExample.poll()); // 23
```

The last node (where 13 used to be) is removed, and then 13 is placed on the top. Through the percolation process, 13 moves down to after the left child of 12 since it's bigger than both 4 and 13.

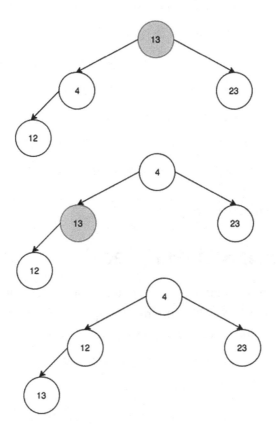

**Figure 16-21.** *Min-heap sort: popping 2 out*

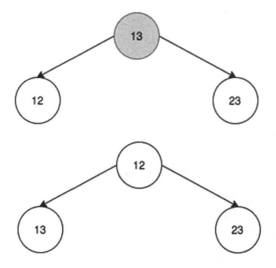

**Figure 16-22.** *Min-heap sort: popping 4 out*

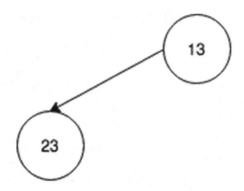

*Figure 16-23.* *Min-heap sort: popping 12 out*

## Descending-Order Sort (Max-Heap)

Figure 16-24 shows the max-heap when all the items have been added to the min-heap, and Figures 16-25 through 16-27 show the max-heap restructuring as items are popped. Finally, when it is empty, the sort is complete.

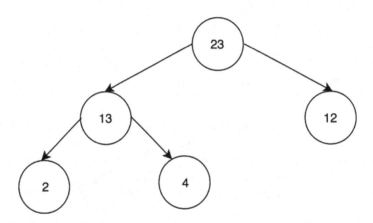

*Figure 16-24.* *Max-heap sort after all items are added*

```
1    var maxHeapExample = new MaxHeap();
2    maxHeapExample.add(12);
3    maxHeapExample.add(2);
4    maxHeapExample.add(23);
5    maxHeapExample.add(4);
6    maxHeapExample.add(13);
```

```
7   maxHeapExample.items; // [23, 13, 12, 2, 4]
8
9   console.log(maxHeapExample.poll()); // 23
10  console.log(maxHeapExample.poll()); // 13
11  console.log(maxHeapExample.poll()); // 12
12  console.log(maxHeapExample.poll()); // 2
13  console.log(maxHeapExample.poll()); // 4
```

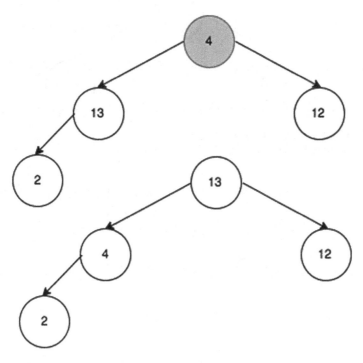

***Figure 16-25.*** *Max sort: popping 23 out*

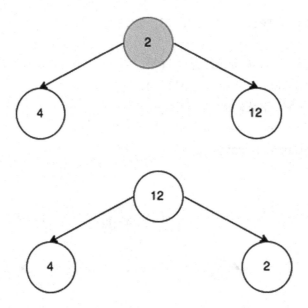

*Figure 16-26. Max sort: popping 13 out*

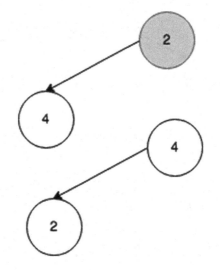

*Figure 16-27. Max sort: popping 12 out*

# Summary

A heap is a tree-like data structure represented using arrays. To get the parent, left child, and right child of a tree's node, you can use the index formula in Table 16-1.

***Table 16-1.*** *Heap Node Index Summary*

| Node | Index |
|---|---|
| (self) | N |
| Parent | (N-1) / 2 |
| Left child | (N*2) + 1 |
| Right child | (N*2) + 2 |

Heaps maintain their structure via *percolation*; when a node is inserted, it "bubbles up" by repeatedly swapping with elements until the proper heap structure is achieved. For a min-heap, this means the *lowest*-valued node at the root. For a max-heap, this means the *highest*-valued node at the root. Heaps work fundamentally by percolation, which allows deletion and insertion in $O(\log_2(n))$ time, as summarized in Table 16-2.

***Table 16-2.*** *Heap Operations Summary*

| Operation | Time Complexity |
|---|---|
| Deletion (leads to "bubble down") | $O(log_2(n))$ |
| Insertion (leads to "bubble up") | $O(log_2(n))$ |
| Heap sort | $O(n\ log_2(n))$ |

# Exercises

You can find all the code for the exercises on GitHub.[1]

---

**KEEP TRACK OF MEDIAN IN STREAM OF NUMBERS**

---

Since this question is in this chapter, that's already a big hint for approaching it. In theory, the solution is fairly simple. Have one min-heap and one max-heap, and then retrieving the median takes only O(1).

For example, let's have a stream of the following integers: 12, 2, 23, 4, 13.

Median, when 12 is inserted, is 12 since that's the only element. When 2 is inserted, there is an even number of items: 2 and 12. Hence, the median is its arithmetic mean, 7 ((12+2)/2). When 23 is inserted, the median is 12. Finally, when 13 is inserted, the median is 12.5, the average of two middle terms (12 and 13).

```
1   medianH.push(12);
2   console.log(medianH.median()); // 12
3   medianH.push(2);
4   console.log(medianH.median()); // 7 ( because 12 + 2 = 14; 14/2 = 7)
5   medianH.push(23);
6   console.log(medianH.median()); // 12
7   medianH.push(13);
8   console.log(medianH.median()); // 12.5
```

```
1    function MedianHeap() {
2        this.minHeap = new MinHeap();
3        this.maxHeap = new MaxHeap();
4    }
5
6    MedianHeap.prototype.push = function (value) {
7        if (value > this.median()) {
8            this.minHeap.add(value);
9        } else {
10           this.maxHeap.add(value);
11       }
```

---

[1]https://github.com/Apress/js-data-structures-and-algorithms

```
12
13      // Re balancing
14      if (this.minHeap.size() - this.maxHeap.size() > 1) {
15          this.maxHeap.push(this.minHeap.poll());
16      }
17
18      if (this.maxHeap.size() - this.minHeap.size() > 1){
19          this.minHeap.push(this.maxHeap.poll());
20      }
21  }
22
23  MedianHeap.prototype.median = function () {
24      if (this.minHeap.size() == 0 && this.maxHeap.size() == 0){
25          return Number.NEGATIVE_INFINITY;
26      } else if (this.minHeap.size() == this.maxHeap.size()) {
27          return (this.minHeap.peek() + this.maxHeap.peek()) / 2;
28      } else if (this.minHeap.size() > this.maxHeap.size()) {
29          return this.minHeap.peek();
30      } else {
31          return this.maxHeap.peek();
32      }
33  }
34
35  var medianH = new MedianHeap();
36
37  medianH.push(12);
38  console.log(medianH.median()); // 12
39  medianH.push(2);
40  console.log(medianH.median()); // 7 ( because 12 + 2 = 14; 14/2 = 7)
41  medianH.push(23);
42  console.log(medianH.median()); // 12
43  medianH.push(13);
44  console.log(medianH.median()); // 12.5
```

## FIND THE *K*TH SMALLEST VALUE IN AN ARRAY

This problem has been explored before in Chapter 10 using quicksort's helper function. Another way to do it is to use a heap. Simply add the elements into a heap and pop it *k*th times. By definition of min-heaps, this returns the *k*th smallest value in the array.

```
1   var array1 = [12, 3, 13, 4, 2, 40, 23]
2
3   function getKthSmallestElement(array, k) {
4       var minH = new MinHeap();
5       for (var i = 0, arrayLength = array.length; i < arrayLength; i++) {
6           minH.add(array[i]);
7       }
8       for (var i = 1; i < k; i++) {
9           minH.poll();
10      }
11      return minH.poll();
12  }
13  getKthSmallestElement(array1, 2); // 3
14  getKthSmallestElement(array1, 1); // 2
15  getKthSmallestElement(array1, 7); // 40
```

## FIND THE KTH LARGEST VALUE IN AN ARRAY

This is the same idea from before just with max-heap.

```
1   var array1 = [12,3,13,4,2,40,23];
2
3   function getKthBiggestElement(array, k) {
4       var maxH = new MaxHeap();
5       for (var i=0, arrayLength = array.length; i<arrayLength; i++) {
6           maxH.push(array[i]);
7       }
8       for (var i=1; i<k; i++) {
9           maxH.pop();
10      }
```

```
11        return maxH.pop();
12    }
13    getKthBiggestElement(array1,2); // 23
14    getKthBiggestElement(array1,1); // 40
15    getKthBiggestElement(array1,7); // 2
```

**Time Complexity:** $O(k log_2(n))$

Here, $n$ is the size of the array since each .pop costs $O(log_2(n))$, which has to be done $k$ times.

**Space Complexity:** $O(n)$

$O(n)$ in memory is needed to store the heap array.

# CHAPTER 17

# Graphs

This chapter covers graphs. Graphs are a versatile way of representing connections between objects. In this chapter, you will learn graph basics, including fundamental terminology and graph types. The chapter will also cover working with these different graph types and methods of representing graphs in data structures that have already been explored. Finally, algorithms for traversing, searching, and sorting graphs are explored to solve problems such as finding the shortest path between two graph nodes.

## Graph Basics

As mentioned in the introduction, *graphs* are visual representations of the connections between objects. Such representations can be of many things and have different applications; Table 17-1 shows some examples.

***Table 17-1.*** *Examples of Graph Applications*

| Application | Item | Connection |
| --- | --- | --- |
| Web site | Web page | Links |
| Map | Intersection | Road |
| Circuit | Component | Wiring |
| Social media | Person | "Friendship"/connection |
| Telephone | Phone number | Landline |

© Sammie Bae 2019
S. Bae, *JavaScript Data Structures and Algorithms*, https://doi.org/10.1007/978-1-4842-3988-9_17

Figure 17-1 shows two examples of simple graphs.

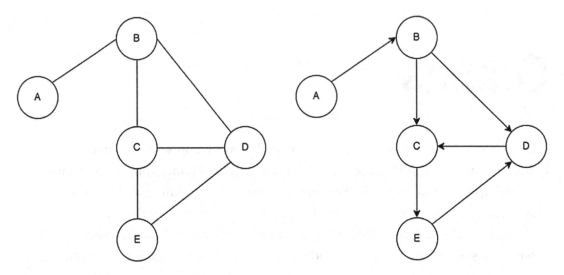

**Figure 17-1.**  *Two examples of graphs*

Before we delve into graphs too deeply, it is useful to introduce some basic terminology and concepts.

- *Vertex*: A vertex is the node from which graphs are formed. In this chapter, a node will be noted as *V* for Big-O analysis. A vertex is represented using a circle, as shown in Figure 17-2.

- *Edge*: An edge is the connection between nodes in a graph. Graphically, it is the "line" between the vertices. It will be noted as *E* for Big-O analysis. An edge is represented using a line, as shown in Figure 17-2.

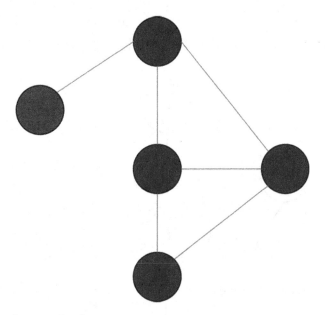

**Figure 17-2.** *Vertices and edges*

- *Degree of vertex*: The degree of a vertex refers to the number of edges on that vertex (node).

- *Sparse graph*: A graph is considered sparse when only a small fraction of possible connections exist between vertices (see Figure 17-3).

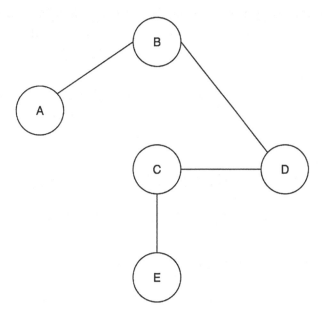

**Figure 17-3.** *Sparse graph*

- *Dense graph*: A graph is considered dense when there are a lot of connections between different vertices (see Figure 17-4).

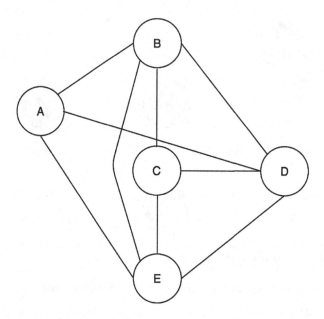

***Figure 17-4.*** *Dense graph*

- *Cyclical graph*: A directed graph is considered cyclical if there is a path that travels from a vertex and back to itself. For example, in Figure 17-5, B can follow the edge to C and then D and then E and then to B again.

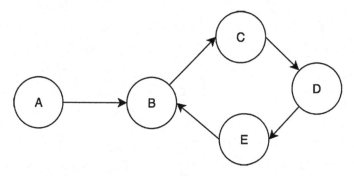

***Figure 17-5.*** *Graph with a cycle on B*

In contrast, Figure 17-6 is an example of a graph that is not cyclical.

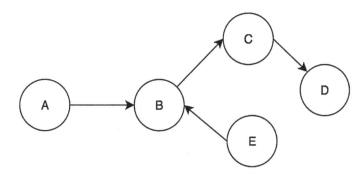

***Figure 17-6.*** *Graph without a cycle*

- *Weights*: Weights are values on the edges. Weights can signify various things depending on the context. For example, weights on a directed graph can represent the distance required to get from node A to B, as shown in Figure 17-7.

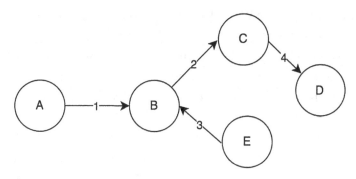

***Figure 17-7.*** *Directed graph with weights*

# Undirected Graphs

*Undirected graphs* are graphs that do not have a direction between edges. The edge implies a mutual connection between the two nodes without a direction. A real-life example of an undirected graph relationship is friendship. Friendship occurs only if both parties mutually acknowledge the relationship. Values of the edges within a friendship graph may indicate how close the friendship is. Figure 17-8 is a simple undirected graph with five vertices and six nondirectional edges with weights.

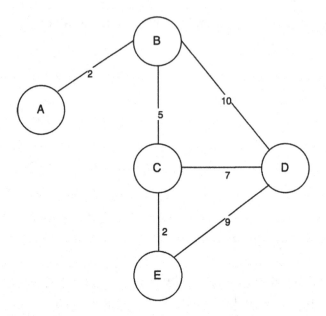

**Figure 17-8.** *Undirected graph with weights*

There are various ways to represent undirected graphs as a data structure class. Two of the most common ways to do this are by using an *adjacency matrix* or an *adjacency list*. The adjacency list uses a vertex as the key for nodes with its neighbors stored into a list, whereas an adjacency matrix is a V by V matrix with each element of the matrix indicating a connection between two vertices. Figure 17-9 illustrates the difference between an adjacency list and an adjacency matrix (This book covers only adjacency lists).

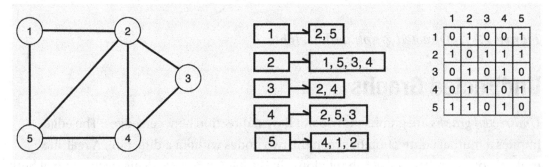

**Figure 17-9.** *Graph (left), adjacency list (middle), and adjacency matrix (right)*

So far, the concepts and definitions of graphs have been discussed. Now, let's actually start implementing these ideas into code and learn how to add and remove edges and vertices.

# Adding Edges and Vertices

In this example, we create a weighted *undirected* graph and add vertices and edges. First, we'll create a new class for an undirected graph. The undirected graph should have an object to store the edges. This is implemented as shown in the following code block:

```
1    function UndirectedGraph() {
2        this.edges = {};
3    }
```

To add edges, vertices (nodes) must be added first. This implementation will take the adjacency list approach by having vertices as objects inside the this.edges object in which edge values are stored.

```
1    UndirectedGraph.prototype.addVertex = function(vertex) {
2        this.edges[vertex] = {};
3    }
```

To add weighted edges into the undirected graph, both vertices in the this.edges objects are used to set the weight.

```
1    UndirectedGraph.prototype.addEdge = function(vertex1,vertex2, weight)
{
2        if (weight == undefined) {
3            weight = 0;
4        }
5        this.edges[vertex1][vertex2] = weight;
6        this.edges[vertex2][vertex1] = weight;
7    }
```

With this, let's add some vertices and edges with the following code:

```
1    var graph1 = new UndirectedGraph();
2    graph1.addVertex(1);
3    graph1.addVertex(2);
```

```
 4    graph1.addEdge(1,2, 1);
 5    graph1.edges;    // 1: {2: 0},  2: {1: 0}
 6    graph1.addVertex(3);
 7    graph1.addVertex(4);
 8    graph1.addVertex(5);
 9    graph1.addEdge(2,3, 8);
10    graph1.addEdge(3,4, 10);
11    graph1.addEdge(4,5, 100);
12  graph1.addEdge(1,5, 88);
```

Figure 17-10 shows the graphical output from this code.

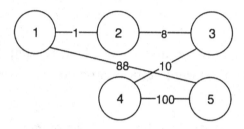

***Figure 17-10.*** *The first undirected graph*

## Removing Edges and Vertices

Continuing with the same example, let's implement the functions for removing edges and vertices for the graph class.

To remove an edge from a vertex, look up the edges object for that vertex in this. edges and delete it using JavaScript's delete operator.

```
1    UndirectedGraph.prototype.removeEdge = function(vertex1, vertex2) {
2        if (this.edges[vertex1] && this.edges[vertex1][vertex2] != undefined) {
3            delete this.edges[vertex1][vertex2];
4        }
5        if (this.edges[vertex2] && this.edges[vertex2][vertex1] != undefined) {
6            delete this.edges[vertex2][vertex1];
7        }
8    }
```

Next, let's delete an entire vertex. One important point to remember is that any time a *vertex is removed, all edges connected to it also must be removed.* This can be accomplished using a loop, as shown in the following implementation:

```
1   UndirectedGraph.prototype.removeVertex = function(vertex) {
2       for (var adjacentVertex in this.edges[vertex]) {
3           this.removeEdge(adjacentVertex, vertex);
4       }
5       delete this.edges[vertex];
6   }
```

With removal now implemented, let's create another undirected graph object similar to the first example but delete some vertices and edges. Vertex 5 is removed first, and the result is shown in Figure 17-11. Vertex 1 is also removed, as shown in Figure 17-12. Finally, Figure 17-13 shows the result when the edge between 2 and 3 is removed.

```
1    var graph2 = new UndirectedGraph();
2    graph2.addVertex(1);
3    graph2.addVertex(2);
4    graph2.addEdge(1,2, 1);
5    graph2.edges;    // 1: {2: 0},  2: {1: 0}
6    graph2.addVertex(3);
7    graph2.addVertex(4);
8    graph2.addVertex(5);
9    graph2.addEdge(2,3, 8);
10   graph2.addEdge(3,4, 10);
11   graph2.addEdge(4,5, 100);
12   graph2.addEdge(1,5, 88);
13   graph2.removeVertex(5);
14   graph2.removeVertex(1);
15   graph2.removeEdge(2,3);
```

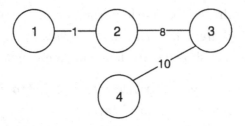

***Figure 17-11.*** *Vertex 5 removed*

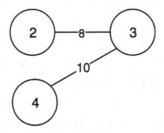

***Figure 17-12.*** *Vertex 1 removed*

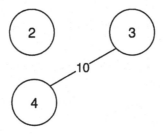

***Figure 17-13.*** *Edge between 2 and 3 removed*

# Directed Graphs

Directed graphs are graphs that *do* have a direction between vertices. Each edge in a directed graph goes from one vertex to another, as shown in Figure 17-14.

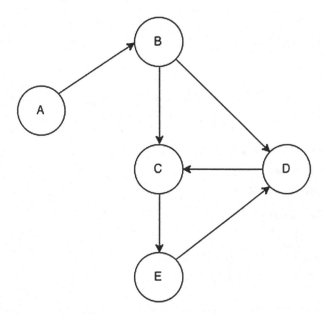

**Figure 17-14.** *Directed graph*

In this example, the E node can "travel" to the D node, and the D node can travel only to the C node.

Now let's implement a weighted directed graph class. The similar adjacency list approach used in the undirected graph implementation will be used. First, the DirectedGraph class is defined with the edges property as shown, and the method of adding the vertex is the same as the implementation from the undirected graph class.

```
1    function DirectedGraph() {
2        this.edges = {};
3    }
4    DirectedGraph.prototype.addVertex = function (vertex) {
5        this.edges[vertex] = {};
6    }
```

Given an edge that starts at the origin vertex and ends at the destination vertex, to add edges into the directed graph, the weight should be set only on the origin vertex, as shown here:

```
1    DirectedGraph.prototype.addEdge = function(origVertex, destVertex, weight) {
2        if (weight === undefined) {
3            weight = 0;
```

```
4        }
5            this.edges[origVertex][destVertex] = weight;
6    }
```

With the functions for adding vertices and edges implemented, let's add some sample vertices and edges.

```
1    var digraph1 = new DirectedGraph();
2    digraph1.addVertex("A");
3    digraph1.addVertex("B");
4    digraph1.addVertex("C");
5    digraph1.addEdge("A", "B", 1);
6    digraph1.addEdge("B", "C", 2);
7    digraph1.addEdge("C", "A", 3);
```

Figure 17-15 shows the edge added between the A and B vertices (line 5). Figure 17-16 illustrates the connections between B and C (line 6), and Figure 17-17 shows the connection between C and A (line 7).

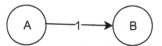

***Figure 17-15.*** *Adding A to B*

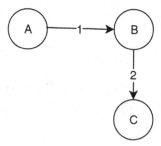

***Figure 17-16.*** *Adding B to C*

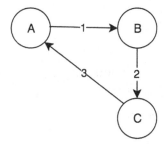

**Figure 17-17.** *Adding C to A*

The implementation for removing a vertex and removing an edge for a directed graph is the same as the implementation seen in the undirected graph except that only the origin vertex in the edges object have to be deleted, as shown here:

```
1   DirectedGraph.prototype.removeEdge = function(origVertex, destVertex) {
2       if (this.edges[origVertex] && this.edges[origVertex][destVertex]
        != undefined) {
3           delete this.edges[origVertex][destVertex];
4       }
5   }
6
7   DirectedGraph.prototype.removeVertex = function(vertex) {
8       for (var adjacentVertex in this.edges[vertex]) {
9           this.removeEdge(adjacentVertex, vertex);
10      }
11      delete this.edges[vertex];
12  }
```

# Graph Traversal

A graph can be traversed in multiple ways. The two most common approaches are breadth-first search and depth-first search. Similarly to how different tree traversal techniques were explored, this section will focus on these two traversal techniques and when to use each of them.

# Breadth-First Search

*Breadth-first search* (BFS) refers to a search algorithm in a graph that focuses on connected nodes and their connected nodes in order. This idea has actually already been explored with trees in Chapter 15 with level-order traversal. Figure 17-18 shows level-order traversal for a binary search tree.

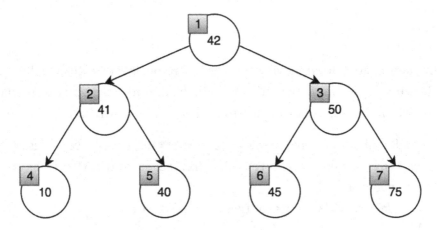

***Figure 17-18.*** *Level-order traversal for binary search tree*

Notice how the order of traversal is by the height from the root node. Notice the similarity with the graph in Figure 17-19.

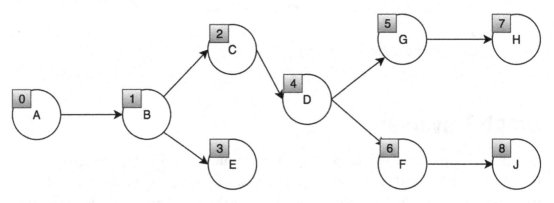

***Figure 17-19.*** *Breadth-first search graph*

Similar to the level-order traversal for the tree data structure, a queue is needed for a BFS. For each node, add each of connected vertices into a queue and then visit each item in the queue. Let's write a generalized BFS algorithm for the graph class.

```
1   DirectedGraph.prototype.traverseBFS = function(vertex, fn) {
2       var queue = [],
3           visited = {};
4
5       queue.push(vertex);
6
7       while (queue.length) {
8           vertex = queue.shift();
9           if (!visited[vertex]) {
10              visited[vertex] = true;
11              fn(vertex);
12              for (var adjacentVertex in this.edges[vertex]) {
13                  queue.push(adjacentVertex);
14              }
15          }
16      }
17  }
18  digraph1.traverseBFS("B", (vertex)=>{console.log(vertex)});
```

**Time Complexity:** $O(V + E)$

The time complexity is $O(V + E)$, where $V$ is the number of vertices and $E$ is the number of edges. This is because the algorithm has to go through every edge and node to traverse the whole graph.

Recall the graph structure in Figure 17-20 from "Undirected Graphs" used earlier in this chapter.

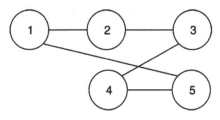

***Figure 17-20.*** *The earlier undirected graph example*

Applying the BFS to the graph, the following is printed: 1, 2, 5, 3, 4.

In Figures 17-21 and 17-22, the lightly shaded node represents the node being currently visited, while the dark node represents that the node has already been visited.

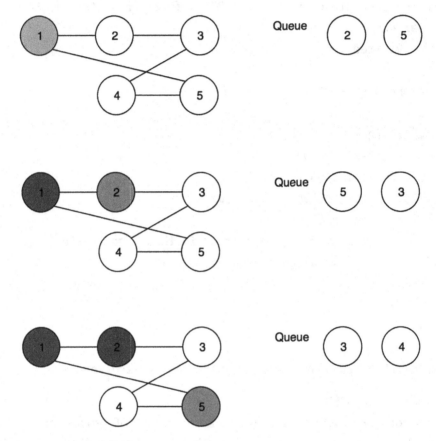

***Figure 17-21.*** *Breadth-first search, part 1*

In Figure 17-21, the breadth-first search starts at the 1 node. Because it has two neighbors, 2 and 5, those are added to the queue. Then, 2 is visited, and its neighbor 3 is added to the queue. 5 is then dequeued, and its neighbor 4 is added to the queue. Finally, 3 and 4 are visited, and the search ends, as shown in Figure 17-22.

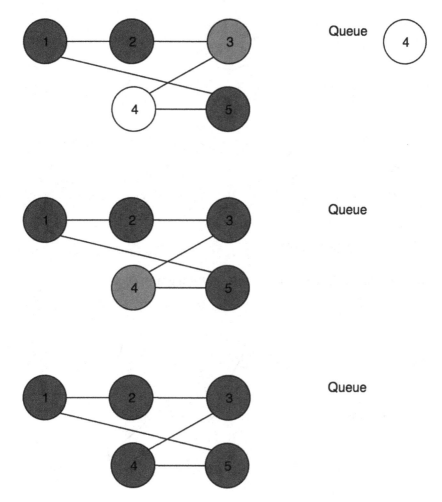

Queue

**Figure 17-22.** *Breadth-first search, part 2*

# Depth-First Search

*Depth-first search* (DFS) refers to a search algorithm in a graph that focuses on traversing deep into one connection before visiting the other connections.

This idea has been explored in Chapter 15 with in-order, post-order, and pre-order traversals in trees. For example, a post-order tree traversal visits the bottom children node before visiting the top root nodes (see Figure 17-23).

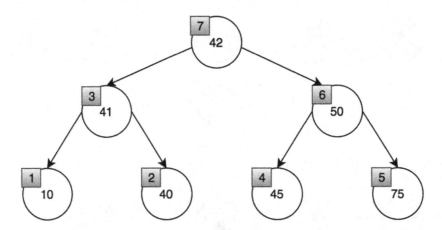

**Figure 17-23.** *Post-order traversal*

Something similar is shown in Figure 17-24 for a graph.

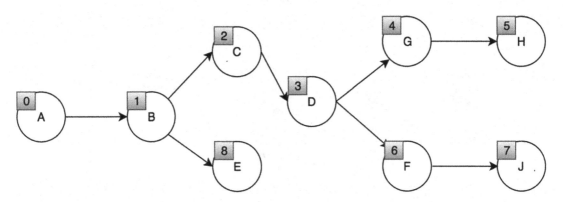

**Figure 17-24.** *Depth-first search graph*

Notice how E is visited last. This is because the search visits all the nodes connected to C in *depth* before visiting E.

Similar to the pre-post, and in-order traversal for the tree data structure, recursion is used to go *deep* into a node until that path is exhausted.

Let's write a generalized DFS algorithm for the graph class.

```
1    DirectedGraph.prototype.traverseDFS = function(vertex, fn) {
2        var visited = {};
3        this._traverseDFS(vertex, visited, fn);
4    }
5
```

```
 6   DirectedGraph.prototype._traverseDFS = function(vertex, visited, fn) {
 7        visited[vertex] = true;
 8        fn(vertex);
 9        for (var adjacentVertex in this.edges[vertex]) {
10            if (!visited[adjacentVertex]) {
11                this._traverseDFS(adjacentVertex, visited, fn);
12            }
13        }
14   }
```

**Time Complexity:** $O(V + E)$

The time complexity is $O(V + E)$ where $V$ is the number of vertices and $E$ is the number of edges. This is because the algorithm has to go through every edge and node to traverse the whole graph. This is the same time complexity as the BFS algorithm.

Again, let's use the graph structure from earlier in the chapter (see Figure 17-25).

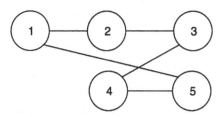

***Figure 17-25.*** *The earlier graph example from Figure 17-20*

Applying the DFS to the graph, the following is printed: 1, 2, 3, 4, 5.

In Figures 17-26 and 17-27, the lightly shaded node represents the node being currently visited, while the dark node represents that the node has already been visited.

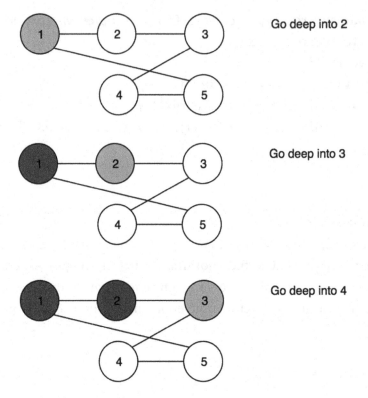

Go deep into 2

Go deep into 3

Go deep into 4

**Figure 17-26.** *Depth-first search, part 1*

In Figure 17-26, the depth-first search starts at the 1 node. Its first neighbor, 2, is visited. Then, 2's first neighbor, 3, is visited. After 3 is visited, 4 will be visited next because it is 3's first neighbor. Finally, 4 is visited followed by 5, as shown in Figure 17-27. Depth-first search always visits the first neighbor recursively.

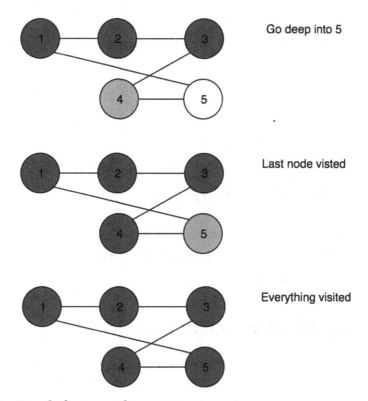

Go deep into 5

Last node visted

Everything visited

**Figure 17-27.** *Depth-first search, part 2*

# Weighted Graphs and Shortest Path

Now that we have covered the basics of graphs and how to traverse them, we can discuss weighted edges and Dijkstra's algorithm, which employs shortest path searches.

## Graphs with Weighted Edges

Recall that edges in a graph represent a connection between the vertices. If edges establish a connection, weight can be assigned to that connection. For example, for a graph that represents a map, the weights on the edges are distances.

It is important to note that the *graphical* length of an edge means nothing with regard to the edge's *weight*. It is purely there for visual purposes. In the implementation and the code, the visual representation is not required. In Figure 17-28, the weights tell us the distances between the cities in a graph representation of five cities. For example, graphically, the distance from City 1 and City 2 is shorter than the distance from City 2 and City 3. However, the edges indicate that the distance from City 1 to City 2 is 50 km, and the distance from City 2 to City 3 is 10 km, which is five times larger.

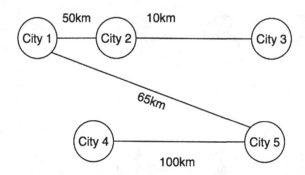

**Figure 17-28.** *Graph representation of five cities*

The most important question for weighted edge graphs is, what is the shortest path from one node to another? There are series of shortest path algorithms for graphs. The one we discuss is Dijkstra's algorithm.

## Dijkstra's Algorithm: Shortest Path

Dijkstra's algorithm works by taking the shortest path at each level to get to a destination. At first, the distance is marked as infinity because some nodes may not be reachable (see Figure 17-29). Then at each traversal iteration, the shortest distance is chosen for each node (see Figures 17-30 and 17-31).

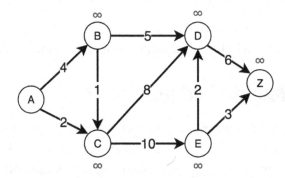

**Figure 17-29.** *Dijkstra stage 1: everything marked as infinity*

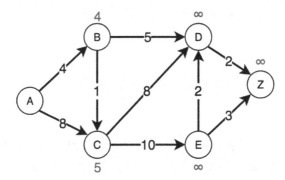

**Figure 17-30.** *Dijkstra stage 2: B and C processed*

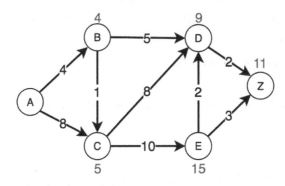

**Figure 17-31.** *Dijkstra stage 3: all nodes now processed*

_extractMin is implemented to compute the neighboring node with the smallest distance for a given vertex. Using the breadth-first search outline to enqueue the neighboring nodes for each vertex as the graph is traversed from the origin to the destination node, the distances are updated and computed.

```
1  function _isEmpty(obj) {
2      return Object.keys(obj).length === 0;
3  }
4
5   function _extractMin(Q, dist) {
6      var minimumDistance = Infinity,
7          nodeWithMinimumDistance = null;
8      for (var node in Q) {
9          if (dist[node] <= minimumDistance) {
10             minimumDistance = dist[node];
```

```
11                    nodeWithMinimumDistance = node;
12                }
13            }
14        return nodeWithMinimumDistance;
15    }
16
17    DirectedGraph.prototype.Dijkstra = function(source) {
18        // create vertex set Q
19        var Q = {}, dist = {};
20        for (var vertex in this.edges) {
21            // unknown distances set to Infinity
22            dist[vertex] = Infinity;
23            // add v to Q
24            Q[vertex] = this.edges[vertex];
25        }
26        // Distance from source to source init to 0
27        dist[source] = 0;
28
29        while (!_isEmpty(Q)) {
30            var u = _extractMin(Q, dist); // get the min distance
31
32            // remove u from Q
33            delete Q[u];
34
35            // for each neighbor, v, of u:
36            // where v is still in Q.
37            for (var neighbor in this.edges[u]) {
38                // current distance
39                var alt = dist[u] + this.edges[u][neighbor];
40                // a shorter path has been found
41                if (alt < dist[neighbor]) {
42                    dist[neighbor] = alt;
43                }
44            }
45        }
```

```
46        return dist;
47    }
48
49    var digraph1 = new DirectedGraph();
50    digraph1.addVertex("A");
51    digraph1.addVertex("B");
52    digraph1.addVertex("C");
53    digraph1.addVertex("D");
54    digraph1.addEdge("A", "B", 1);
55    digraph1.addEdge("B", "C", 1);
56    digraph1.addEdge("C", "A", 1);
57    digraph1.addEdge("A", "D", 1);
58    console.log(digraph1);
59    // DirectedGraph {
60    // V: 4,
61    // E: 4,
62    // edges: { A: { B: 1, D: 1 }, B: { C: 1 }, C: { A: 1 }, D: {} }}
63    digraph1.Dijkstra("A"); // { A: 0, B: 1, C: 2, D: 1 }
```

**Time Complexity:** $O(V^2 + E)$

The algorithm here is similar to the BFS algorithm but requires the _extractMin method, which is $O(n)$ in time complexity. Because of this, the time complexity is $O(V^2 + E)$ because all neighbor vertices of the node currently being traversed have to be checked during the _extractMin method. This algorithm can be improved using a priority queue for the extract min, which would yield $O(log_2(V))$ _extractMin and hence yield an overall time complexity of $O(E + V) * O(log2(V)) = O(E \, log_2(V))$. This can be even more optimized by using a Fibonacci heap, which has constant time to compute _extractMin. However, for simplicity, neither a Fibonacci heap nor a priority queue was used for this demonstration.

# Topological Sort

For a directed graph, it can be important to know which node should be processed first for various applications. An example of this is a task scheduler where one task depends on a previous task being done. Another example is a JavaScript library dependency manager where it has to figure out which libraries to import before others. The topological sorting algorithm implements this. It is a modified DFS that uses a stack to record the order.

Put simply, it works by performing DFS from a node until its connected nodes are recursively exhausted and by adding it to the stack until the connected nodes are all visited (see Figure 17-32).

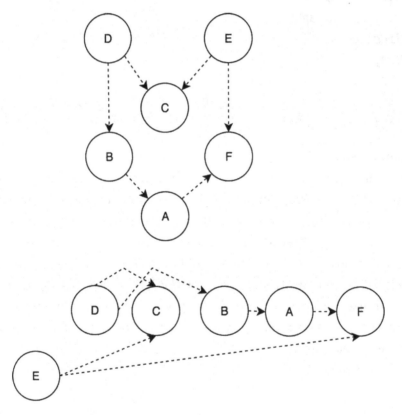

***Figure 17-32.*** *Topological sort*

Topological sorting has a visited set to ensure that the recursive call does not result in an infinite loop. For a given node, that node is added to the visited set, and its neighbors that have not been visited are visited in the next recursive call. At the end of the recursive call, unshift is used to add the current node's value to the stack. This ensures that the order is chronological.

```
1    DirectedGraph.prototype.topologicalSortUtil = function(v, visited, stack) {
2        visited.add(v);
3
4        for (var item in this.edges[v]) {
5            if (visited.has(item) == false) {
6                this.topologicalSortUtil(item, visited, stack)
7            }
8        }
9        stack.unshift(v);
10   };
11
12   DirectedGraph.prototype.topologicalSort = function() {
13       var visited = {},
14           stack = [];
15
16
17       for (var item in this.edges) {
18           if (visited.has(item) == false) {
19               this.topologicalSortUtil(item, visited, stack);
20           }
21       }
22       return stack;
23   };
24
25   var g = new DirectedGraph();
26   g.addVertex('A');
27   g.addVertex('B');
28   g.addVertex('C');
29   g.addVertex('D');
30   g.addVertex('E');
```

```
31    g.addVertex('F');
32
33    g.addEdge('B', 'A');
34    g.addEdge('D', 'C');
35    g.addEdge('D', 'B');
36    g.addEdge('B', 'A');
37    g.addEdge('A', 'F');
38    g.addEdge('E', 'C');
39    var topologicalOrder = g.topologicalSort();
40    console.log(g);
41    // DirectedGraph {
42    // V: 6,
43    // E: 6,
44    // edges:
45    //  { A: { F: 0 },
46    //     B: { A: 0 },
47    //     C: {},
48    //     D: { C: 0, B: 0 },
49    //     E: { C: 0 },
50    //     F: {} } }
51    console.log(topologicalOrder); // [ 'E', 'D', 'C', 'B', 'A', 'F' ]
```

**Time Complexity:** O($V + E$)

**Space Complexity:** O($V$)

The topological sort algorithm is simply DFS with an extra stack. Therefore, the time complexity is the same as DFS. Topological sorting requires O($V$) in space because it needs to store all the vertices in the stack. This algorithm is powerful for scheduling jobs from given dependencies.

# Summary

This chapter discussed different types of graphs, their properties, and how to search and sort them. A graph, composed of vertices and connected via edges, can be represented as a data structure in many different ways. In this chapter, an adjacency list was used to represent the graph. If the graph is dense, it is better to use a matrix-based representation of a graph instead. In a graph's edges, weights signify the importance (or the lack thereof) of the connected vertices. Moreover, by assigning weights to edges, Dijkstra's shortest path algorithm was implemented. Finally, graphs are versatile data structures with various use cases and interesting algorithms.

Table 17-2 shows some key properties of the graphs.

***Table 17-2.*** *Graph Properties Summary*

| Property | Description |
|----------|-------------|
| Dense | There are a lot of connections between different vertices. |
| Sparse | Only a small fraction of possible connections exist between vertices. |
| Cyclical | There is a path that takes vertices back to themselves. |
| Uncyclical | There is a no path such that vertices can be taken back to themselves. |
| Directed | Graphs have a direction between edges. |
| Undirected | Graphs do not have a direction between edges. |

Table 17-3 summarizes the graph algorithms.

***Table 17-3.*** *Graph Algorithm Summary*

| Algorithm | Description/Use Case | Time Complexity |
|-----------|----------------------|-----------------|
| BFS | Traverses the graph by visiting neighbor nodes one level at a time | $O(V + E)$ |
| DFS | Traverses the graph by going deep into each neighbor node one at a time | $O(V + E)$ |
| Dijkstra | Finds the shortest path from one vertex to the rest of the other vertices | $O(V^2 + E)$ |
| Topological Sort | Sorts the directed graph; for job scheduling algorithms | $O(V + E)$ |

# CHAPTER 18

# Advanced Strings

This chapter will cover more advanced string algorithms than the previous chapters have discussed. They should be easier to understand now that you have learned about some other data structures. Specifically, this chapter will focus on string searching algorithms.

## Trie (Prefix Tree)

A *trie* is special type of tree used commonly for searching strings and matching on stored strings. At each level, nodes can branch off to form complete words. For example, Figure 18-1 shows a trie of the words: *Sammie, Simran, Sia, Sam*. Each ending node has a boolean flag: isCompleted. This indicates that the word ends in this path. For example, *m* in *Sam* has endOfWord set to true. Nodes with endOfWord set to true are shaded in Figure 18-1.

© Sammie Bae 2019

S. Bae, *JavaScript Data Structures and Algorithms*, https://doi.org/10.1007/978-1-4842-3988-9_18

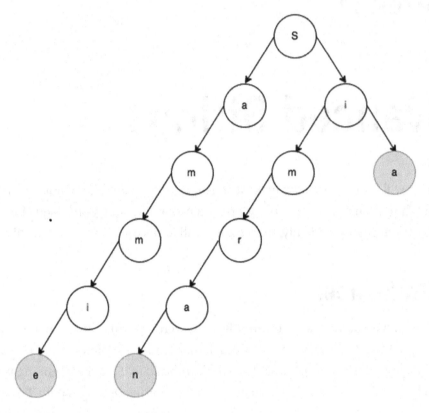

***Figure 18-1.*** *Trie of Sammie, Simran, Sia, Sam*

A trie is implemented using a nested object where each level has its direct children as keys. A trie node can be formed by using an object to store the children. The trie has a root node that is instantiated in the constructor of the Trie class, as shown in the following code block:

```
1   function TrieNode() {
2       this.children = {}; // table
3       this.endOfWord = false;
4   }
5
6   function Trie() {
7       this.root = new TrieNode();
8   }
```

To insert into the trie, the child trie node is created on the root if it does not exist already. For each character in the word being inserted, it creates a child node if the character does not exist, as shown in the following code block:

```
1   Trie.prototype.insert = function(word) {
2       var current = this.root;
3       for (var i = 0; i < word.length; i++) {
4           var ch = word.charAt(i);
5           var node = current.children[ch];
6           if (node == null) {
7               node = new TrieNode();
8               current.children[ch] = node;
9           }
10          current = node;
11      }
12      current.endOfWord = true; //mark the current nodes endOfWord as true
13  }
```

To search inside a trie, each character of the word must be checked. This is done by setting a temporary variable of current on the root. The current variable is updated as each character in the word is checked.

```
1   Trie.prototype.search = function(word) {
2       var current = this.root;
3       for (var i = 0; i < word.length; i++) {
4           var ch = word.charAt(i);
5           var node = current.children[ch];
6           if (node == null) {
7               return false; // node doesn't exist
8           }
9           current = node;
10      }
11      return current.endOfWord;
12  }
13  var trie = new Trie();
14  trie.insert("sammie");
```

```
15    trie.insert("simran");
16    trie.search("simran"); // true
17    trie.search("fake") // false
18    trie.search("sam") // false
```

To delete an element from a trie, the algorithm should traverse the root node until it reaches the last character of the word. Then, for each node that does not have any other children, the node should be deleted. For example, in a trie with *sam* and *sim*, when *sim* is deleted, the *s* node in the root stays intact, but *i* and *m* are removed. The recursive implementation in the following code block implements this algorithm:

```
1    Trie.prototype.delete = function(word) {
2        this.deleteRecursively(this.root, word, 0);
3    }
4
5    Trie.prototype.deleteRecursively = function(current, word, index) {
6        if (index == word.length) {
7            //when end of word is reached only delete if currrent.end Of
             Word is true.
8            if (!current.endOfWord) {
9                return false;
10           }
11           current.endOfWord = false;
12           //if current has no other mapping then return true
13           return Object.keys(current.children).length == 0;
14       }
15       var ch = word.charAt(index),
16           node = current.children[ch];
17       if (node == null) {
18           return false;
19       }
20       var shouldDeleteCurrentNode = this.deleteRecursively(node, word,
         index + 1);
21
22       // if true is returned then
23       // delete the mapping of character and trienode reference from map.
```

```
24        if (shouldDeleteCurrentNode) {
25            delete current.children[ch];
26            //return true if no mappings are left in the map.
27            return Object.keys(current.children).length == 0;
28        }
29        return false;
30   }
31   var trie1 = new Trie();
32   trie1.insert("sammie");
33   trie1.insert("simran");
34   trie1.search("simran"); // true
35   trie1.delete("sammie");
36   trie1.delete("simran");
37   trie1.search("sammie"); // false
38   trie1.search("simran"); // false
```

**Time Complexity:** $O(W)$

**Space Complexity:** $O(N*M)$

Time complexity is $O(W)$ for all operations (insert, search, delete), where $W$ is the length of the string being searched because each character in the string is checked. The space complexity is $O(N*M)$, where $N$ is the number of words inserted into the trie and $M$ is the length of the longest character. Hence, a trie is an efficient data structure when there are multiple strings with common prefixes. For searching one specific *string pattern* in one specific *string*, a trie is not efficient because of the additional memory required to store the strings in the tree-like structure.

For a pattern search in a single target string, the Boyer–Moore algorithm and the Knuth–Morris–Pratt (KMP) algorithm are useful and are covered later in this chapter.

# Boyer–Moore String Search

The Boyer–Moore string search algorithm is used to power the "find" tool used in text editor applications and web browsers, like the one in Figure 18-2.

***Figure 18-2.*** *Find tool commonly seen in many applications*

The Boyer–Moore string search algorithm allows linear time in search by skipping indices when searching inside a string for a pattern. For example, for the pattern *jam* and the string *jellyjam*, visualization of brute-force comparison is shown in Figure 18-3. It should be noted that in the fourth iteration when *j* is compared with *m*, since *j* is shown in the pattern, skipping ahead by 2 would be valid. Figure 18-4 shows an optimized iteration cycle where the number of string comparisons is limited by skipping ahead when the string at the index exists in the pattern.

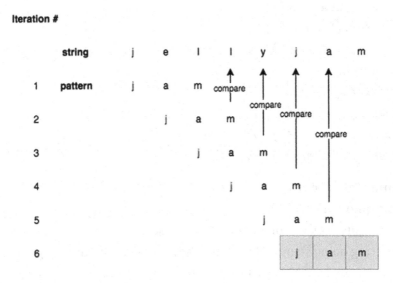

**Figure 18-3.** *Brute-force pattern match iterations*

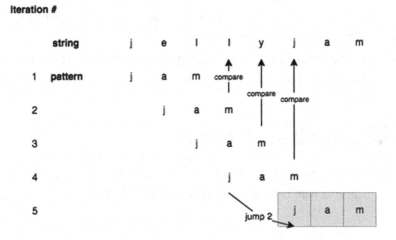

**Figure 18-4.** *Boyer–Moore Skipping Indices*

To implement this skip rule, you can build a "bad match table" structure. The bad match table indicates how much to skip for a given character of a pattern. Some examples of various patterns and its corresponding bad match table are shown here:

| Pattern | Bad Match Table |
|---------|-----------------|
| *jam*   | {j: 2, a: 1, m: 3} |
| *data*  | {d: 3, a: 2, t: 1} |
| *struct* | {s: 5, t: 4, r: 3, u: 2, c: 1} |
| *roi*   | {r: 2, o: 1, i: 3} |

For the *roi* example, r:2 indicates that if r is not found in the string, the index should skip by 2. This bad match table can be implemented with the following code block:

```
function buildBadMatchTable(str) {
    var tableObj = {},
        strLength = str.length;
    for (var i = 0; i <  strLength - 1; i++) {
        tableObj[str[i]] = strLength - 1 - i;
    }
    if (tableObj[str[strLength-1]] == undefined) {
        tableObj[str[strLength-1]] = strLength;
    }
    return tableObj;
}
buildBadMatchTable('data');     // {d: 3, a: 2, t: 1}
buildBadMatchTable('struct');   // {s: 5, t: 4, r: 3, u: 2, c: 1}
buildBadMatchTable('roi');      // {r: 2, o: 1, i: 3}
buildBadMatchTable('jam');      // {j: 2, a: 1, m: 3}
```

Using this bad match table, the Boyer–Moore string search algorithm can be implemented. When scanning the input string for the pattern, if the current string being looked at exists in the bad match table, it skips over by the bad match table value associated with the current string. Otherwise, it is incremented by 1. This continues until either the string is found or the index is greater than the difference of the pattern and string lengths. This is implemented in the following code block:

```
function boyerMoore(str, pattern) {
    var badMatchTable = buildBadMatchTable(pattern),
        offset = 0,
        patternLastIndex = pattern.length - 1,
        scanIndex = patternLastIndex,
        maxOffset = str.length - pattern.length;

    // if the offset is bigger than maxOffset, cannot be found
    while (offset <= maxOffset) {
        scanIndex = 0;
        while (pattern[scanIndex] == str[scanIndex + offset]) {
            if (scanIndex == patternLastIndex) {
                // found at this index
                return offset;
            }
            scanIndex++;
        }
        var badMatchString = str[offset + patternLastIndex];
        if (badMatchTable[badMatchString]) {
            // increase the offset if it exists
            offset += badMatchTable[badMatchString]
        } else {
            offset += 1;
        }
    }
    return -1;
}
boyerMoore('jellyjam','jelly');  // 5. indicates that the pattern starts at
                                 //    index 5
boyerMoore('jellyjam','jelly');  // 0. indicates that the pattern starts at
                                 //    index 0
boyerMoore('jellyjam','sam');    // -1. indicates that the pattern does not
                                 //     exist
```

**Best Case:**

In the best case, all the characters in the pattern are the same, and this consistently produces shifts by $T$, where $T$ is the length of the pattern. Hence, O($W/T$) is the best time complexity where $W$ is the string where the pattern is being searched. The space complexity is O($1$) since only 1 value is stored into the bad match table.

**Time Complexity:** O($T/W$)

**Space Complexity:** O($1$)

**Worst Case:**

In the worst case, the string has the pattern at the end of the string, and the preceding part is all unique characters. An example of this is a string of *abcdefgxyz* and pattern of *xyz*. In this case, $T*W$ string comparisons are done.

**Time Complexity:** O($T*W$)

**Space Complexity:** O($T$)

All the characters in the pattern and the string are the same. An example of such a case is the string *bbbbbb* and the pattern *bbb*. This case cannot use the skip mechanism to its fullest because the index will always be incremented by 1. Space complexity in this case is $T$ because the pattern could have all unique characters.

# Knuth–Morris–Pratt String Search

Chapter 4 discussed the native `String.prototype.indexOf` function. A naive implementation of the `String.prototype.indexOf` function was included as an exercise for that chapter. A better (*faster*) implementation uses the Knuth–Morris–Pratt (KMP) string search algorithm. The following implementation of the KMP algorithm returns all indices where the pattern is present.

The KMP string searching algorithm searches for occurrences of the "word" $W$ within an input "text," which is $T$, by utilizing the observation that the occurrence of a mismatch contains sufficient information about where the next match could begin. This helps to skip re-examination of previously matched characters. A prefix array has to be built to indicate how many indices it has to backtrack to get the same prefix. For the string *ababaca*, the prefix building looks like the following:

**At current index 0**, there is no string to compare to, and the prefix array value is initialized to 0.

> array index 0 1 2 3 4 5 6
>
> character a b a b a c a
>
> prefix array 0

**At current index 1**:

- The character is b.

- The previous prefix array value, prefix[0], is 0.

Compare index 0 to the current index: *a* (at index = 0) and *b* (at index = 1) mismatch. prefix[1] is set to 0:

> Array index 0 1 2 3 4 5 6
>
> Character a b a b a c a
>
> Prefix array 0 0

**At current index 2**:

- The character is *a*.

- The previous prefix array value, prefix[1], is 0.

Compare the index and to the current index: *a* (at index = 0) and *a* (at index = 2) match.

prefix[2] is set to 1 (incremented from prefix[1]):

> Array index 0 1 2 3 4 5 6
>
> Character a b a b a c a
>
> Prefix array 0 0 1

**At current index 3**:

- The character is *b*.

- The previous prefix array value, prefix[2], is 1.

Compare index 1 and the current index: $b$ (at index = 1) and $b$ (at index = 3) match. prefix[3] is set to 2 (incremented from prefix[2]):

Array index 0 1 2 3 4 5 6

Character a b a b a c a

Prefix array 0 0 1 2

**At current index 4:**

- The character is $a$.

- The previous prefix array value, prefix[3], is 2.

Compare index 2 and the current index: $a$ (at index = 2) and $a$ (at index = 4) match. prefix[4] is set to 3 (incremented from prefix[3]):

Array index 0 1 2 3 4 5 6

Character a b a b a c a

Prefix array 0 0 1 2 3

**At current index 5:**

- The character is c.

- The previous prefix array value, prefix[4], is 3.

Compare index 3 and the current index: $b$ (at index = 3) and $c$ (at index = 5) mismatch.
prefix[5] is set to 0:

Array index 0 1 2 3 4 5 6

Character a b a b a c a

Prefix array 0 0 1 2 3 0

**At current index 6:**

- The character is $c$.

- The previous prefix array value, prefix[5], is 0.

Compare from index 0 and current index: *a* (at index = 0) and *a* (at index = 5) match. prefix[6] is set to 1 (incremented from prefix[5]):

Array index 0 1 2 3 4 5 6

Character a b a b a c a

Prefix array 0 0 1 2 3 0 1

The function in the following code block illustrates this algorithm to build a prefix table:

```
function longestPrefix(str) {
    // prefix array is created
    var prefix = new Array(str.length);
    var maxPrefix = 0;
    // start the prefix at 0
    prefix[0] = 0;
    for (var i = 1; i < str.length; i++) {
        // decrement the prefix value as long as there are mismatches
        while (str.charAt(i) !== str.charAt(maxPrefix) && maxPrefix > 0) {
            maxPrefix = prefix[maxPrefix - 1];
        }
        // strings match, can update it
        if (str.charAt(maxPrefix) === str.charAt(i)) {
            maxPrefix++;
        }
        // set the prefix
        prefix[i] = maxPrefix;
    }
    return prefix;
}
console.log(longestPrefix('ababaca')); // [0, 0, 1, 2, 3, 0, 1]
```

With this prefix table now, KMP can be implemented. KMP search iterates through the string and the pattern to be searched for index by index. Whenever there is a mismatch, it can use the prefix table to compute a new index to try.

When the pattern's index reaches the length of the pattern, the string is found. This is implemented in detail in the following code block:

```
function KMP(str, pattern) {
    // build the prefix table
    var prefixTable = longestPrefix(pattern),
        patternIndex = 0,
        strIndex = 0;

    while (strIndex < str.length) {
        if (str.charAt(strIndex) != pattern.charAt(patternIndex)) {
            // Case 1: the characters are different

            if (patternIndex != 0) {
                // use the prefix table if possible
                patternIndex = prefixTable[patternIndex - 1];
            } else {
                // increment the str index to next character
                strIndex++;
            }

        } else if (str.charAt(strIndex) == pattern.charAt(patternIndex)) {
            // Case 2: the characters are same
            strIndex++;
            patternIndex++;
        }

        // found the pattern
        if (patternIndex == pattern.length) {
            return true
        }
    }
    return false;
}
KMP('ababacaababacaababacaababaca', 'ababaca'); //  true
KMP('sammiebae', 'bae'); //  true
KMP('sammiebae', 'sammie'); //  true
KMP('sammiebae', 'sammiebaee'); // false
```

315

**Time Complexity:** $O(W)$

**Space Complexity:** $O(W)$

Preprocessing a word of length $W$ requires both $O(W)$ time and space complexity.

**Time Complexity:** $O(W + T)$

Here, $W$ is the "word" in the $T$ (the main string being searched).

# Rabin–Karp Search

The Rabin–Karp algorithm is based on hashing to find the specified pattern in text. While KMP is optimized to skip redundant checks during the search, Rabin–Karp seeks to speed up the equality of the pattern of the substring via a hash function. To do this efficiently, the hash function must be O(1). Specifically for the Rabin-Karp search, the Rabin fingerprint hashing technique is used.

## The Rabin Fingerprint

The Rabin fingerprint is calculated via the following equation: $f(x) = m_0 + m_1 x + \ldots + m_{n-1} x^{n-1}$ where $n$ is the number of characters being hashed and $x$ is some prime number.

This is a simple implementation, as shown in the following code block. An arbitrary prime number of 101 was set for this example. Any high prime number should work well in this case. However, be aware that if the $x$ is too high, it could cause integer overflow because $x^{n-1}$ grows quickly. The endLength argument indicates to what string index the hash should be calculated. It should be defaulted to the length of str if the argument is not passed.

```
1 function RabinKarpSearch() {
2     this.prime = 101;
3 }
4 RabinKarpSearch.prototype.rabinkarpFingerprintHash = function (str,
   endLength) {
5     if (endLength == null) endLength = str.length;
6     var hashInt = 0;
7     for (var i=0; i < endLength; i++) {
8         hashInt += str.charCodeAt(i) * Math.pow(this.prime, i);
9     }
10    return hashInt;
```

```
11 }
12 var rks = new RabinKarpSearch();
13 rks.rabinkarpFingerprintHash("sammie"); // 1072559917336
14 rks.rabinkarpFingerprintHash("zammie"); // 1072559917343
```

As shown in the previous code block result, the hashes from *sammie* and *zammie* are unique because they are two different strings. The hash value allows you to quickly, in constant time, check whether two strings are the same. As an example, let's look for *am* inside *same*. Since *am* is only two characters long, when you scan the text, *sa*, *am*, and *me* are formed from *same* and compute the hash as shown here:

```
1    rks.rabinkarpFingerprintHash("sa"); // 9912
2    rks.rabinkarpFingerprintHash("am"); // 11106
3    rks.rabinkarpFingerprintHash("me"); // 10310
```

This is a sliding hash calculation. How can this be done efficiently? Let's analyze it mathematically. Recall that for this example the $x$ is 101. In addition, the character code for $s$, $a$, $m$, and $e$ are 115, 97, 109, and 101, respectively.

$$\text{sa: } f(x) = m_0 + m_1 x = 115 + (97)*(101) = 9912$$

$$\text{am: } f(x) = m_0 + m_1 x = 97 + (109)*(101) = 11106$$

$$\text{me: } f(x) = m_0 + m_1 x = 109 + (101)*(101) = 10310$$

To get the hash value from *sa* to *am*, you must subtract the first term, divide the remaining by the prime number, and then add the new term. This recalculation algorithm is implemented in the following code block:

```
1 RabinKarpSearch.prototype.recalculateHash = function (str, oldIndex,
  newIndex, oldHash, patternLength) {
2     if (patternLength == null) patternLength = str.length;
3     var newHash = oldHash - str.charCodeAt(oldIndex);
4     newHash = Math.floor(newHash/this.prime);
5     newHash += str.charCodeAt(newIndex) * Math.pow(this.prime,
      patternLength - 1);
6     return newHash;
7 }
8 var oldHash = rks.rabinkarpFingerprintHash("sa"); // 9912
9 rks.recalculateHash("same", 0, 2, oldHash, "sa".length); //  11106
```

Lastly, two different strings can still have the same hash value although it's unlikely. Therefore, there needs to be a function to check that two strings are equal given the start index and end index for both strings. This is implemented in the following code block:

```
1 RabinKarpSearch.prototype.strEquals = function (str1, startIndex1,
                                                          endIndex1,
2                                                         str2, startIndex2,
                                                          endIndex2) {
3     if (endIndex1 - startIndex1 != endIndex2 - startIndex2) {
4         return false;
5     }
6     while ( startIndex1 <= endIndex1
7            && startIndex2 <= endIndex2) {
8         if (str1[startIndex1] != str2[startIndex2]) {
9             return false;
10        }
11        startIndex1++;
12        startIndex2++;
13    }
14    return true;
15 }
```

Then, the main Rabin–Karp search function is implemented by calculating the starting hash and then recalculating the hashes in a sliding manner until the pattern is found or the end of the string is reached.

```
1 RabinKarpSearch.prototype.rabinkarpSearch = function (str, pattern) {
2     var T = str.length,
3         W = pattern.length,
4         patternHash = this.rabinkarpFingerprintHash(pattern, W),
5         textHash = this.rabinkarpFingerprintHash(str, W);
6
7     for (var i = 1; i <= T - W + 1; i++) {
8         if (patternHash == textHash &&
9             this.strEquals(str, i - 1, i + W - 2, pattern, 0, W - 1)) {
10            return i - 1;
11        }
```

```
12          if (i < T - W + 1) {
13                  textHash = this.recalculateHash(str, i - 1, i + W - 1,
                    textHash, W);
14              }
15      }
16
17      return -1;
18 }
19
20 var rks = new RabinKarpSearch();
21 rks.rabinkarpSearch("SammieBae", "as"); // -1
22 rks.rabinkarpSearch("SammieBae", "Bae"); // 6
23 rks.rabinkarpSearch("SammieBae", "Sam"); // 0
```

**Preprocessing Time Complexity:** O($W$)

The preprocessing time complexity $W$ is the length of the "word."

**Matching Time Complexity:** O($W + T$)

At most, this algorithm iterates through the sum of length $T$ and length $W$, where $T$ is the string being searched for.

# Applications in Real Life

The Rabin–Karp algorithm can be used for detecting plagiarism. With a source material, this algorithm can search through a paper submission for instances of phrases and sentences from the source material (and ignoring grammar details like punctuation by omitting punctuation characters during the preprocessing phase). This problem is impractical for single-search algorithms because of the large set of sought (input) phrases and sentences. The Rabin–Karp algorithm is also used in other string matching applications such as looking for a specific sequence in large DNA data.

# Summary

This chapter returned to the topic of strings and looked at more advanced examples and searching on string patterns. The chapter discussed several different types.

- Trie is great for multiple searches and prefix pattern matching.

- Boyer–Moore, with assumption that the absence of a match at the end means no need to match the beginning, tries to match the last character of the pattern instead of the first; this allows large "jumps" (spaces between indexes) and works better when the text is larger.

- The KMP algorithm searches for occurrences of the pattern in a string by observing that when a mismatch occurs, the pattern itself has sufficient information to determine the index in the string where the next match could begin. Hence, the KMP algorithm is better for small sets.

Table 18-1 summarizes the different search algorithms.

***Table 18-1.***  *Single String Search Summary*

| Algorithm | Preprocessing Time Complexity | Matching Time Complexity | Space Complexity |
|---|---|---|---|
| Naive | None | $O(W * T)$ | None |
| Boyer–Moore | $O(W + T)$ | $O(T/W)$ best case $O(W * T)$ worst case | $O(1)$ |
| KMP | $O(W)$ | $O(T)$ | $O(W)$ |
| Rabin–Karp | $O(W)$ | $O(W + T)$ | $O(1)$ |

# CHAPTER 19

# Dynamic Programming

Dynamic programming involves breaking down problems into their subproblems. By solving for the optimal subproblems and saving those results into memory to access them whenever a repeated problem needs to be solved, the algorithmic complexity decreases significantly. Implementing dynamic programming algorithms requires higher-level thinking about the problem's patterns. To explain dynamic programming, let's re-examine the Fibonacci sequence that was discussed in Chapter 8. Then the chapter will cover the rules of dynamic programming and walk you through some examples to make the concepts more concrete.

## Motivations for Dynamic Programming

The code for the Fibonacci sequence has already been determined to be the following:

```
function getNthFibo(n) {
    if (n <= 1) {
        return n;
    } else {
        return getNthFibo(n - 1) + getNthFibo(n - 2);
    }
}
getNthFibo(3);
```

Recall that the recursive implementation of this algorithm is $O(2^n)$. This is an exponential runtime, which is impractical for real-world applications. Upon closer examination, you will notice that much of the same computation is repeated. As shown in Figure 19-1, when getNthFibo for 6 is called, the calculation for 4, 3, 2, and 1 are repeated multiple times. Knowing this, how can you make this algorithm more efficient?

© Sammie Bae 2019
S. Bae, *JavaScript Data Structures and Algorithms*, https://doi.org/10.1007/978-1-4842-3988-9_19

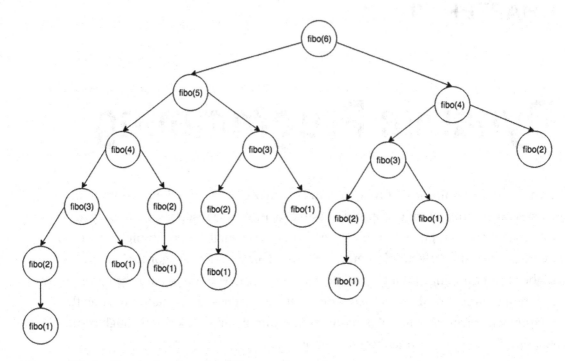

**Figure 19-1.** *Recursion tree for Fibonacci numbers*

Using a hash table, once the Fibonacci number has been computed, it can be stored like the following implementation:

```
1   var cache={};
2   function fiboBest(n){
3       if(n<=1)return n;
4       if(cache[n])return cache[n];
5       return (cache[n]=fiboBest(n-1)+fiboBest(n-2));
6   }
7   fiboBest(10); // 55
```

This is known as *overlapping subproblems*. Calculating the Fibonacci sequence for 6 requires calculating the Fibonacci sequence for 4 and 5. Hence, the Fibonacci sequence for 5 overlaps with the fourth Fibonacci sequence calculation. This problem also has an optimal substructure, which refers to the fact that the optimal solution to the problem contains optimal solutions to its subproblems.

With this, let's now formalize what dynamic programming is.

# Rules of Dynamic Programming

*Dynamic programming* (DP) is the method of storing values that were already calculated and using those values to avoid any recalculations (typically in a recursive algorithm). This method can be applied only to those problems with *overlapping subproblems* and *optimal substructure*.

## Overlapping Subproblems

Similar to divide and conquer in recursion, DP combines solutions on subproblems. DP is used when solutions for subproblems are needed multiple times. It stores subproblem solutions typically in a hash table, an array, or a matrix, and this is referred to as *memoization*. DP is useful for solving problems in which there are many repeated subproblems.

An example of this can be seen with the Fibonacci sequence recursive method. It can be observed that some numbers such as 3 will be recalculated many times.

A hash table can be used to store results to avoid any recalculations. Doing this reduces the time complexity from $O(2^n)$ to just $O(n)$, which is an immense change. Calculating $O(2^n)$ with a realistically large enough $n$ can take literally years to compute.

## Optimal Substructure

An optimal substructure is when the optimal solution of a problem can be found by using the optimal solutions of its subproblems.

For example, the shortest path finding algorithms have optimal substructures. Consider finding the shortest path for traveling between cities by car. If the shortest route from Los Angeles to Vancouver passes through San Francisco and then Seattle, then the shortest route from San Francisco to Vancouver must pass through Seattle as well.

## Example: Ways to Cover Steps

Given a distance, $n$, count the total number of ways to cover $n$ number of steps with one, two, and three steps. For example, when $n=3$, there are four combinations (ways), shown here:

1.  1 step, 1 step, 1 step, 1 step

2.  1 step, 1 step, 2 steps

3.   1 step, 3 steps

4.   2 steps, 2 steps

Here's the function for achieving the count:

```
1    function waysToCoverSteps(step){
2        if (step<0) return 0;
3        if (step==0) return 1;
4
5        return waysToCoverSteps(step-1)+waysToCoverSteps(step-2)+
         waysToCoverSteps(step-3 );
6    }
7    waysToCoverSteps(12);
```

**Time Complexity:** $O(3^n)$

This recursive method has a large time complexity. To optimize the time complexity, simply cache the result and use it instead of recalculating the values.

```
1    function waysToCoverStepsDP(step) {
2        var cache = {};
3        if (step<0) return 0;
4        if (step==0) return 1;
5
6        // check if exists in cache
7        if (cache[step]) {
8            return cache[step];
9        } else {
10           cache[step] = waysToCoverStepsDP(step-1)+waysToCoverStepsDP
             (step-2)+waysToCoverStepsDP(step-3);
11           return cache[step];
12       }
13   }
14   waysToCoverStepsDP(12);
```

**Time Complexity:** $O(n)$

This shows the power of dynamic programing. It improves time complexity immensely.

# Classical Dynamic Programming Examples

This section will explore and solve some of the classical dynamic programming problems. The first one that will be explored is the knapsack problem.

## The Knapsack Problem

The knapsack problem is as follows:

> Given $n$ weights and the values of items, put these items in a knapsack of a given capacity, $w$, to get the maximum total value in the knapsack.

## Optimal Substructure

For every item in the array, the following can be observed:

- The item is included in the optimal subset.

- The item is not included in the optimal set.

The maximum value must be one of the following:

1. (excluding the Nth item): max value obtained with n-1 items

2. (including the Nth item): max value obtained with n-1 items minus the Nth item (can only work if the weight of the Nth item is smaller than W)

## Naive Approach

The naive approach implements the described optimal substructure recursively, as shown here:

```
1    function knapsackNaive(index, weights, values, target) {
2        var result = 0;
3
4        if (index <= -1 || target <= 0) {
5            result = 0
6        } else if (weights[index] > target) {
7            result = knapsackNaive(index-1, weights, values, target);
```

```
8            } else {
9                // Case 1:
10               var current = knapsackNaive(index-1, weights, values, target)
11               // Case 2:
12               var currentPlusOther = values[index] +
13                   knapsackNaive(index-1, weights, values,
                     target - weights[index]);
14
15               result = Math.max(current, currentPlusOther);
16           }
17       return result;
18   }
19   var weights = [1,2,4,2,5],
20       values  = [5,3,5,3,2],
21       target = 10;
22   knapsackNaive(4,weights, values, target);
```

**Time Complexity:** $O(2^n)$

Figure 19-2 shows the recursion tree for a knapsack capacity of 2 units and 3 items of 1 unit weight. As the figure shows, the function computes the same subproblems repeatedly and has an exponential time complexity. To optimize this, you can have the results based on the item (reference via index) and target (weight: $w$).

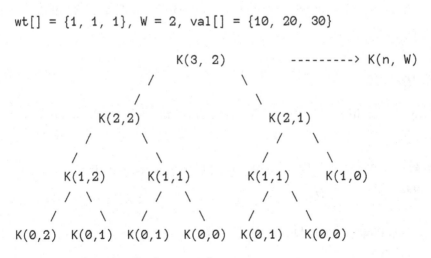

**Figure 19-2.** *Recursion tree for knapsack*

# DP Approach

As discussed, the following DP implementation stores the result of the knapsack using the current array index and target as a key to a JavaScript object for later retrieval. For recursive calls that have already been calculated, it will use the stored result, and this reduces the time complexity of the algorithm significantly.

```
1   function knapsackDP(index, weights, values, target, matrixDP) {
2       var result = 0;
3
4       // DP part
5       if (matrixDP[index + '-' + target]){
6           return matrixDP[index + '-' + target];
7       }
8
9       if (index <= -1 || target <= 0) {
10          result = 0
11      } else if (weights[index] > target) {
12          result = knapsackDP(index - 1, weights, values, target,
                matrixDP);
13      } else {
14          var current = knapsackDP(index-1, weights, values, target),
15              currentPlusOther = values[index] + knapsackDP(index-1,
                weights, values, target - weights[index]);
16          result = Math.max(current, currentPlusOther);
17      }
18      matrixDP[index + '-' + target] = result
19      return result;
20  }
21  knapsackDP(4, weights, values, target, {});
```

**Time Complexity:** O($n*w$)

Here, $n$ is the number of items, and $w$ is the capacity of the knapsack.

**Space Complexity:** O($n*w$)

This algorithm requires an $n$ times $w$ combination to store the cached results inside matrixDP.

The next DP question that will be studied is another classic.

# Longest Common Subsequence

Given two sequences, find the length of the longest subsequence where a subsequence is defined as a sequence that appears in relative order without necessarily being contiguous. For example, *sam, sie, aie*, and so forth, are subsequences of *sammie*. A string has $2^n$ possible subsequences where $n$ is the length of the string.

As a real-world example, let's consider a generalized computer science problem that appears in main domains such as bioinformatics (DNA sequencing). This algorithm is also how the diff functionality (file comparison to output difference between files) is implemented in version control and operating systems.

## Naive Approach

Letting str1 be the first string of length $m$, str2 be the second string of length $n$, and LCS be the function, the naive approach can first consider the following pseudocode:

1.  if last characters of both sequences match (i.e. str1[m-1] == str2[n-1]):
2.      result = 1 + LCS(X[0:m-2], Y[0:n-2])
3.  if last characters of both sequences DO NOT match (i.e. str1[m-1] != str2[n-1]):
4.      result = Math.max(LCS(X[0:m-1], Y[0:n-1]),LCS(X[0:m-2], Y[0:n-2]))

With this recursive structure in mind, the following can be implemented:

```
1   function LCSNaive(str1, str2, str1Length, str2Length) {
2       if (str1Length == 0 || str2Length == 0) {
3           return 0;
4       }
5
6       if (str1[str1Length-1] == str2[str2Length-1]) {
7           return 1 + LCSNaive(str1, str2,
8                               str1Length - 1,
9                               str2Length - 1);
10      } else {
11          return Math.max(
12              LCSNaive(str1, str2, str1Length, str2Length-1),
13              LCSNaive(str1, str2, str1Length-1, str2Length)
14          );
```

```
15          }
16     }
17
18     function LCSNaiveWrapper(str1, str2) {
19          return LCSNaive(str1, str2, str1.length, str2.length);
20     }
21     LCSNaiveWrapper('AGGTAB', 'GXTXAYB'); // 4
```

**Time Complexity:** $O(2^n)$

Figure 19-3 shows the recursion tree for SAM and BAE (visually cut off at a height of 3). As you can see, ('SA', 'BAE') is repeated.

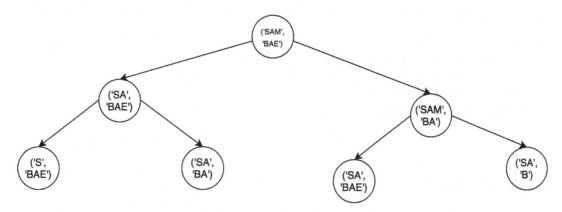

***Figure 19-3.*** *Recursion tree for longest common string length*

## DP Approach

The recursive structure described can be translated into a table/cache where the rows each represent a character in str1 and the columns each represent a character in str2. Each item in a matrix at a row, *i*, and a column, *j*, represents LCS(str1[0:i], str2[0:j]).

```
1     function longestCommonSequenceLength(str1, str2) {
2          var matrix = Array(str1.length + 1).fill(Array(str2.length +
           1).fill(0)),
3               rowLength = str1.length + 1,
4               colLength = str2.length + 1,
5               max = 0;
6
```

```
7            for (var row = 1; row < rowLength; row++) {
8                for (var col = 1; col < colLength; col++) {
9                    var str1Char = str1.charAt(row - 1),
10                       str2Char = str2.charAt(col - 1);

12                   if (str1Char == str2Char) {
13                       matrix[row][col] = matrix[row - 1][col - 1] + 1;
14                       max = Math.max(matrix[row][col], max);
15                   }
16               }
17           }
18           return max;
19       }
20   longestCommonSequenceLength('abcd', 'bc');
```

**Time Complexity:** $O(m * n)$
**Space Complexity:** $O(m * n)$
Here, $m$ is the length of str1, and n is the length of str2.

# Coin Change

Given a value/money $n$ and an unlimited supply of each coin of different values, S = {S1, S2, .. Sm}, of size $M$, how many ways can the change be made without considering the order of the coins?

Given $N=4$, $M=3$, and $S = \{1,2,3\}$, the answer is 4.

1.   1,1,1,1,
2.   1,1,2
3.   2,2
4.   1,3

# Optimal Substructure

You can observe the following about the number of coin changes:

1)   Solutions without Mth coin
2)   Solutions with (at least) one Mth coin

Given that coinChange(S, M, N) is a function to count the number of coin changes, mathematically it can be rewritten as follows by using the two observations from earlier:

coinChange(S, M, N) = coinChange(S, M-1, N) + coinChange(S, M, N-Sm)

## Naive Approach

The naive approach can implement the described algorithm using recursion, as shown here:

```
1    // Returns the count of ways we can sum coinArr which have
2    // index like: [0,...,numCoins]
3    function countCoinWays(coinArr, numCoins, coinValue){
4        if (coinValue == 0) {
5            // if the value reached zero, then only solution is
6            // to not include any coin
7            return 1;
8        }
9        if (coinValue < 0 || (numCoins<=0 && coinValue >= 1)) {
10            // value is less than 0 means no solution
11            // no coins left but coinValue left also means no solution
12            return 0;
13        }
14        //
15        return countCoinWays(coinArr,numCoins-1, coinValue) +
16            countCoinWays(coinArr,numCoins, coinValue-coinArr[numCoins-1]);
17    }
18    function countCoinWaysWrapper(coinArr, coinValue) {
19        return countCoinWays(coinArr, coinArr.length, coinValue);
20    }
21    countCoinWaysWrapper([1,2,3],4);
```

**Time Complexity:** $O(n^m)$
**Space Complexity:** $O(n)$

Here, $m$ is the number of available types of coins, and $n$ is the desired currency to convert into change.

## Overlapping Subproblems

You can see from the recursion tree in Figure 19-4 that there are lots of overlapping subproblems.

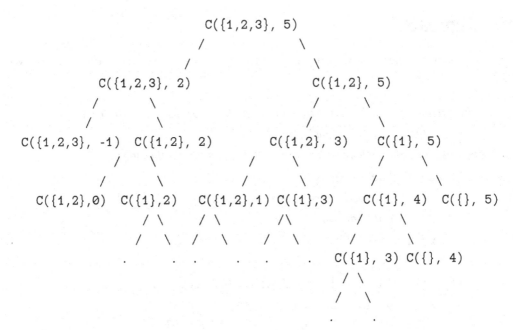

***Figure 19-4.*** *Recursion tree for longest coin change*

To account solve for this, a table (matrix) can be used to store already computed results.

## DP Approach

The matrix for the DP approach has the coinValue number of rows and the numCoins number of columns. Any matrix at *i* and *j* represent the number of ways given a coinValue of *i* and a numCoins of *j*.

```
1    function countCoinWaysDP(coinArr, numCoins, coinValue) {
2         // creating the matrix
3         var dpMatrix = [];
4
5         for (var i=0; i <= coinValue; i++) {
6             dpMatrix[i] = [];
```

```
7           for(var j=0; j< numCoins; j++) {
8               dpMatrix[i][j] = undefined;
9           }
10      }
11
12      for (var i=0; i < numCoins; i++) {
13          dpMatrix[0][i] = 1;
14      }
15
16      for (var i=1; i < coinValue + 1; i++) {
17          for (var j=0; j < numCoins; j++) {
18              var temp1 = 0,
19                  temp2 = 0;
20
21              if (i - coinArr[j] >= 0) {
22                  // solutions including coinArr[j]
23                  temp1 = dpMatrix[i - coinArr[j]][j];
24              }
25
26              if (j >= 1) {
27                  // solutions excluding coinArr[j]
28                  temp2 = dpMatrix[i][j-1];
29              }
30
31              dpMatrix[i][j] = temp1 + temp2;
32          }
33      }
34      return dpMatrix[coinValue][numCoins-1];
35  }
36
37  function countCoinWaysDPWrapper(coinArr, coinValue) {
38      return countCoinWaysDP(coinArr, coinArr.length, coinValue);
39  }
40  countCoinWaysDPWrapper([1,2,3],4);
```

**Time Complexity:** $O(m * n)$

**Space Complexity:** $O(m * n)$

Here, $m$ is the number of available types of coins, and $n$ is the desired currency to convert into change.

# Edit (Levenshtein) Distance

The edit distance problem considers the following:

> Given a string (str1) of length $m$ and another string (str2) of length $n$, what is the minimum number of edits to convert str1 into str2?

The valid operations are the following:

1. Insert

2. Remove

3. Replace

## Optimal Substructure

If each character is processed one by one from each str1 and str2, the following is possible:

```
1.   the characters are the same:
       do nothing
2.   the characters are different:
       consider the cases recursively:
           Insert:      for m    and n-1
           Remove:      for m-1 and n
           Replace:     for m-1 and n-1
```

## Naive Approach

The naive approach can implement the described substructure recursively, as shown here:

```
1    function editDistanceRecursive(str1, str2, length1, length2) {
2        // str1 is empty. only option is insert all of str2
3        if (length1 == 0) {
```

```
4            return length2;
5        }
6        // str2 is empty. only option is insert all of str1
7        if (length2 == 0) {
8            return length1;
9        }
10
11       // last chars are same,
12       // ignore last chars and count remaining
13       if (str1[length1-1] == str2[length2-1]) {
14           return editDistanceRecursive(str1, str2,
15                                       length1-1, length2-1);
16       }
17
18       // last char is not the same
19       // there are three operations: insert, remove, replace
20       return 1 + Math.min (
21           // insert
22           editDistanceRecursive(str1, str2, length1, length2-1),
23           // remove
24           editDistanceRecursive(str1, str2, length1-1, length2),
25           // replace
26           editDistanceRecursive(str1, str2, length1-1, length2-1)
27       );
28   }
29
30   function editDistanceRecursiveWrapper(str1, str2) {
31       return editDistanceRecursive(str1, str2, str1.length, str2.length);
32   }
33
34   editDistanceRecursiveWrapper('sammie','bae');
```

**Time Complexity:** $O(3^m)$

The time complexity of the naive solution is exponential, and the worst case is when no characters in the two strings match. This makes sense because each call has three calls (insert, remove, replace).

Again, you can see that the same problems are solved over and over again (see Figure 19-5). This can be optimized by constructing a matrix that stores the already-computed results of subproblems.

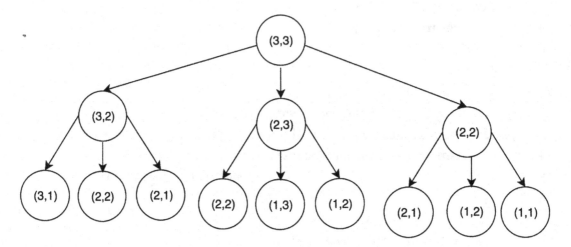

**Figure 19-5.** *Recursion tree for edit distance*

## DP Approach

The dynamic programming approach will construct a matrix with the dimensions str1 and str2. The base case is when *i* or *j* is equal to 0. In other cases, it is 1 + min(insert, remove, replace) just like the recursive approach.

```
1    function editDistanceDP(str1, str2, length1, length2) {
2        // creating the matrix
3        var dpMatrix = [];
4        for(var i=0; i<length1+1; i++) {
5            dpMatrix[i] = [];
6            for(var j=0; j<length2+1; j++) {
7                dpMatrix[i][j] = undefined;
8            }
9        }
10
11       for (var i=0; i < length1 + 1; i++) {
12           for (var j=0; j < length2 + 1; j++) {
13               // if first str1 is empty,
```

```
14                    // have to insert all the chars of str2
15                    if (i == 0) {
16                        dpMatrix[i][j] = j;
17                    } else if (j == 0) {
18                        dpMatrix[i][j] = i;
19                    } else if (str1[i-1] == str2[j-1]) {
20                        // if the same, no additional cost
21                        dpMatrix[i][j] = dpMatrix[i-1][j-1];
22                    } else {
23                        var insertCost = dpMatrix[i][j-1],
24                            removeCost = dpMatrix[i-1][j],
25                            replaceCost= dpMatrix[i-1][j-1];
26
27                        dpMatrix[i][j] = 1 + Math.min(insertCost,removeCost,
                          replaceCost);
28                    }
29                }
30        }
31        return dpMatrix[length1][length2];
32   }
33
34   function editDistanceDPWrapper(str1, str2) {
35        return editDistanceDP(str1, str2, str1.length, str2.length);
36   }
37
38   editDistanceDPWrapper('sammie','bae');
```

**Time Complexity:** $O(m * n)$

**Space Complexity:** $O(m * n)$

Here, $m$ is the length of str1, and $n$ is the length of str2.

# Summary

Dynamic programming can be utilized to optimize an algorithm if the following conditions are satisfied:

- *Optimal substructure*: The optimal solution to the problem contains optimal solutions to its subproblems.

- *Overlapping subproblems*: The solutions for subproblems are needed multiple times.

To store the already computed solutions to a subproblem, a matrix or a hash table is typically used; this is because both provide $O(1)$ lookup time. Doing this, the time complexity can be improved from exponential (e.g., $O(2^n)$) to polynomial time (e.g., $O(n^2)$).

# CHAPTER 20

# Bit Manipulation

Bit manipulation is an advanced topic that JavaScript developers typically do not need to know. Low-level programming languages such as C take advantage of these operators. However, you should learn a bit about bit manipulation if you want to implement high-performance server-side code.

Understanding bit manipulation requires some knowledge of digital logic. Any introductory course in discrete math or circuits would be helpful to understand these concepts.

## Bitwise Operators

Here are the bitwise operators in JavaScript:

- `&` :   AND
- `|` :   OR
- `~` :   NOT
- `^` :   XOR
- `<<`:   Left shift
- `>>`:   Right shift
- `>>>`:  Zero-fill right shift

---

**Note**   Recall from Chapter 3 that all numbers are represented with 32 bits (meaning there are 32 1s and 0s). When converting from decimal numbers (base 10) to binary (base 2), it is important to keep this in mind.

---

© Sammie Bae 2019
S. Bae, *JavaScript Data Structures and Algorithms*, https://doi.org/10.1007/978-1-4842-3988-9_20

# AND

The AND operator is true when both bits are 1. The & (ampersand) is used for the AND operator.

| a | b | a AND b |
|---|---|---------|
| 0 | 0 | 0 |
| 0 | 1 | 0 |
| 1 | 0 | 0 |
| 1 | 1 | 1 |

In bitwise operations, the numbers are in binary representation. For example, 9 in binary is 1001, and 5 in binary is 101.

For each bit, the AND operation has to be performed:

```
9:        0 0 0 0 0 0 0 0 0 0 0 0 0 0 0 0 0 0 0 0 0 0 0 0 0 0 0 1 0 0 1
5:        0 0 0 0 0 0 0 0 0 0 0 0 0 0 0 0 0 0 0 0 0 0 0 0 0 0 0 0 1 0 1
9 & 5:    0 0 0 0 0 0 0 0 0 0 0 0 0 0 0 0 0 0 0 0 0 0 0 0 0 0 0 0 0 0 1 = 1
```

```
1   console.log(9 & 5); // prints 1
```

Here's another example:

```
40 in base 10 = 100010 in base 2
41 in base 10 = 100011 in base 2
```

```
40:        0 0 0 0 0 0 0 0 0 0 0 0 0 0 0 0 0 0 0 0 0 0 0 0 0 1 0 0 0 1 0
41:        0 0 0 0 0 0 0 0 0 0 0 0 0 0 0 0 0 0 0 0 0 0 0 0 0 1 0 0 0 1 1

40 & 41:   0 0 0 0 0 0 0 0 0 0 0 0 0 0 0 0 0 0 0 0 0 0 0 0 0 1 0 0 0 1 0 =  40
```

# OR

The OR operator is when either bit is 1. The | (pipe) is used for the OR operator.

| a | b | a OR b |
|---|---|--------|
| 0 | 0 | 0 |
| 0 | 1 | 1 |
| 1 | 0 | 1 |
| 1 | 1 | 1 |

Let's use 9 | 5 and 40 | 41 as examples.

```
9:      0 0 0 0 0 0 0 0 0 0 0 0 0 0 0 0 0 0 0 0 0 0 0 0 0 0 0 0 1 0 0 1
5:      0 0 0 0 0 0 0 0 0 0 0 0 0 0 0 0 0 0 0 0 0 0 0 0 0 0 0 0 0 1 0 1
9 | 5:  0 0 0 0 0 0 0 0 0 0 0 0 0 0 0 0 0 0 0 0 0 0 0 0 0 0 0 0 1 1 0 1 = 13
```

Here's another example:

```
40:      0 0 0 0 0 0 0 0 0 0 0 0 0 0 0 0 0 0 0 0 0 0 0 0 0 0 1 0 0 0 1 0
41:      0 0 0 0 0 0 0 0 0 0 0 0 0 0 0 0 0 0 0 0 0 0 0 0 0 0 1 0 0 0 1 1
40 & 41: 0 0 0 0 0 0 0 0 0 0 0 0 0 0 0 0 0 0 0 0 0 0 0 0 0 0 1 0 0 0 1 1 = 41
```

# XOR

XOR means "exclusive or." It evaluates to true only when one of the bits is 1. The ^ (caret) is used for the XOR operator.

| a | b | a XOR b |
|---|---|---------|
| 0 | 0 | 0 |
| 0 | 1 | 1 |
| 1 | 0 | 1 |
| 1 | 1 | 0 |

```
9:       0 0 0 0 0 0 0 0 0 0 0 0 0 0 0 0 0 0 0 0 0 0 0 0 0 0 0 0 1 0 0 1
5:       0 0 0 0 0 0 0 0 0 0 0 0 0 0 0 0 0 0 0 0 0 0 0 0 0 0 0 0 0 1 0 1
9 ^ 5:   0 0 0 0 0 0 0 0 0 0 0 0 0 0 0 0 0 0 0 0 0 0 0 0 0 0 0 0 1 1 0 0 = 12

40:      0 0 0 0 0 0 0 0 0 0 0 0 0 0 0 0 0 0 0 0 0 0 0 0 0 0 1 0 0 0 1 0
41:      0 0 0 0 0 0 0 0 0 0 0 0 0 0 0 0 0 0 0 0 0 0 0 0 0 0 1 0 0 0 1 1
40 ^ 41: 0 0 0 0 0 0 0 0 0 0 0 0 0 0 0 0 0 0 0 0 0 0 0 0 0 0 0 0 0 0 0 1 =  1
```

# NOT

The NOT operator inverses all bits. The ~ (tilde) is used for the NOT operator. Please do not confuse the NOT operator with the negative operator. Once the bits are inverted, the numbers in 32-bit follow.

| a | NOT a |
|---|-------|
| 0 | 1 |
| 1 | 0 |

Let's take 9 and 5 as an example:

```
9:    0 0 0 0 0 0 0 0 0 0 0 0 0 0 0 0 0 0 0 0 0 0 0 0 0 0 0 0 1 0 0 1
~9:   1 1 1 1 1 1 1 1 1 1 1 1 1 1 1 1 1 1 1 1 1 1 1 1 1 1 1 1 0 1 1 0 = -10

5:    0 0 0 0 0 0 0 0 0 0 0 0 0 0 0 0 0 0 0 0 0 0 0 0 0 0 0 0 0 1 0 1
~5:   1 1 1 1 1 1 1 1 1 1 1 1 1 1 1 1 1 1 1 1 1 1 1 1 1 1 1 1 1 0 1 0 = -6
```

# Left Shift

In left shift, all the bits are shifted to the left, and any excess bits shifted off to the left are discarded. The << (double left-angle brackets) is the operator of left shift.

```
9:        0 0 0 0 0 0 0 0 0 0 0 0 0 0 0 0 0 0 0 0 0 0 0 0 0 0 0 0 1 0 0 1
9 << 1: 0 0 0 0 0 0 0 0 0 0 0 0 0 0 0 0 0 0 0 0 0 0 0 0 0 0 0 1 0 0 1 0 = 18
9 << 2: 0 0 0 0 0 0 0 0 0 0 0 0 0 0 0 0 0 0 0 0 0 0 0 0 0 0 1 0 0 1 0 0 = 36
```

Left shift often multiplies elements by 2 for each shift. This is because binary is a base 2 system, implying a left shift is equal to multiplying all the digits by 2. However, the shift can cause the bit to overflow and reduce the value.

```
1073741833:            0 1 0 0 0 0 0 0 0 0 0 0 0 0 0 0 0 0 0 0 0 0 0 0 0 0 0 0 0 0 1
0 0 1
1073741833 << 2:  0 0 0 0 0 0 0 0 0 0 0 0 0 0 0 0 0 0 0 0 0 0 0 0 0 0 0 0 1 0 0
1 0 0 = 36
```

# Right Shift

In right shift, all the bits are shifted to the right, and any excess bits shifted off to the right are discarded. The >> (double right angle brackets) is the operator for right shift.

```
9:         0 0 0 0 0 0 0 0 0 0 0 0 0 0 0 0 0 0 0 0 0 0 0 0 0 0 0 0 1 0 0 1
9 >> 1:    0 0 0 0 0 0 0 0 0 0 0 0 0 0 0 0 0 0 0 0 0 0 0 0 0 0 0 0 0 1 0 0 = 4

-9:        1 1 1 1 1 1 1 1 1 1 1 1 1 1 1 1 1 1 1 1 1 1 1 1 1 1 1 1 0 1 1 1
-9 >> 2:   1 1 1 1 1 1 1 1 1 1 1 1 1 1 1 1 1 1 1 1 1 1 1 1 1 1 1 1 1 1 0 1 = -3
```

In this example, shifting divided the 9 by 2 (integer division). This is because, again, binary is a base 2 system.

## Zero-Fill Right Shift

In zero-fill right shift, all the bits are shifted to the right, and any excess bits shifted off to the right are discarded. However, the sign bit (the leftmost bit) becomes a 0 before the shift, and this results in a non-negative number. The >>> (triple right brackets) is the operator for the zero-fill right shift.

```
-9:         1 1 1 1 1 1 1 1 1 1 1 1 1 1 1 1 1 1 1 1 1 1 1 1 1 1 1 1 0 1 1 1
-9 >>> 1:   0 1 1 1 1 1 1 1 1 1 1 1 1 1 1 1 1 1 1 1 1 1 1 1 1 1 1 1 0 1 1 =
            2147483643
```

In this example, shifting divided the 9 by 2 (integer division). This is because, again, binary is a base 2 system.

To have a better understanding of why these operations work, it is recommended to take an introductory digital logic course in school or online. In the end, everything consists of 1s and 0s because a transistor in a computer can have only two states: on and off.

# Number Operations

This section will cover how to perform addition, subtraction, multiplication, division, and modulus using bitwise operators.

## Addition

Adding binary numbers is no different from adding decimal numbers. The rule that children learn in the second grade is the same: add up two numbers and carry 1 to next digit if it exceeds 10.

The function that implements this is as follows. You can find all the code on GitHub.[1]

```
1    function BitwiseAdd(a, b){
2        while (b != 0) {
3            var carry = (a & b);
```

---

[1]https://github.com/Apress/js-data-structures-and-algorithms

```
4               a = a ^ b;
5               b = carry << 1;
6           }
7       return a;
8   }
9
10  console.log(BitwiseAdd(4,5)); // 9
```

Here are two examples in detail:

```
bitwiseAdd(4, 5);
4:              0 0 0 0 0 0 0 0 0 0 0 0 0 0 0 0 0 0 0 0 0 0 0 0 0 0 0 0 0 1 0 0
5:              0 0 0 0 0 0 0 0 0 0 0 0 0 0 0 0 0 0 0 0 0 0 0 0 0 0 0 0 0 1 0 1
sum = 4 ^ 5 =   0 0 0 0 0 0 0 0 0 0 0 0 0 0 0 0 0 0 0 0 0 0 0 0 0 0 0 0 0 0 0 1
= 1 (base 10)
carry = (a & b) << 1
a & b =         0 0 0 0 0 0 0 0 0 0 0 0 0 0 0 0 0 0 0 0 0 0 0 0 0 0 0 0 0 1 0 0
(a & b) << 1 =  0 0 0 0 0 0 0 0 0 0 0 0 0 0 0 0 0 0 0 0 0 0 0 0 0 0 0 0 1 0 0 0
= 8 (base 10)

bitwiseAdd(1, 8);
1:              0 0 0 0 0 0 0 0 0 0 0 0 0 0 0 0 0 0 0 0 0 0 0 0 0 0 0 0 0 0 0 1
8:              0 0 0 0 0 0 0 0 0 0 0 0 0 0 0 0 0 0 0 0 0 0 0 0 0 0 0 0 1 0 0 0

sum = 1 ^ 8 = 0 0 0 0 0 0 0 0 0 0 0 0 0 0 0 0 0 0 0 0 0 0 0 0 0 0 0 0 1 0 0 1
= 9 (base 10)

carry =    (a & b) << 1
a & b =    0 0 0 0 0 0 0 0 0 0 0 0 0 0 0 0 0 0 0 0 0 0 0 0 0 0 0 0 0 0 0 0
-> return 9 (a)
```

## Subtraction

Subtraction is the difference of two numbers. However, you can also think of it as adding a negative number. Here's an example: 5 - 4 = 5 + (-4).

Therefore, first create a negate function using the NOT operator. In binary, subtracting a negative binary number from a positive one is obtained by inverting all the bits and adding 1. This is implemented in the following code block:

```
1    function BitwiseNegate(a) {
2        return BitwiseAdd(~a,1);
3    }
4
5    console.log(BitwiseNegate(9)); // -9
6    // negation with itself gives back original
7    console.log(BitwiseNegate(BitwiseNegate(9))); // 9
8
9    function BitwiseSubtract(a, b) {
10       return BitwiseAdd(a, BitwiseNegate(b));
11   }
12
13   console.log(BitwiseSubtract(5, 4)); // 1
```

## Multiplication

Multiplying numbers in base 2 follows the same logic as multiplying numbers in base 2; multiply the numbers, carry anything over 10 to the next digit, and then multiply the next digit with the shifted base (in the case of decimals, multiply by 10 each time you shift the digit). For example, 12 times 24 is done by first multiplying 2 and 4, then 10 and 4, then shifting the digit to 2 (20 now), multiplying 20 and 2, and then multiplying 20 times 10. Finally, add those values up to obtain 288.

```
    12
    24
------
    48
    24
------
   288
```

In binary:

```
      0 1 1 0 0
      1 1 0 0 0
------------------
              0 0 0 0 0
            0 0 0 0 0
          0 0 0 0 0
      0 1 1 0 0
    0 1 1 0 0
---------------
    1 0 0 1 0 0 0 0 0
```

The following code block illustrates this implementation, and it also handles negative numbers:

```
1    function BitwiseMultiply(a, b) {
2        var m = 1,
3            c = 0;
4
5        if (a < 0) {
6            a = BitwiseNegate(a);
7            b = BitwiseNegate(b);
8        }
9        while (a >= m && b) {
10           if (a & m) {
11               c = BitwiseAdd(b, c);
12           }
13           b = b << 1;
14           m = m << 1;
15       }
16       return c;
17   }
18   console.log(BitwiseMultiply(4, 5)); // 20
```

# Division

Division can be thought of as the number of times you can subtract b from a, given a/b. For example, 4/2 = 2 because 4-2-2 = 0. Using this property, bitwise division can be implemented as follows:

```
1   function BitwiseDividePositive(a, b) {
2       var c = 0;
3
4       if (b != 0) {
5           while (a >= b) {
6               a = BitwiseSubtract(a, b);
7               c++;
8           }
9       }
10      return c;
11  }
12  console.log(BitwiseDividePositive(10, 2)); // 5
```

This is relatively simple for positive numbers. The while loop can keep subtracting, and a counter variable can store how many times b subtracted a. However, what about for negative numbers? -10 /2 = -5, but we cannot subtract 2 from -10 because the while loop would go on forever. To avoid this, convert both the numbers into positive numbers. Doing this, we have to keep track of the sign.

| a | b | a * b |
|---|---|-------|
| + | + | +     |
| + | - | -     |
| - | + | -     |
| - | - | +     |

If negative is represented as 1 and positive as 0, this is the same table as an XOR table:

| a | b | a * b |
|---|---|-------|
| 0 | 0 | 0     |
| 0 | 1 | 1     |
| 1 | 0 | 1     |
| 1 | 1 | 0     |

The division algorithm is shown next. This function subtracts b from a until it is zero. Again, negative numbers have to be handled appropriately at the end with a negation helper function.

```
1    function BitwiseDivide(a, b) {
2        var c = 0,
3            isNegative = 0;
4
5        if (a < 0) {
6            a = BitwiseNegate(a); // convert to positive
7            isNegative = !isNegative;
8        }
9
10       if (b < 0) {
11           b = BitwiseNegate(b); // convert to positive
12           isNegative = !isNegative;
13       }
14
15       if (b != 0) {
16           while (a >= b) {
17               a = BitwiseSubtract(a, b);
18               c++;
19           }
20       }
21
22       if (isNegative) {
23           c = BitwiseNegate(c);
24       }
25
26       return c;
27   }
28
29   console.log(BitwiseDivide(10, 2)); // 5
30   console.log(BitwiseDivide(-10, 2)); // -5
31   console.log(BitwiseDivide(-200, 4)); // -50
```

# Summary

This chapter covered the basics of bit manipulation in JavaScript. Bit manipulation is used for high-performance numerical operations. Using bitwise operators is much faster than using the native methods in the Math class. With JavaScript advancing into server-side programming with Node.js, more efficient code is needed. To consolidate the concepts from this chapter, Table 20-1 summarizes bitwise operators and their usage.

***Table 20-1.***  *Bit Manipulation Summary*

| Operator | Operation | Use Case |
|---|---|---|
| & | AND | 1 when both bits are 1 |
| \| | OR | 1 when either bit is 1 |
| ~ | NOT | Inverts all the bits |
| ^ | XOR | 1 when *only* one of the bits is 1 |
| << | Left shift | Shifts to the left, and any excess bits are shifted off |
| >> | Right shift | Shifts to the right, and any excess bits are shifted off |
| >>> | Zero-fill right shift | Shifts to the right, and any excess bits are shifted off and the sign bit comes 0 |

# Index

## A

Access queue, 170–171

Access stacks, 166–167

Algorithm

    Boyer–Moore string search, 307

    KMP string search, 311

    Rabin–Karp search, 316

AND operator, 340

Arrays

    access, 54

    deletion, 54

    exercises

        matrix rotation, 79–81

        path finding, 75–79

        spiral print, 71–73

        tic-tac-toe check, 73–74

    functional array methods, 67

    helper functions, 57

    insertion, 53–54

    iteration, 54

    K-sorted arrays, 66–67

    largest value, 270

    median of two sorted

        arrays, 63–65

    multidimensional arrays, 68

    .slice() function, 62–63

    smallest value, 270

Ascending-Order sort, 261–264

.atob() function, 42

## B

Base64 encoding, 42–43

Big-O notation

    coefficient rule, 5–6

    complexities, 2–3

    fundamental rules, 4

    master theorem, 106–107

    $O(n)$ algorithm, 2

    polynomial rule, 8

    product rule, 7–8

    recurrence relations, 105–106

    sum rule, 6

Binary heap

    max-heap, 254–257

    percolation

        bubble up/down, 250

        implementation, 253–254

AVL trees

    deletion, 230–231

    double rotation

        rotate left right, 227

        rotate right left, 225–226

    insertion, 229–230

    result, 231–232

    single rotation

        rotate left, 222–223

        rotate right, 223, 225

    tree balancing, 228

© Sammie Bae 2019
S. Bae, *JavaScript Data Structures and Algorithms*, https://doi.org/10.1007/978-1-4842-3988-9

Printed in the United States
By Bookmasters